Before Tomorro\

Before Tomorrow

Epigenesis and Rationality

Catherine Malabou

Translated by Carolyn Shread

polity

First published in French as *Avant demain. Épigenèse et rationalité*
© Presses Universitaires de France, 2014

This English edition © Polity Press, 2016

Polity Press
65 Bridge Street
Cambridge CB2 1UR, UK

Polity Press
350 Main Street
Malden, MA 02148, USA

ISBN-13: 978-0-7456-9150-3
ISBN-13: 978-0-7456-9151-0 (pb)

A catalogue record for this book is available from the British Library.

Typeset in 10.5 on 12 pt Sabon by
Servis Filmsetting Ltd, Stockport, Cheshire
Printed and bound in Great Britain by CPI Group (UK) Ltd, Croydon

The publisher has used its best endeavours to ensure that the URLs for external websites referred to in this book are correct and active at the time of going to press. However, the publisher has no responsibility for the websites and can make no guarantee that a site will remain live or that the content is or will remain appropriate.

Every effort has been made to trace all copyright holders, but if any have been inadvertently overlooked the publisher will be pleased to include any necessary credits in any subsequent reprint or edition.

For further information on Polity, visit our website:
politybooks.com

CONTENTS

TRANSLATOR'S FOREWORD

Epigenesis of Her Texts

> Tomorrow, the order of precedence between program and its translation will be inverted.
>
> Catherine Malabou

With every new Malabou translation comes a fresh understanding of my practice and another translation manifesto. Working with her – especially this time, where for over a year the author has been the translator's partner in transforming her text – translation has assumed its plasticity, its change, its accident, and, now, its epigenetic function. As Malabou analyzes the epigenesis of Kant's notion of rationality in *Before Tomorrow*, I am led to consider how, in translation, her own texts undergo a process of epigenesis: that is, the biological process of cellular differentiation. Which parts are sloughed off and which undergo maturation? How does Malabou develop in her arrival in English? Does the move into the Anglophone context allow for a development of that which is premature or impeded in French? Where else is she going? Who will retranslate her work tomorrow?

In the sinews of her rigorous and unrelenting tracking of Kantian philosophy, Malabou proposes that "critique itself, from the *Critique of Pure Reason* to the *Critique of the Power of Judgment*," is subject to "*epigenetic development*" (156). Drawing again on the sciences that other continental philosophers have turned their backs on, she finds the most exciting movements of our era and brings to life biology. She confronts the moment when Kant is to be relinquished by speculative realists by uncovering in his work the resources she needs to open "the chink of a farewell" (xiii). She will bring in the life force of new frontiers in biology, for "the time has come to say

viii

it: transcendental epigenesis is epigenesis *of* the transcendental itself" (158). That which we thought was set in stone will be rocked by a new focus, shattered, then regrounded, differently: "The transcendental is subject to epigenesis – not to foundation" (158).

Beyond all the trying genetic investigations, always in search of a lost, inaccessible, founding origin, Malabou's book on Kant acknowledges frankly that "epigenesis can produce" (50), even if it builds on moving grounds. For our part, as translation theorists, we have been thinking translation in genetic terms and therefore failing to account for, or recognize, epigenetic productivity. Yet translation is epigenesis. After the afterlife and after survival, the plastic life of the text. As translators, "we now all have a new word"[1] for our art, something to help us explain how it is that texts are not complete until they are translated. How it is that texts bear the program to translate, the need to develop their parts in translation. That translation is generative, not as "a succession or connection of events taking place in a linear fashion starting from a given, identifiable point" (175), but rather, more holistically, as "the temporality of a synthetic continuum within which all of the parts are presented together in a movement of growth whereby the whole is formed through self-differentiation" (178). Translation is that process in which the text self-differentiates and thereby grows, develops, matures.

Malabou deploys new biological paradigms to read Kant, and in turn, reading her, I propose that we adopt epigenesis in translation studies to better describe the plasticity of the translating process. But is this any different from the multiplicity of metaphors that the discipline has already developed? The proposal and contestation of metaphors is integral to our field, from Lori Chamberlain's foundational "Gender and the Metaphorics of Translation" (1988) to James St André's recent essay collection, *Thinking through Translation with Metaphors* (2014).[2] Analogical thinking seemingly corresponds to our relational practices. But epigenesis is different. Just as Malabou is sensitive to the fact that her argument rides on being more than a "rhetorical artifice," that her parsing of Kant's phrase in paragraph 27 of the *Critique of Pure Reason*, "as it were a system of epigenesis of pure reason," must be more, for "if it turns out that epigenesis is only an image with nothing other than an exoteric, pedagogic, or illustrative role, then my entire elaboration is meaningless" (181). Indeed. To say *what is* goes far beyond *as it were*, and at this point, translation studies, too, must go beyond analogy to talk mechanics, life systems.

The slow seismic shifting or the shock of the quake. The moment in a translation when words slip, leap, echo, fly. Epigenesis: is that what translation is? Is that how we rid ourselves of the genetic paradigm that has shackled us to the original? Is it here, again, translating Malabou, that I find an answer to my questions about how to frame translation? It is – and I don't think it's just a translator's conceit. Even as the authors' closest readers, we, translators, work at the surface, determined to achieve the moment where "their difference disappears right into their contact" (157). We translate and retranslate, conscious that "epigenesis marks the current valency of the meeting point between the old and the new, the space where they reciprocally interfere with and transform one another" (158). Epigenetics describes how specific genes are activated or deactivated in response to environmental variants – the gene expression that is the transcription and translation of genetic code. The epigenesis of translation is about how texts turn off and on to speak to their audience, to react to their specific contact point. And so here, with a translation that is at once biological and textual, I find that epigenesis, then, is the meaning in translation.

Carolyn Shread

Epigignomai: (1) to be born after (*oi epigignomenoi*, the descendants); (2) to arise, to take place; (3) to add.

All evolution is epigenetic.

Georges Canguilhem[1]

Hence natural things which we find possible only as ends constitute the best proof of the contingency of the world-whole.

Immanuel Kant[2]

PREFACE

Why write another book on Kant? Why add to the already extensive list of dissertations, monographs, and articles written on him even today?

Quite simply, because, working behind the screen of all this recognition and celebration, my plan is to trace out the opposite, namely the chink of a farewell. A break with Kant is in the works in contemporary continental philosophy. Under the banner of "speculative realism," a new approach to the world, thinking, and time puts into question a number of postulates considered untouchable since the *Critique of Pure Reason*: the finitude of knowledge, the phenomenal given, the *a priori* synthesis as the originary relation between subject and object, the entire structural apparatus said to guarantee the universality and necessity of the laws of both nature and thought, in a word, the "transcendental." And the rallying cry of new post-critical thought is *relinquish the transcendental*.

This relinquishing has been on the cards for some time. Initiated by Hegel, it marched on unrelenting until we reached the destruction and deconstruction of metaphysics. From Hegel to Heidegger, then from Heidegger to Derrida and Foucault, the transcendental was interrogated on the grounds of its rigidity, its permanence, its purported role as the condition *sine qua non* of thinking. To bring time, as did Heidegger, or history, as did Foucault, into the transcendental was already a way of relinquishing it. But that's not all. The neurobiological revolution of the late 1980s, which must at last be acknowledged, and which brought to light a set of questions that are not entirely germane to the analytic tradition, also undermined any notion of the transcendental. Recent discoveries about how the brain functions have, in their own way, challenged the supposed invariability of laws of thought.

How, then, should we situate speculative realism, given that it views itself as even more radical than the deconstruction of metaphysics and cognitivism? And amidst all these upheavals, what happens to Kantian philosophy, or, for that matter, philosophy itself?

I believe that it is important to formulate a response to these questions by presenting a panorama of the ultra-contemporary philosophical landscape, where several major readings of Kant are being staged in terms of three questions: time; the relation between thinking and the brain; and the contingency of the world.

Of course, the indispensable counterweight to this exploration is the response of Kant himself to his own posterity.

I have constructed this response here around *epigenesis*, a figure that Kant summons in the *Critique of Pure Reason* in reference to the gestation of the categories. In biology, epigenesis designates the growth of the embryo through the gradual differentiation of cells – as opposed to preformation, which assumes that the embryo is fully constituted from the start. I develop the thesis that, far from being simply a rhetorical artifice, epigenesis applies to the transcendental itself. The transcendental grows, develops, transforms, and evolves. This evolution is such as to ensure that it spans the centuries separating the epigenetism of the eighteenth century from contemporary epigenetics.

Thus, the transcendental begins life anew.

After *The Future of Hegel*,[1] the time has come to write on Kant's future. The next task will be to return to the relation between epigenesis and dialectic.

*

I wish to thank Monique Labrune and John Thompson, my publishers in France and the UK, for their patience and confidence. I also thank Øystein Brekke for his invaluable aid, both philosophical and bibliographic; this book owes much to our exchanges between Paris and Oslo. Étienne Balibar also provided me with books that were nowhere to be found, and I would like to express my gratitude and enduring friendship to him here. Lastly, I am deeply grateful to my translator and friend Carolyn Shread, and to Steve Howard, from Kingston University, who so generously reread the translation. Without their scrutiny and expertise, this project would not have come to light.

INTRODUCTION

Assessment: An Unstable Kant

Three questions

Three questions lie at the origin of this book, three addresses to contemporary continental philosophy that seek to reveal in it, as their negative or paradoxical echo, the outlines of three areas of incomprehensible silence.

The first question concerns time. Why has the question of time lost its status as the leading question of philosophy? Why did it simply disappear after *Being and Time*, and why did Heidegger himself go so far as to confirm, in his late work, the need to leave behind the question of time as such? In *On Time and Being*, he even asserted that "time" ends up "vanishing *(verschwinden)*" as a question.[1] Indeed, no one asks this question anymore, no one has taken up the problem by trying to develop afresh a decisive concept of temporality, be it with or against Heidegger.

The second question concerns the relation between reason and the brain: why does philosophy continue to ignore recent neurobiological discoveries that suggest a profoundly transformed view of brain development and that now make it difficult, if not unacceptable, to maintain the existence of an impassable abyss between the logical and the biological origin of thinking? Can we continue to claim, without further examination, as Paul Ricœur does in his interviews with Jean-Pierre Changeux, that "the brain is [nothing but] the *substrate* of thought [. . .] and that thought is the *indication* of an underlying neuronal structure"?[2] How should we understand this intractable and systematic resistance to a possible reformulation of

1

rational activity as the dispositions of the brain? Isn't it urgent to face the question today, rather than allowing it to slip entirely out of the field of philosophy?

The third question concerns Kant's status. This is the first time that the authority of Kant – the guarantor, if not the founder, of the identity of continental philosophy – has been so clearly up for discussion, from within this same philosophical tradition. The *a priori* character of causal necessity, on which Kant builds the principle of the validity of knowledge and the stability of nature, is openly in question today. Quentin Meillassoux's book *After Finitude* – which might be better read as "after Kant" – was a thunderbolt that toppled the statue of "correlation."[3] "Correlation" is what Meillassoux terms the *a priori* synthesis in critical philosophy, that is, a structure of originary co-implication of subject and object that ensures the strict equivalence of the laws of the understanding and the laws of nature and thereby guarantees their "necessity and strict universality."[4] Meillassoux states that "correlationism consists in disqualifying the claim that it is possible to consider subjectivity and objectivity independently of one another."[5] He explains: "[T]he central notion of modern philosophy since Kant seems to be that of *correlation*. By 'correlation,' we mean the idea according to which we only ever have access to the correlation between thinking and being, and never to either term considered apart from the other." We can therefore describe as correlationist "any current of thought which maintains the unsurpassable character of the correlation so defined."[6] In a move explicitly defined as post-critical, *After Finitude* asserts the urgency of thinking antecedence, the "prior," before and beyond the *a priori*, before the synthesis that would impose its form as the only possible form of the world.

Since the world started well before "us," it could, in fact, be entirely indifferent to "us," to "our" structures of cognition and thinking. Likewise, it could be indifferent to its own necessity and could therefore prove to be absolutely contingent. This radical contingency calls for the development of a new philosophical thought. While Kant calls the study of the possibility of *a priori* knowledge "transcendental," the thinking to come must proceed purely and simply via "the relinquishing of transcendentalism."[7]

Meillassoux's book enjoyed a very rapid international uptake. The term "speculative realism," which, rightly or wrongly, is now attached to the philosophical position presented in his work, is all the rage, on the tip of every student's, every researcher's, tongue. Yet no one has undertaken the task of discussing or assessing the implications of the immense provocation involved in the proposal that we relinquish the transcendental. No one has yet thought to ask what continental philosophy might become after this "break."[8]

Break with what? According to Meillassoux, synthesis – or "correlation" – cannot, in the last instance, be legitimized, nor can it legitimate anything whatsoever, contrary to what Kant claims to have proven with the transcendental deduction. From that point on, causal necessity remains without any true grounding, in other words, without necessity. To break with the transcendental thus implies no less than to break in two the deductive solidarity between synthesis and natural order.

The a priori *and the condition of possibility*

However innovative and surprising it may be, Meillassoux's intervention in fact serves to confirm what can only be called a tradition of reading, even as it claims to be taking its leave from this tradition. His greatest contribution, his true innovation, is to give a lost edge back to this tradition. It serves to return us to the question of what to do with Kant, how to inherit from him, thereby making this a defining issue for philosophical contemporaneity.

What tradition are we referring to? Initiated by Hegel, reworked and reoriented in the twentieth century, across the range of its instances, this tradition comprises all the interpretations of Kant that observe a fundamental instability of the transcendental. This observation inevitably leads if not to relinquishing Kant, then at least to reading him against himself, paradoxically, in order to secure the deductive force of the critique. We have to recognize that any serious reading of transcendental idealism in fact always tends, thematically or otherwise, to point to and indeed run the risk of exacerbating, what may appear as its lack of foundation.

"Unstable" means both off-balance and changeable. Immediate objections arise: is it really possible to apply this term to the "transcendental," which, according to Kant, is precisely what confers on the rational edifice the solidity of its foundations? The multiple meanings of "transcendental" in the Kantian lexicon, some of which are contradictory, do not obscure the fact that Kant offers some very simple and entirely unambiguous definitions in the Introduction to the *Critique of Pure Reason*.[9] He writes that the transcendental can be understood either as a pure and simple synonym of *a priori*, "*absolutely* independent of all experience,"[10] or – if one wishes to distinguish it from the *a priori* – as the characteristic not of all *a priori* cognition, but of that which "is occupied not so much with objects

3

but rather with our mode of cognition of objects insofar as this is to be possible *a priori*."[11] "Transcendental" thus refers to the "possibility of cognition or its use *a priori*."[12] The lexicon of the transcendental is therefore one and the same as the condition of possibility. These definitions are unequivocal.

If relinquish the transcendental we must, it is nevertheless, as Meillassoux demonstrates, less because of *definitional* than *foundational* problems. The pure forms of thought, categories, judgments, principles, in fact appear to be simply established by decree:

> Kant maintains that it is impossible to derive the forms of thought from a principle or system capable of endowing them with absolute necessity. These forms constitute a "primary fact" which is only susceptible to description and not to deduction (in the genetic sense). And if the realm of the in-itself can be distinguished from the phenomenon, this is precisely because of the facticity of these forms, the fact that they can only be described, for if they were deducible, as is the case with Hegel, theirs would be an unconditional necessity that abolishes the possibility of there being an in-itself that could differ from them.[13]

Relinquishing the transcendental thus implies also relinquishing the *a priori* itself, weighing the doubt regarding the manner in which Kant undertakes the deduction of the *a priori* character of the structures of thinking and cognition – categories, judgments, principles – by taking them precisely as "conditions of possibility."

Here again, Meillassoux radicalizes a problem frequently raised in the past, regarding the fact that while the transcendental is defined as an originary condition, it cannot explain its origin, Kant simply asserts that it is *a priori*, that there is the *a priori*. A true deduction would have to show how the transcendental forms itself, how it constitutes itself as the condition of the forms of thought. Yet, paradoxically, this act of self-positing, self-formation, or self-legitimation is lacking in the transcendental deduction. The synthesis is a fact. Derrida had already commented on this: in *Glas* we read: "[T]he transcendental has always been, strictly, a *transcategorial*, what could be received, formed, terminated, in none of the categories intrinsic to the system."[14] It "assures the system's space of possibility" without this overhanging position being able to itself account for its own possibility. The transcendental, Derrida also says, is thus "excluded" from the system, which appears to be imposed on it from the outside.

This type of questioning also affects the nature of antecedence contained in the term *a priori*. "Independent of all experience" means prior to all experience. But what exactly is the meaning of this anteriority? What legitimacy, what value, does its primacy hold? In other words, how is the *a priori* founded, if indeed it founds itself? These questions have been raised on numerous occasions. The idea proposed in *After Finitude* of another possible world, one that is indifferent to "us," does not come out of nowhere. It reinforces a set of suspicions regarding the circularity of the *a priori* and the transcendental.

Is the transcendental innate or fabricated?

Let's take this thought a little further. One way or another these difficulties have always been related to what appeared to be a lack of clarity at the border between the innate and acquired *a priori* in Kant's thought. This phenomenon is all the more paradoxical in that the outline of this boundary is one of the touchstones of critical philosophy. Kant himself says as much: while they are given before all experience, the *a priori* forms of cognition are not exactly innate. In *Kant's Inaugural Dissertation of 1770* we read that the categories find their source "in the very nature of the pure understanding," but certainly not "as innate notions."[15]

We should instead understand that *a priori* elements are *acquired*. But since they are also not derived from experience, they must be considered more precisely as *originarily acquired*. Subsequently, Kant stated in 1790 that

> The *Critique* [*of Pure Reason*] admits absolutely no divinely implanted (*anerschaffene*) or innate (*angeborene*) *representations*. It regards them all, whether they belong to intuition or to concepts of the understanding, as *acquired*. There is, however, an original acquisition (*Erwerbung*) (as the teachers of the natural right formulate it), consequently also of that which previously did not exist, and therefore did not pertain to anything before the act. Such is, as the *Critique* shows, *first of all*, the form of things in space and time, *secondly*, the synthetic unity of the manifold in concepts; for neither of these is derived by our faculty of knowledge from the objects given to it as they are in themselves, but rather it brings them out of itself *a priori*.[16]

We must, of course, return to the idea of original acquisition (*acquisitio originaria*). For the moment, we'll focus on the logical problem it both contains and attempts to resolve. Original acquisition relates to the in-between of experience and the given of birth. Kant states clearly that there is no antecedence without this logical intermediary space where the circular structure of the *a priori* sits along with the transcendental. The original acquisition contradicts innatism precisely because it is an acquisition. It takes place and takes time while also having neither space nor time because it is originary.

Can this paradoxical legal case really come to the rescue of the possibility of the condition of possibility? It seems that for many readers it cannot: transcendental instability and ambiguity result directly in the poorly defined character of just such an in-between. Some claim that Kant is more "innatist" than he admits. Moreover, the statement that follows the passage cited above appears to justify their suspicion, for he goes on to say: "There must, however, be a ground in the subject which makes it possible for these representations to originate in this and no other manner, and which enables them to be related to objects which are not yet given. And it is this ground, at the very least, that is innate."[17] He says it. The constitution of our cognitive power is thus and not otherwise. The "peculiar constitution of [our] cognitive faculties"[18] is innate.

Meanwhile, other scholars firmly assert that, on the contrary, in critical philosophy one must acknowledge the work of a type of "genesis" of the *a priori*. If the *a priori* does not mean innate, then it must be that the *a priori* constitutes itself – and thus, in that case, borrows from experience! The idea had already occurred to Kant's contemporaries: perhaps what Kant did was to hide a productive power of manufacture behind the notion of the *a priori*. The suspicion of a form of labor inherent in the *a priori* was articulated by Schlosser in 1795 when he described the Kantian system as a "manufacturing industry for the production of mere forms (*Formgebungsmanufaktur*)."[19] But Kant defended himself against this interpretation straight away, responding that for the *a priori* "it is not an arbitrary *form-giving* undertaken *by design,* or even *machine-made* (on behalf of the state), but [. . . an] industrious and careful work of the subject, his own faculty (of reason)."[20] This work before "machine-made" manufacture, this industry before the handling, and this designing before the shaping, immediately reintroduce the risk of innatism. How do we defend the idea of "pure labor" without assimilating it, quite simply, to a lack of labor, to mystery, to a gift, once more?

The question arises again: how can this "before" that Kant names the *a priori* – neither innate nor shaped – find its foundation within itself without leaning constantly in one direction or another? Isn't the validity of the transcendental secretly threatened again by the disequilibrium of such an in-between, always fated to borrow something from the two extremes it rejects?

Definitive or in default?

The link between our three initial areas of investigation – time; taking the brain into account in thinking; the fate of a philosophy of radical contingency – appears in a surprising manner here, at the site of a similar problem. With the transcendental, Kant brings to light a specific mode of identification of rationality that, through the logic of an incredible coincidence, is at once definitive and in default. It is definitive, for this mode of identification confers its specificity on continental philosophy.[21] At the same time, it is in default, for this same philosophy constantly observes the founding insufficiency and must therefore, in order to continue to exist, either attempt to reinforce the transcendental, or reject it so as to find its own origin elsewhere – which, as we shall see, in a sense amounts to one and the same. Today, time, the biology of thinking, and contingency appear as the three most meaningful expressions of this complex relation to Kantian reason, a relation of simultaneous debt and separation. The three initial questions correspond to three different ways of relinquishing the transcendental: a conservative relinquishing (time); a relinquishing that does not recognize the debt (the brain); a relinquishing as an awareness of legacy (contingency).

Time

Let me explain. Reading Kant against himself in order to better find him again is Heidegger's declared intent in *Kant and the Problem of Metaphysics*, where he goes so far as to slice Kant in half by separating the two editions of the *Critique of Pure Reason*.[22] Heidegger claims that in the first edition, Kant justifies the founding formation of the *a priori* by bringing to light its temporal structure. This perspective suggests perfectly that the transcendental refers to all the structures of "transcendence," by which thinking departs from itself in order to "meet" what it encounters. This type of "ecstasy" assumes a prior orientation towards the object, a "before" that is none other than the mark of primordial temporality. Temporality thus saves the *Critique* from the assault of an artificial foundation.

And how does temporality enable Kant to elude the dual trap of innatism and manufactured production, a trap that differs in its expression, but is identical in its effect? Heidegger argues that in the first edition, temporality is unfolded in the in-between that is the playing field of the transcendental imagination. The imagination is truly the formative instance of the transcendental, which produces

Def'n

not transcendtl (

the "pure view" of everything that comes to meet it as the horizon of transcendence itself. The imagination is effectively defined as "the formative self-giving of that which gives itself,"[23] but without this act proceeding from a "doing," and at the same time without the act being annulled in the already done of an innate giving. The imagination produces images, yet these images are not artifacts for once again we are outside the alternative of innate or fabricated. Such images are in fact not beings, the register in which this alternative holds us captive. Insofar as they are pure images of time, "the pure intuitions in their representing cannot allow any beings to spring forth."[24] Instead they cause time to appear as the ontological ground of objectivity, the unity of what is, what occurs, and what is coming as the originary condition of any encounter with the object.

We have seen that Kant asserts the innate nature of the constitution of our cognitive power, in other words, the partitioning of this constitution into the two "stems" of sensibility and the understanding. But now the intermediary role of the imagination, which simultaneously ensures the "original unification" of sensibility and the understanding, opens the slit of an ontological formation into the artificial obscurity of their innateness.[25]

Heidegger explains that "originality" should not be understood in ontic or psychological terms, and that it does not refer to given presence, or even to the innateness of these images. The original can only be understood as that which does "spring forth."[26] There may be an innateness to stems, but for the root there is neither innateness nor fabrication. In fact, if it were not thus, transcendental philosophy would offer nothing but a fake version of grounding. Heidegger acknowledges this point:

> If the established ground (*der gelegte Grund*) does not have the character of a floor or base which is at hand (*ein vorhandener Boden*), but if instead it has the character of a root (*Wurzel*), then it must be ground in such a way that it lets the stems out from itself, lending them support and stability. With that, however, we have already attained the direction we sought, by means of which the originality of the Kantian ground-laying can be discussed within its own particular problematic. This ground-laying becomes more original if it does not simply take the already-laid ground in stride, but if instead it unveils how this root is the root for both stems. But this means nothing less than that pure intuition and pure thinking lead back to the transcendental power of imagination.[27]

If we follow the reasoning of the first edition, the questions of the priority of the innate or the acquired would then be nothing but quar-

rels about ontic or "anthropological" priority, incapable of masking
the ontological primacy of the temporalization of time, figured in and
through pure images of the productive imagination. Time is the root
that thereby proves to be the "essential unity" of thinking.[28] Time is
not then the "nature" of thinking, but rather its "essence" and hence
its true source, which brings it to light "in its springing forth."[29] Time
is thus the root that makes it possible to avoid reducing the transcendental to the stem.

As we know, Heidegger nevertheless considered that in the second
edition of the *Critique of Pure Reason*, the productive and tempo-
ralizing imagination loses its status as the root of transcendence.
It no longer sits between sensibility and the understanding. The *a
priori* synthesis thereby loses its time. The act of connection is now
attributed to the understanding alone. Kant "shrank back" before the
overly bold conception that represented the grounding of objectivity
in an act that formed images.[30] "The transcendental power of the
imagination is deleted as a particular grounding faculty and [. . .]
its function is taken over by the understanding as mere spontaneity
[. . .]."[31] Later he writes: "While in the first edition, all synthesis, i.e.
synthesis as such, sprang forth from the power of imagination as a
faculty which is not reducible to sensibility or the understanding, in
the second edition the understanding alone now assumes the role of
origin for all synthesis."[32]

The discourse of logic and science in the second edition consequently obscures the ontological audacity of the first. With the
elimination of the prime role of the imagination, the formative
power of the transcendental thus also disappears. The question of an
unstable and arbitrary ground re-emerges. If, at the origin, there is
no longer any forming of images of the origin, doesn't the origin then
become a mere presupposition? A given without a formative act, or,
conversely, the result of manufacture? Kant certainly continues to
accord the imagination a role in the second edition, but a diminished
one. Heidegger explains that for Kant, "if the entire ground-laying
is not thereby to collapse into itself, then certainly the accomplish-
ments of its transcendental grounding according to the first edition
must still be maintained."[33] Yet does this ground-laying, maintained
"by the force of things," remain a ground-laying? Instability and
ambiguity are back. It is thus a matter, after Kant and for Kant, of
taking up the question of time again in order to take it still further;
this reconsideration also implies a removal of the instability and
ambiguity of the transcendental. And, in the end, this amounts to
relinquishing it.

The brain

It might be surprising to find the neurobiological approach to rationality dealt with here as a philosophical approach from the outset and given the same status as the other interpretations. But I wish to emphasize the point that even negatively, even as a rejection, this approach contains resources for a genuine rereading of Kant. Continental philosophers are wrong to ignore it, or to simply relegate this reading to the analytic tradition.

From the perspective of contemporary neurobiologists, there is no shadow of a doubt that what Kant calls "transcendental" is just the generic name for a set of predetermined cognitive processes, whatever he might say about it and whatever philosophers such as Heidegger may claim. The Kantian *a priori* is quite simply innate. Kant could never prove otherwise, nor could he go beyond this conception.

But, contrary to what is too often assumed, contemporary neurobiologists claim that the elements of cognition are not in fact innate. These elements develop and appear as a result of the constant interaction between the internal milieu and the environment. This type of interaction fundamentally defines rationality as adaptability – an adaptive power that the transcendental, without a formative force and without the ability to be formed, can neither account for nor describe.

In *The Good, the True and the Beautiful*, Jean-Pierre Changeux claims that the two "stems" of cognition, sensibility and the understanding, have been opposed to one another throughout the history of philosophy and hence gave rise to the quarrel of empiricism and rationalism.[34] Changeux argues that rationalism corresponds to the most current form of philosophical "innatism." He claims that the "*rationalist* or *innatist* point of view" finds its most extreme expression in "Descartes, who writes: 'I find in myself an infinity of ideas of certain things' and also 'it does not seem [to me] as though I were learning anything new, but rather as though I were remembering what I had previously known – that is, that I am perceiving things which were already in my mind.'"[35] Meanwhile, according to Changeux, Kant "adopts a similar attitude" and pushes it to its extreme.[36] Critical rationalism is, without doubt, an extreme form of innatism.

Indeed, the transcendental is not an internal generator of variety. Without evolution, without the ability to form and transform, it is fixed – as if the pure elements of thought and cognition came ready-packaged in the mind. To understand Changeux's reasoning, it is important to see that for him the logical antecedence of the *a priori* is

10

the philosophical equivalent of genetic determinism in biology. The circularity of the *a priori* and the transcendental seems analogous to a program – an analogy that prohibits and condemns the neurobiological view of rationality. In fact, synaptic development is never the mere implementation of a program or code. On the contrary, it "includ[es] the spontaneous activity in the nervous system in addition to activity provoked by interaction with the environment."[37] One of the fundamental issues in contemporary neurobiology is "the elucidation of the still poorly understood relationship between the human genome and the phenotype of the brain,"[38] between program and individuation. This relation opens the playing field of *epigenesis*, the differentiated development that takes the middle ground between genetic determinism and the "environmental selective imprint" on the individual.[39] The origin of thinking flows from this relation, rather than from the program itself, as would still be the case in Kant. Only an epigenetic view of the "shaping of neural connections"[40] enables a break with innatism: this, then, is the unexpected consequence of a neurobiologization of the *a priori*. Once again, the transcendental is relinquished.

Contingency

According to Meillassoux, any dispute about the origin of the subject of correlation or synthesis is pointless. Whether innate or acquired, synthesis cannot mask or limit the contingency that presides over its establishment. Once again, in the end transcendental structures appear as facts and therefore cannot explain their own formation. The invariants of reason have no reason. This is why, according to Meillassoux, "if contingency consists in knowing that worldly things could be otherwise, facticity just consists in not knowing why the correlational structure has to be thus."[41] The problem is that "in insisting upon the facticity of correlational forms, the correlationist is *not* saying that these forms could actually change; he is merely claiming that we cannot think why it should be impossible for them to change, nor why a reality wholly other than the one that is given to us should be proscribed *a priori*."[42] Thus transcendental philosophy, which ought to think its own facticity and open itself to the new concept of an *a priori* contingency, implying the transformability as much of the laws of nature as of the principles of reasoning, ultimately closes itself off to this outcome and supports the stability of forms without proof. The inquiry into the true nature of stems and roots, and the determination of their origin – ontological or biological – changes nothing in terms of the problem of their factuality.

11

We must therefore instigate the "break"[43] so as to expose think-ing to "the Great Outdoors" of radical contingency, an outdoors to which it can no longer "correlate."[44] The philosophy to come discovers "everything's capacity-to-be-other or capacity-not-to-be."[45] It finds the form of its discourse in mathematics. Indeed, in the twentieth century, mathematics initiated an overhaul of classic concepts of quantity and necessity, illuminating the impossibility of totalizing the possible and of thereby assigning a stability, along with a universal and permanent invariability, to the order of the world. Mathematics thus exploded the structure of synthetic *a priori* judgments more effectively than could any philosophical deconstruc-tion. At the same time, mathematics allowed the articulation of an entirely different concept of the possible from the one contained in the notion of "condition of possibility." The de-transcendentalization of mathematics, in other words, its post-Kantian future, thus presents as the future of philosophy. This is in no way a denial of the legacy of Kantianism, for as Meillassoux acknowledges, "we cannot but be heirs of Kantianism."[46] But again this recognition coincides with a relinquishing.

Suspect spontaneity

Ontology and temporality, the biology of reason, the mathematics of contingency: these three directions of thinking all emphasize the opacity of the Kantian concept of spontaneity.

Kantian spontaneity is unable to support itself, maintain its role as initiative, or exhibit the autonomy of its formation. It will always be paradoxically derived. Rooted in time, biologically determined, or quite simply contingent.

To question spontaneity – which is just another way of expressing the relinquishing of the transcendental – clearly amounts to aiming for the heart of Kantian philosophy as a whole. In fact, spontaneity characterizes not only the activity of the understanding for Kant, but also that of reason. The spontaneity of the understanding gives birth to the categories, while ideas are born of a pure spontaneity of reason.[47] Now, this spontaneity of reason is both theoretical and practical. In Kant, "reason creates the idea of a spontaneity, which could start to act from itself, without needing to be preceded by any other cause that in turn determines it to action according to the law of causal connection."[48] This spontaneity brings us back to "freedom in the cosmological sense," to the "faculty of beginning a state *from itself*, the causality of which does not in turn stand under another cause determining it in time in accordance with the law of nature."[49] In the end, spontaneity characterizes life, the organizing force of the living being, which is the object of teleological judgment in the *Critique of the Power of Judgment.*

To suggest that spontaneity might be impure is thus to threaten the entire critical philosophy and deprive it of its most powerful weapon: the reduction of the origin, the very concept of origin, to a series of structures – the "I think," the categorical imperative, and the architecture of judgment, so many pure forms that are without any substantiality, property, or particular characteristic. Kantian spontaneity presents itself as this springing forth which, in its purity and suddenness, without duration or attributable date, cuts short the regression towards a full, essential origin, and carves out the space of its autonomy in an ontological flesh that consequently explodes. This type of space is precisely the space of the transcendental, the space of a formal reduction of beginnings.

To bring the transcendental back to a fundamental ambiguity by assigning it the value of an artificial base – innate or fabricated – therefore amounts to challenging this reduction. It implies that it could, in fact, retain certain metaphysical commitments from which it claims, however, to free itself, namely innatism or *a priori* manufacture. It undermines the purity of the link that is established in the system of the three *Critiques* between thinking, freedom, and life. We know that reconsideration of these principles is tantamount to a radical dismantling of Kantianism. In Kant there is certainly a logic of facts, but what contemporary readings are aiming at is a sort of accidental facticity due to the unsteady nature of the foundation. The fact that the foundation is poorly constructed. In very different, often incompatible, ways, the approaches discussed nevertheless all result in the decision to drown spontaneity in a more ancient past than subjectivity. For Heidegger, it is an ontological past with no beginning; for the neuroscientists, it is the night of a biological and evolutionary past; meanwhile, Meillassoux evokes ancestrality without human ancestors.

Indeed, Meillassoux argues that we should stop asking ourselves what antecedence the *a priori* names and consider that the appearance of thinking, the will, and even life are nothing more than events like any other in the long succession of ages in the formation of the Earth. A series of upheavals that arise without privilege against the background of a non-human "ancestral" past, prior to both reason and life. A past without the value of an origin and without any transcendental ambition, the past of all synthesis, more ancient than the *a priori.* This past, then, frees the philosophy to come from the impossible task of foundation and simultaneously opens the possibility *"to discourse about a past where both humanity and life are absent."*[50]

Ontology, neurobiology, mathematics: the aporia

Clearly, the three avenues that we have just opened up all converge on the elaboration of *another* rationality. This rationality goes beyond the critique of reason and refuses to legitimate thinking simply on the grounds of the exposition of its intrinsic conditions of possibility: philosophical discourse can no longer result from the consciousness of laws, nor can concepts or judgments be founded on the "spontaneity of thinking."[51] Instead, it is a matter of understanding from which non-conscious, not necessarily human and not programmed, formative instances thinking derives. The philosophical turn from the twentieth to the twenty-first century is thus notable for the in-depth search for the origin of thinking outside of consciousness and will. This is what all the attempts to break with the Kantian transcendental have in common.

At the same time, we have to admit – and this is the key point – that all these attempts to relinquish the transcendental are at a dead end. The temporalization, biologization, and mathematization of the transcendental *relinquish their object as they relinquish the transcendental*, in other words, time, the scientific perspective on the life of thinking, and contingency, respectively. We shall see that the concept of time has not survived its non-transcendental future. Destruction-deconstruction has become bogged down in the infinite poetization of a dreary messianic temporality. The idea of a gradual development of reason leads only to an acritical reductionism and positivism that can but repel the continental philosopher who entertains the idea of exploring it. As for "speculative realism," it is ultimately incapable of offering the slightest content – be it theoretical or practical – to the idea of radical contingency.

A new dialectical arena has arisen in which the destructive-deconstructive line of thought and the demand of the "real" inherent in the new injunction calling for a return to science confront each other, but without really meeting. This injunction itself conveys the conflict between mathematics and biology.

Negotiating with Kant

Given these observations, it will not be a matter here of attempting to "reconstruct" the transcendental or of "returning" to Kant. I do not seek to assert the intransgressible nature of his philosophy without discussion. Why would I? No, I do not seek to prove that the transcendental is intact or that it must be restored. What I am saying is that *the relinquishing of Kant must be negotiated with him, not against him.* Indeed, as I shall attempt to show, in Kant himself we find, at the heart of the *Critique,* the orchestration of an encounter between the transcendental and that which resists it. This encounter is not about the divide between the transcendental and the empirical; instead it is the confrontation of the transcendental and that which organizes itself without it. This is the theme of the third *Critique,* specifically in its second part: the confrontation with life.

The living being has *no transcendental status.* The *Critique of the Power of Judgment* considers the consequences of this intrusion of the non-transcendental into critical rationality. The connection between thinking, freedom, and life is a connection that undergoes transformation as a result of the confrontation between the transcendental and that which is indifferent to it. The encounter with life – the contact point between the transcendental and this indifference to the transcendental – also reveals a modifiability in the structure of categories within Kantianism, one that enables the opening of another way between innatism and fabrication.

I suggest that it is only by initiating a discussion with a certain evolution of the transcendental in Kant's philosophy that the three questions of time, a natural origin of reason, and the radicalness of contingency have a future.

Rereading Kant through his posterity and challenging him in this way, my goal is to ascertain whether or not he can allow philosophy to reorient itself in thinking the origin, reformulating antecedence, and understanding what is at stake in contemporary ontology, mathematics, and neurobiology. Once again, we have no choice but to acknowledge that neither fundamental ontology, nor biological reductionism, nor "speculative realism" manages to successfully answer the current demand for a rigorous post-critical philosophical rationality. This post-critical crisis of reason must therefore be brought back to the dialogue with Kant and, in return, we must force Kantian thought to speak about its own founding validity, to measure the force of its "before" in terms of the demands of its tomorrows.

This, then, is the main idea directing this work, a dual project that involves returning to, and closely exploring, the difference described above between the innate, the acquired, and *a priori*. The dialogue between Kant and his posterity will draw its strength precisely from the resources of this difference.

Long before Jean-Pierre Changeux, the difference between the innate and acquired *a priori* led Kant to speak about an *epigenesis of reason*, as early as in the *Critique of Pure Reason*, and, as Kant is perfectly well aware, this difference is what puts the transcendental on shaky ground right from the start.

On the "System of the Epigenesis of Pure Reason"

"System of the *epigenesis* of pure reason."[52] This phrase, which appears in §27 of the *Critique of Pure Reason* and thus belongs to the second edition, succinctly expresses, before the phrase "original acquisition," and in a more striking and provocative manner, the problems described above.

In this paragraph in the Transcendental Deduction, Kant exposes the question of the origin of "correlation," that is, as he says, the necessity of the agreement (*Übereinstimmung*) that connects the categories to the objects of experience *a priori*. The questions I discussed earlier lie at the center of his analysis. Kant claims that this agreement cannot be innate, which forces us to consider that categories are "implanted [*eingepflanzte*] in us along with our existence."[53] But nor can the agreement come from experience and derive from an empirical source. We must therefore opt for another approach: a pure production of the categories. This is the point where Kant has recourse to an analogy: the analogy of the biological process of epigenesis. He declares that, if correctly understood, the *a priori* agreement between the categories and experience opens what amounts to "as it were a system of the *epigenesis* of *pure* reason [*gleichsam ein System der Epigenesis der reinen Vernunft*]."[54]

From the Greek *epi*, which means "above," and *genesis*, "genesis" or "constitution," epigenesis refers to a mode of embryonic development through the successive addition of parts that are born from one another. Aristotle uses the term *"epigenesis"* for the first time in *Generation of Animals* to refer to the formation of the living being.[55] He writes:

In the early stages the parts [of the body] are all traced out in outline; later on they get their various colours and softnesses and hardnesses,

16

for all the world as if a painter were at work on them, the painter being Nature. Painters, as we know, first of all sketch in the figure of the animal in outline, and after that go on to apply the colours.[56]

Modern usage of the term begins in 1650 with William Harvey, who, in his 1651 book *Observations on the Generation of Animals*, presents epigenesis as characteristic of an organism in which "all parts are not fashioned simultaneously, but emerge in their due succession and order." In fact, Harvey continues, "the formative faculty [. . .] acquires and prepares its own material for itself."[57] Later, in the early eighteenth century, Maupertuis and Buffon argued for the superiority of epigenetism over preformationism, thereby instigating the conflict that became central to the midcentury.[58] The theory of growth through epigenesis – embryonic formation by progressively becoming more complex – is opposed to the preformationist theory that claims that the embryo is a fully constituted being, a miniature individual whose growth, which is only quantitative, consists solely in the unveiling of organs and already-formed parts.

Clearly Kant is referring to this conflict in §27, taking the side of the epigenetic conception of "agreement." In fact, he contrasts epigenesis with "a kind of *preformation-system* of pure reason," which assumes the existence of a "pre-established harmony" between our cognitive structures and their objects and defines categories as innate "subjective predispositions." Countering this view, Kant claims that the relation of the categories to objects develops through self-differentiation, as do all embryos. Epigenesis, the concept that finally achieved widespread favor at the end of the eighteenth century, then becomes the privileged biological figure of the spontaneity of the understanding: there is therefore a transcendental formation of the elements of thinking. This assertion cuts short both innatism and the fabrication argument: transcendental formation develops as a living individual and is not produced artificially.

However, §27 does not settle the difficulties raised previously with regard to the question of origin. In fact, it appears even to exacerbate them. How is it possible to argue for the existence of *a priori* epigenesis without contradiction? Are we not back at the strange idea of a "pure" labor, a labor before labor, an acquisition without a process? These are the alternatives: either *a priori* epigenesis is nothing but a certain kind of preformation that requires a return to innate predispositions – but again, how can we think a pure development without annulling the very idea of development? – or epigenesis is not pure and includes experience, that is, adventure and surprise, in its process.

17

Yet Kant is adamant: the relation of the categories to the objects of experience is not innate, nor can it take anything whatsoever from experience. He points to the coincidence between differential growth and the *a priori*: this is the vertiginous problem presented by the transcendental deduction. In spite of everything, does Kant eventually manage to resolve it to reveal a founding transformability in the transcendental?

By following the thread of epigenesis, focusing on all the investigations to which it gives rise, and facing up to all the contradictions and even logical impossibilities it produces, I take on the task of answering this question. The intrication of epigenesis – biological life – and the transcendental is my topic. I shall demonstrate that this intrication, which starts as an analogy, ultimately becomes an intimate relation at the heart of the critical project. Is this still to read Kant against himself? Perhaps, but it is also my way of showing that we cannot do without him, especially when it is a matter of relinquishing him.

Methodological Principles

Starting from the *Critique of Pure Reason* and the problem of the origin of pure concepts of the understanding – their spontaneity – I shall continue with the historical-practical meaning of epigenesis and end with the immense question that the teleological critique of judgment presents the transcendental.

My argument adopts the rhythm of growth of epigenesis itself. I start therefore with a textual embryo – the body of §27 – in order to follow the morphological development of the problem to other places in the Kantian corpus where different occurrences of the motif of epigenesis appear in a process of increasing conceptual complexity.

My second methodological decision involves not starting directly with Heidegger, Meillassoux, or neurobiological analyses, but rather ending up there. In order to do so, I shall start with several important readings of §27, which already question the foundational stability of the transcendental. The interpretative trajectory is therefore also epigenetic, starting with specific readings in order to progress on to more general interpretations, so as to establish both a cartography and a diagnosis of Kant's reception today.

The decision to read Kant through these interpretations may appear to be provocative, but remember that it is from the point of view of Kant's critical posterity, from his *a posteriori* development, that I set about treating epigenesis *a priori*! This approach is motivated by the

18

fact that these interpretations all cause the pendulum to swing one way or another between innatism and preformationism, on the one hand, and experience and the *a posteriori*, on the other. Concertinaed time, the indecision of necessity, the biologization of reason, the slit of contingency, these obstacles, oscillations, and impossibilities to deciding one way or another will thus all appear and reappear continuously during this exploration. Should we therefore conclude that epigenesis is a symptom of the ultimately unstable nature of *a priori* necessity? Is this the ferment of an inevitable dislocation of critical philosophy that must lead us to "relinquishing" it to its contingency today? Or will we discover, through the figure of transcendental epigenesis, a new dimension of time, an unexpected anticipation of brain epigenesis, and another logic of foundation?

Will the enigma opened within the transcendental tissue by epigenesis prove the lack of unity and coherence of Kantian thought, or will it reveal a failure of perspective by contemporary philosophy, which, while believing that it is reading Kant, in fact is reading nothing but itself?

— 1 —

PARAGRAPH 27 OF THE
CRITIQUE OF PURE REASON

Presentation of the Initial Problem:
The Origin of the Categories

In the *Critique of Pure Reason*, Kant makes reference to two specific tropes to depict the coincidence between the constitution of cognition and the systematic organization of reason, namely architecture and generation (*Erzeugung*): the edifice under construction and the engendering of the living being. The "system" thus draws its unity simultaneously from an architectonic coherence and from "grow[ing] internally," thereby allying the solidity of foundations with the intrinsic solidarity of the parts of an organism.[1] The figure of "epigenesis" enables Kant to account for the fact that the engendering of the categories and the engendering of the system are not separable and that the whole that they form develops "like an animal body."[2] Epigenesis makes manifest both the *a priori* productivity of the understanding and the architectonic tendency of reason. Thus the Transcendental Deduction and the Architectonic of Pure Reason complement one another perfectly.

Kant introduces the figure of epigenesis in the second edition of the *Critique of Pure Reason* in order to respond to objections the work received from the time of its publication in 1781. These objections were already concerned with the stability of the transcendental ground. In *Metaphysical Foundations of Natural Science* (1786), Kant mentions these objections, all of which relate to the status of the deduction. In a note, he mentions the existence of a "review" in which "Prof. Ulrich" expresses doubts about the value of the "principal basis" granted to the deduction. Kant acknowledges that these

20

doubts are legitimate and states that "*without an entirely clear and sufficient deduction of the categories* the system of the *Critique of Pure Reason* totters on its foundation."[3] Indeed,

> all use of pure reason can never extend to anything other than objects of experience, and, since nothing empirical can be the condition of *a priori* principles, the latter can be nothing more than principles of the *possibility of experience* in general. This alone is the true and sufficient basis for the determination of the limits of pure reason, but not the solution to the problem how experience is now possible by means of these categories, and only through these categories alone.[4]

The initial question is therefore the legitimation of the *a priori* agreement between the categories and the objects of experience.

Paragraph 27 of the *Critique of Pure Reason* responds to this specific challenge and illuminates the interdependence of two primary structures: first, the *a priori* origin of the pure concepts of the understanding; second, the *a priori* origin of the relation of these concepts to objects of experience. The epigenesis analogy allows Kant to prove and explain that the categories, which contain the principles of the possibility of all experience in general, apply to appearances *a priori*, meet them, and are well and truly their form. The analogy must therefore supply the adequate representation of their objective reference. Kant argues that this reference can come only from a *generative production*, the work of the spontaneity of the understanding. The validity of the system of rationality as a whole depends on the nature and solidity of this relation. It must be neither innate nor constructed.

Equivocal Generation, Preformation, and Epigenesis

What type of production is it, then? The problem is clearly articulated in §27: "[T]here are only two ways in which a *necessary* agreement (*Übereinstimmung*) of experience with the concepts of its objects can be thought: either the experience makes these concepts possible or these concepts make experience possible." Only the second conception is valid, and this conception opens "as it were a system of the *epigenesis* of pure reason."[5]

Let us examine the "two ways" that Kant goes on to further present in the paragraph by adding a "middle way" in-between them. As a result, there are in fact three ways, which correspond analogically to three biological theories of generation: (1) equivocal generation (*generatio aequivoca*); (2) preformation; (3) epigenesis.

*generation
of life on a certain
species of life?*

Of the "two ways [. . .] the first" makes experience the source of concepts. Kant states right away that this path leads nowhere. He says: "The first [way] is not the case with the categories (nor with pure sensible intuition); for they are *a priori* concepts, hence independent of experience."[6] The biological equivalent of this unacceptable possibility is *equivocal generation*: "[T]he assertion of an empirical origin [of the categories] would be a sort of *generatio aequivoca*."[7] This theory, which was already largely superseded in Kant's day, explains the appearance of life through the spontaneous differentiation of inorganic matter. It assumes that there is a different nature between the origin of generation – inert matter – and the generative principle – the vital initiative. If the transcendental deduction followed this "way," we would have to accept that the *a priori* amounts to an inorganic origin out of which the living categories miraculously appear. Like the categories themselves, the agreement between the categories and objects would arise *ex nihilo*. Obviously, it is impossible for Kant to adopt this "way." The spontaneity of the understanding is not the same type as the spontaneity of this generation, even if it, too, is called spontaneous. This approach postulates the existence of a birth foreign to its source, offspring born of nothing. By contrast, the categories are well and truly the categories *of* the understanding, born of it and belonging wholly to it. Equivocal generation, which contradicts the very idea of generation, is a theoretical monstrosity that warrants no further consideration.

The "middle way" between equivocal generation and epigenesis is preformation. According to this system,

> the categories were neither *self-thought* (*selbtsgedacht*) *a priori* first principles of our cognition nor drawn from experience, but were rather subjective predispositions for thinking (*Anlagen zum Denken*), implanted in us along with our existence by our author in such a way that their use would agree exactly with the laws of nature along which experience runs (a kind of *preformation-system* of pure reason).[8]

To accept the preformationist "way" amounts to thinking that the pure elements of cognition are innate logical tendencies, placed in us by God and arranged in such a way that their use corresponds exactly to their objects. From this perspective, right from the start the concepts and appearances "to which they apply" match each other thanks to a divine decision, in a relation of perfect coincidence, a relation of "pre-established harmony." Following this "middle way" produces the assertion that the mind is originally "predisposed," according to the economy of a relation settled in advance, to apprehend appearances according to certain laws. The laws of nature, like the law of causality, for example, would thus be imposed on our understanding arbitrarily.

Hume and Pre-established Harmony

Kant associates the first "way" of equivocal generation with the empiricist position, which corresponds to a first skeptical thesis. The inseparable pair of the first, the "middle way" is a *second* skeptical thesis. Who represents this second thesis?

The representative here is the result of a hybrid of two philosophers, Crusius and Hume.[9] A note in the *Prolegomena* (1786) helps identify the first philosopher.[10] Paragraph 36 of this text discusses the same problem as §27 of the *Critique of Pure Reason*. Kant states:

> [A]greement, and indeed necessary agreement, between the principles of possible experience and the laws of the possibility of nature, can come about only from one of two causes: either these laws are taken from nature by means of experience, or, conversely, nature is derived from the laws of the possibility of experience in general and is fully identical with the mere universal lawfulness of experience.[11]

Kant also adds that the first hypothesis, which is entirely contradictory, is defended by Crusius. His note is as follows:

> Crusius alone knew of a middle way: namely that a spirit who can neither err nor deceive originally implanted these natural laws in us. But, since false principles are often mixed in as well – of which this man's system itself provides not a few examples – then, with the lack of sure criteria for distinguishing an authentic origin from a spurious one, the use of such a principle looks very precarious, since one can never know for sure what the spirit of truth or the father of lies may have put into us.[12]

We cannot go into the certainly very unfair nature of these comments in the present context, but what is interesting is that in the *Metaphysical Foundations of Natural Science* the figure of Crusius is replaced by Hume. In this work, Kant recognizes that the problem of the validity of the foundation of the "agreement" is one that "has great importance" and that it relates back to an "obscurity that attaches to [his] earlier discussions in this part of the deduction [§27]."[13] This is when Hume appears. Contrary to his claim, the solution to this problem is certainly not about "taking refuge in a pre-established harmony to explain the surprising agreement of appearances with the laws of the understanding, despite their having entirely different sources from the former. This remedy would be much worse than the evil it is supposed to cure, and, on the contrary, actually cannot help at all."[14]

The preformationist theory of "implantation" is thus attributed here to Hume, who, in Section V of *An Enquiry Concerning Human Understanding*, in fact develops the hypothesis of a "pre-established harmony" between *a priori* knowledge and the order of nature.[15] He writes: "Here, then, is a kind of pre-established harmony between the course of nature and the succession of our ideas; and though the powers and forces by which the former is governed be wholly unknown to us, yet our thoughts and conceptions have still, we find, gone on in the same train with the other works of nature."[16]

Kant's response is the same in the *Critique of Pure Reason* as in the *Metaphysical Foundations of Natural Science*. The thesis of a preformed agreement destroys all the objective necessity of the categories. To follow this path thus amounts to accepting that the link between cause and effect "remains only *subjectively necessary*."[17] In other words, it is to claim that it is purely "contingent." Kant goes on to argue that this is what Hume is saying "when he calls this mere illusion from custom."[18]

Pre-established harmony undermines categorial necessity. If the agreement is predetermined, then the understanding can only accept it as a fact, since it does not form it, which also suggests that this agreement is arbitrary, that it might have been entirely other. Kant continues: "[I]n [the case of pre-established harmony], the categories would lack the *necessity* that is essential to their concept. For, e.g., the concept of cause, which asserts the necessity of a consequent under a presupposed condition, would be false if it rested only on a subjective necessity, arbitrarily implanted in us [. . .]."[19] Settled by divine decree, this innate agreement "arbitrarily implanted in us" would kidnap the origin from the spontaneity of the understanding, which would then do nothing more than receive it.

The Third Way

This leaves the only possible "way": epigenesis. If the categories do not come from experience, and if they do not contain the reference to objects "within themselves" either, through some innate virtue, then how can we be sure that they refer to something? How do we legitimate the *a priori* character of the objective reference?

The answer is as follows: the agreement must be thought by analogy with an embryo developing *by itself*, through the process of gradual cellular differentiation and complexification. Epigenesis presents the two-fold advantage of being able to counter any idea of a "pre-established" harmony, since it concerns autonomous development, and also any idea of empirical derivation, since development must nevertheless conform to the outline offered in advance (*a priori*) of the specific type to which it defers.

At the time of Kant, a distinction was still commonly made between the "*eductus*," produced by preformation, and the "*productus*," the result of epigenesis. The "eduction" is simply the "grown up" development of the individual that is already constituted in the egg. Conversely, the theory of epigenesis assumes that the reality of the "produced" is constituted through self-differentiation and gradual growth starting from an amorphous mix of germs.[20] François Duchesneau explains that

> for nearly a century (1672–1759) [. . .] preformationist theories of generation had reigned virtually without contest. These theories excluded any model of self-organization of life and any concept of specific force able to explain the emergence of complex structures since a primordial amorphous state emerged from the mixing of [germs]. In the mid-eighteenth century, preformationism still existed in extensively modified forms among scholars such as Albrecht von Haller and Charles Bonnet, [even if] Kant appeared to be unaware of these more sophisticated versions, directing his critique rather at the theories belonging to the previous century and to the historical context defined by the speculations of Malebranche and Leibniz during the emergence of preformationism.[21]

The triumph of epigenesis, which supplies the indispensable background to the Kantian position, takes off in 1759 with Caspar Friedrich Wolff's *Theoria generationis*, followed by Blumenbach's hypothesis of the "formative drive (*Bildungstrieb*)," developed in 1780.[22]

At a later point, I shall, of course, address the important question of Kant's relation to the biologists of his time, but for now what is important to emphasize is the fact that epigenesis offers him an escape from the two impasses of equivocal generation and preformationism and thus allows him to bring to light the generative force proper to thought. The agreement between the categories and objects can only be thought as the product of a dynamic, creative, and self-forming relation. It can come neither from a prior accord (preformationism) nor from a magical animation of the inorganic (equivocal generation). The understanding imposes, of itself, a form on the given and

25

how is epigenesis different from this?

thereby constitutes knowledge as the product of its own activity. It is therefore legitimate to argue that "the categories contain (*erhalten*) the grounds of the possibility of all experience in general from the side of the understanding."[23]

We must, then, understand the term "contain" not as the expression of an already constituted and amassed treasure that asks only to pour out before our eyes, but, quite on the contrary, as the germ of an organism that must develop in order to come into existence. The categories are the pure seeds of experience.

— 2 —

CAUGHT BETWEEN SKEPTICAL
READINGS

erhalten

Predispositions

The problem of the purity and transcendental stability of the spontaneously formative origin has still to be resolved. It's only digging
itself in deeper.

"Contain" is a strange verb. Doesn't it evoke the idea of predisposition in spite of everything? A passage from the Analytic of Concepts
seems to confirm that this is the case. Kant writes:

> We will therefore pursue the pure concepts into their first germs and
> predispositions (*Keime und Anlagen*) in the human understanding,
> where they lie ready (*vorbereitet liegen*), until with the opportunity of
> experience they are finally developed (*bis sie endlich bei Gelegenheit der
> Erfahrung entwickelt . . . werden*) and exhibited (*dargestellt*) in their
> clarity by the very same understanding, liberated from the empirical
> conditions attaching to them.[1]

If it is true that the categories "lie ready" in the mind, ready to serve
experience, waiting to unwrap their germ in a sense, then how can
Kant prove that they are not innate and that the true source of their
agreement with objects is not a kind of "pre-established harmony"?

It does seem that the skeptical argument, in its two-fold form,
immediately traps the Kantian position. First, it proves to be far more
difficult than it appeared to ensure that the epigenetic thesis is truly
distinct from the preformationist thesis in the realm of the transcendental. Second, granting experience too great a role in the so-called
"pure" generation in an attempt to prove that Kant is not preformationist runs the risk of leaning towards the skeptical argument that

27

asserts the empirical derivation of the objective reference. Readings of §27, including those that seek to defend its logic, constantly oscillate between these two tendencies, thus dragging the "way" opened by Kant into the spiral of skeptical becoming.

Again, the difficulty is how to justify and support the idea of an *a priori* epigenesis without contradiction. Of course, biological epigenesis occurs according to a necessary order; there is no improvisation in the development of the embryo. In this sense it is possible to argue for the idea of *a priori* necessity for epigenetic growth. But since epigenesis is a qualitative, rather than a quantitative, development, it is impossible for it to unfold without having an essential, unexpected dimension, despite it all. This, then, is what makes recourse to the analogy problematic: biological epigenesis is incompatible with the idea of pure development. So why does Kant choose epigenesis as the most faithful image of categorial generation?

"Formation without Preformation"

It's no help to try to relativize the analogy or minimize its role by claiming that in the end it's nothing more than a metaphor. Without exception, all the commentators of §27 claim that it is not possible to describe Kant's recourse to epigenesis as a mere rhetorical device.[2] Epigenesis is a model of development that Kant has in mind throughout his work, and it is clear that the use he makes of it is never illustrative. The fact that this model underwent modifications or corrections in the course of his work in no way detracts from its importance. The problem is that it is easier to understand Kant's engagement with biological epigenetism than with transcendental epigenetism! Paragraph 81 of the *Critique of the Power of Judgment* is well known for its defense of the biological theory of epigenesis as a system of "generations by production," brilliantly developed by Blumenbach, in opposition to the "individual preformation" system. Kant writes: "No one has done more for the proof of this theory of epigenesis as well as the establishment of the proper principles of its application [. . .] than Privy Councilor Blumenbach."[3] The support for epigenesis in the third *Critique* is entirely coherent with the analysis of the organized being as natural end proposed throughout the critique of teleological judgment. And yet epigenesis appears to counter the very idea of the *a priori*!

Let's examine this problem further. If the generation of the agreement between the categories and objects of experience finds its analogical expression in epigenesis, then it must be admitted that there is a transcendental equivalent of the tendency which forms the organism in biology. This "formative tendency" is the subject of the famous §65 in the *Critique of the Power of Judgment*, in which Kant writes:

> An organized being is thus not a mere machine, for that has only a *motive* power, while the organized being possesses in itself a *formative force* (*bildende Kraft*), and indeed one that it communicates to the matter, which does not have it (it organizes the latter): thus it has a self-propagating formative force, which cannot be explained through the capacity for movement alone (that is, mechanism).[4]

If we accept, as we do here, that at the time of the second edition of the *Critique of Pure Reason* Kant was already on the way to the definitive concept of epigenesis that he employed in 1790, then we may well consider that the problem presented by §27 is indeed what we can call, following François Duchesneau, the existence of a "*transcendental formative drive.*"[5]

Once again, I hear the retort claiming that this force is nothing but another way of describing the "formative spontaneity of the understanding," which is said to engender by itself the agreement between the rules or pure elements of cognition and the objects of experience, between the *a priori* and the *a posteriori*. But this type of response exacerbates the difficulty rather than appeasing it. Indeed, insofar as it is formative, how can this spontaneity avoid seeing itself transformed in return by what it engenders, without following a plan or predestination? How can it escape the subsequent effect of birth, the unpredictable final form of that which was no more than an embryonic bud? How can it not take into consideration the retroactive action of the result on the origin, the metamorphosis of the germ in the germ itself, without entirely depriving the engendered forms of their autonomy?

In other words, how can we think together the *a priori* necessity that presides over transcendental formation and the role of chance inscribed in the formation of the living being? The initial outline, followed by the repercussion of the *a posteriori*?

Embryonic Development is Necessarily Unpredictable

In a 1962 essay, Georges Canguilhem shed light on this difficulty in a remarkable fashion. He suggested that epigenesis is "a forming without preformation."[6] By contrast, "contrary to common sense, [preformationism] implies that the germ is already what one day it is destined to become."[7] But, in order to prove the legitimacy of Canguilhem's thesis and to deny this predeterminism, those who argue in favor of epigenesis must emphasize the role of the unforeseeable at work in all generative becoming. They must demonstrate that the individual who will be born will necessarily be surprising. That this individual cannot be born *before tomorrow*. If embryonic growth has to respect an order, it is equally true that all life in gestation is "the conquest of its figure, volume, and form." And this achievement includes a dimension of contingency. If "there is no future for a preformed being,"[8] there is at least the unpredictable in epigenetic development.

Referring to Wolff's most important work, *Theoria generationis*, Canguilhem writes:

> There are typical processes in *formatio* that are irreducible to any system of prefiguration, whatever hypotheses one may wish it to satisfy: this is the case, for example, in the doubling of a layer, the closing of an organ that was initially open, the soldering of two layers in a tube.[9]

But "we know not how to engender a tear or a duplication."[10] Epigenesis cannot be thought without its accidents, anomalies, and occasional failures. "There is no single development that can pass as a synopsis of developments."[11] As much as to say, again, that since epigenesis is always simultaneously individualizing and individualized, it cannot be entirely foreseen. As Alain Boyer also comments, "[E]ven if the form of an organ were potentially innate, it would still have to receive empirical, energetic or informational elements in order to develop according to its own logic [. . .]."[12]

And so we find ourselves back at square one. Doesn't speaking of *a priori* epigenesis amount to obliterating this unpredictability or surprise? Can *a priori* epigenesis be anything other than a simple unfolding of predefined forms? In other words, can *a priori* epigenesis be truly different from a preformation?

In some respects, the preformationist argument eludes the biological field and appears instead as an unwarranted mathematization of the living being. Embryonic development is conceived on the model of the topological occurrence of forms: formation by deformation continues from the same structure. The development of a preformed structure assumes that the increased size of the parts occurs according to the rules of perfect homeothety and homeomorphy. Preformationism thus substitutes the paradigm of geometric transformation for the mode of organic growth.

In asserting the *a priori* character of the epigenesis of the relation of the categories to their objects, and by dismissing the aleatory ahead of time, can Kant ultimately escape this reduction of heterogeneity in the developments of form? Must the engendering of the relation between the categories and experience thus occur in the elastic mode of a constant formation-deformation, with each object coming to alter the initial categorial form for a time by stretching it out in order to confirm its structure once it is coupled with it?

Yet, if it is necessary to break with this topological and elastic conception of development caused by preformationism, if we must think a free development of forms, wouldn't we immediately run into the other side of the skeptics' thesis, the one that asserts the role of the unexpected and the irreducibility of the *a posteriori* that are constitutive of epigenesis?

We certainly understand that Kant wants to escape the two traps of innatism and empiricism by showing both that the spontaneity of the understanding derives from no divine decree and that it is this force of free production that does not, however, allow experience – by which we mean the power of the outside – to become mixed up in its source.

The problem is that the biological translation of the metaphysical positions also appears to distort the situation. Does epigenesis really have a place in the transcendental deduction? Shouldn't it be countered and reduced to preformationism so as to save the transcendental from the risk of adventure? Or perhaps, so as to protect it from all preformationism, should we instead emphasize its derived nature? In both cases, it appears that we cannot but admit its fundamental ambiguity.

Readings and Contradictions

As all these readings of §27 indicate, contradictions constantly emerge and appear to be so many *a posteriori* expressions of an impossibility inherent to Kantianism. It is as if the instability of the transcendental were revealed in the series of exegetical stalemates generated by the analogy. Whatever their guiding principle, project, or purpose, all the readings – even those that argue vigorously against it – lead to a skeptical conclusion that seems to prove Hegel correct in thinking that critical philosophy is the ultimate expression of modern skepticism and that sees the same "style of skepticism" in the *Critique of Pure Reason* as that which is found in Hume.[13]

In fact, it is not readily apparent that there are two very distinct

31

camps here: the skeptics and the Kantians. Of course, as we shall see, there are resolutely skeptical readings of epigenesis that immediately wrench it away from the *a priori* and the transcendental. The neurobiological reading is one of the most striking examples of this. But the skeptical approach also contaminates readings that wish to remain faithful to Kant. Kantian critics who seek to justify the validity of *a priori* epigenesis constantly come up against the impossibility of establishing the correct measure for the relation of the transcendental and experience. Either they go too far in rejecting experience, arguing that epigenesis in Kant can be reduced again to a certain kind of preformation and claiming that the agreement should be viewed as already existing as a germ that does not transform. Or else they go too far in the role they attribute to experience in the constitution of agreement, claiming that contingency is at work in the *a priori* one way or another. In each and every case, we end up back with skepticism.

Further Methodological Details

The constitution of the agreement cannot be thought in the mathematical (topological) or mechanical models, but, as Kant says, it must instead be thought in an organic model. Now, if it is true that an organism forms by transforming, rather than by unfolding, then we must accept that the transcendental, too, is endowed with a certain transformability. Not only does it have a formative force, it also has the power of being formed. If the *a priori* is not innate, then, in a sense, it must *be born*, it must engage in the process of generative metamorphosis. The fundamental question raised by §27 is, then, the possible mutability of the transcendental.

The challenge is for this mutability of the transcendental not to contradict its *a priori* nature. The readings of §27 perceive this challenge very clearly, but they do not manage to resolve it, and this is what gives rise to the decision to relinquish Kant. This is entirely understandable. How can this kind of changeability be asserted without immediately disfiguring Kantianism and dragging it down the skeptical path? And yet, how can it not be acknowledged? How can we fail to take seriously the epigenetic analogy and reduce the origin of the agreement to the unfolding of a prior and preformed accord? Is it possible to read Kant without mutilating him one way or another, by giving the transcendental too much or too little as a creative resource? These are the aporetic directions with which we must engage before exploring Kant's response to the main question put to him by posterity.

At this point in the analysis, it is time to specify the investigative method at work in the arguments that follow. I seek to address the three exegetical directions discussed in the introduction (time, cerebral reason, contingency), starting with the multiple approaches to §27, all of which identify the instability and ambiguity of the transcendental as a symptom and therefore lead slowly but surely towards a relinquishing of Kant. It is important to show that the current situation calling Kantianism into question was prepared for throughout the twentieth century by a series of local and more ambitious interpretations, all of which concluded, one way or another, that the transcendental had failed.

I shall organize these interpretations along two main tracks: the critical track and the skeptical track, even if, as I have just shown, the line between them always tends to blur.

The critical track will also be split. On the one side we will have the readings of epigenesis that conclude with Kant's preformationism, on the other we will have the more open readings, such as those of Gérard Lebrun in *Kant et la fin de la métaphysique*[14] and Foucault's masterful analysis in "What Is Enlightenment?,"[15] which, as I shall explain, concludes with the need for an experimentation of the transcendental. Following a close analysis of §27, this track will gradually see the motif of epigenesis develop into a reflection on freedom and history.

The second track explores the hypothesis of a biologization of the transcendental as the legacy of Humean thought. The key reading for this approach is Jacques Bouveresse's article on §27 of the *Critique of Pure Reason* entitled "Le problème de l'*a priori* et la conception évolutionniste des lois de la pensée."[16] This argument will be extended through the cognitivist approach to the cerebral origin of the categories of thought. The conclusions produced by this approach claim that the *a priori* and the transcendental quite simply do not exist. The engendering of the categories of thought is always derived. If epigenesis exists, this can only be within an evolutionary and adaptive conception of truth.

This hypothesis must be fully explored, until the point where we breach the gulf that separates eighteenth-century *epigenesis* from contemporary *epigenetics* that claim the incompressible role of outside influences on the development of life. As we have seen, the paradigmatic example of epigenetic development is brain development. Drawing on contemporary descriptions of this development,

I shall push the Kantian thesis to its limit: what if, in the end, the agreement of the categories of thought with the real were simply the fruit of biological adaptation, an evolutionary process at the origin of the theory that some neurobiologists call "mental Darwinism"? What would happen to the *a priori* in the context of adaptive contingency and the assimilation of reason to the brain?

Curiously, once again we shall see that although their arguments conflict, the conclusions resulting from all the readings lead to the same observation: the idea of transcendental epigenesis is indefensible.

If skepticism does turn out to be the uninteriorized contradiction of Kantian philosophy, must we then conclude with Meillassoux that what Kant bequeaths us is perhaps only the need to further explore "Hume's problem," to claim the absoluteness of contingency beyond skepticism?

Following these investigations, we shall then return to the three initial orientations: ontological (Heidegger), cognitivist (Changeux), and realist (Meillassoux).

Again, the questions presented in §27 call for nothing less than the meaning of Kantianism as a whole, which is why I take them here as starting points. The figure of epigenesis – irreducible to a simple rhetorical device – in fact determines the fate of the transcendental, the problem that lies at the core of my reading of these readings.

— 3 —

THE DIFFERENCE BETWEEN
GENESIS AND EPIGENESIS

Why such insistence on the aporetic nature of readings of §27? To answer this question, we must examine the general meaning of the concept of epigenesis more closely.

As previously mentioned, the prefix *"epi"* means "above." "Epigenesis" therefore means literally "above genesis" or "over genesis." This literal meaning is initially very difficult to understand: just what does this "over genesis" mean? To explain it, we often transform "above" into "after." Isn't epigenesis just a development that follows a first genesis, a first source, one that takes off from it? The embryo does form starting from the seed, *after* it. Epigenesis thus appears commonly as a second genesis, one that takes place after engendering. According to an order of priority that is at once logical and ontological, paradoxically the "above" therefore appears to situate it *below* genesis.

Epigenesis and Epicenter

But let's examine this "above" a little more closely. The geological meaning of the prefix *"epi"* is very illuminating and comes to our rescue. It helps us understand "above" not as an extension that comes "over" something else, but as a *surface effect*.

In geology, the "epicenter" is the point of projection of the "hypocenter," the underground site where an upheaval emerges on the surface of the earth. The hypocenter is the underground "focus" of an earthquake, while the epicenter is its surface event. The epicenter lies exactly on a vertical line extending upwards from the underground focus.[1] The task of determining the position of

35

the epicenter, the place where destruction is the greatest, is called "localization."

This meaning of "surface" is not excluded from the semantics of epigenesis. Indeed, contemporary epigenetics actually studies the transformation mechanisms at work *on the surface* of DNA molecules during transcription. We shall return later to a more detailed discussion of the importance of these mechanisms.

For the moment, suffice it to say that all epigenesis also necessarily comes to light starting from a focus that corresponds to a hypocenter. The philosophical question, then, is that of knowing how to read epigenesis. Should it be related systematically to its focus, explained by its before, its "underground," which would then be viewed as its foundations? And should it be made secondary through this, turned into an "epiphenomenon" that minimizes its radical potential? Does recognizing epigenesis mean penetrating its underground? If so, the problem is that the reading proposed is a genetic reading, and is no longer strictly epigenetic.

But the point is that *epigenesis is not genesis*. To grant its own logic, we must remain on the surface in some way – which does not mean being superficial, but rather working where *it occurs*, at the contact point between underground and ground. We have to be able to locate the epicenter and remain at the impact point. In this way, of course, it would be possible to look below later on, but only *after* and without this changing anything that has occurred. In the case of an earthquake, in many ways the epicenter becomes primary vis-à-vis the hypocenter.

If we follow the epicentric logic, as we must, we then conclude that the seat of the "system of the epigenesis of pure reason" should not be sought *below*, in the shadows of a burying as if the circularity of the *a priori* and the transcendental needed to explain something more ancient and deeper than itself. The spontaneity defined by Kant refers precisely, and conversely, to the idea of a founding by the epicenter. *I suggest here that this founding at the point of contact – unlike the founding by the root or focus – corresponds exactly to the Kantian conception of the origin.*

This means that questions about the stability of the transcendental should not be questions that sound, questions that seek to determine the innate nature of the cognitive power or, conversely, its mysterious makeup. Stability cannot be traced back to the focus. In Kant the transcendental is a surface structure.

It is striking to note that, by contrast, the readings of Kant that we shall examine all follow a genetic order. It is only from this genetic

36

order that they draw conclusions about the instability or facticity of the transcendental foundation. By pointing to the necessary inadequacy of these readings – a genesis simply cannot account for an epigenesis – I seek to gradually reveal the possibility of an *epigenetic reading of Kantian epigenesis,* one that does not sacrifice epigenesis to that which supposedly remains hidden beneath it.

Kant is actually very clear on this point: reason is a ground (*Boden*) whose solidity must be ensured without digging. Thus, when he speaks about morals in the Transcendental Dialectic, he says:

> [W]e now concern ourselves with a labor less spectacular but nevertheless not unrewarding: that of making the terrain for these majestic moral edifices level and firm enough to be built upon; for under this ground there are all sorts of passageways, such as moles might have dug, left over from reason's vain but confident treasure hunting, that make every building insecure.[2]

Should we point out that ground without treasure is nothing? Should we object that the lack of underground depth reveals the principled uprooting of the transcendental that can hold up only via artificial means? This is what is at stake in the discussion; the challenge is to understand how a surface can be foundational and to what extent epigenesis can prove to be more fruitful than genesis.

To start, it would be best to explore blockages in genetic readings so as to gradually illuminate the fact that the decision to relinquish the transcendental comes directly from a confusion between genesis and epigenesis.

These readings do have some legitimacy. Isn't the genetic temptation immediately prompted by the problem presented in §27, which is a problem of origin, namely the origin of the categories and their relation to objects? Are we not encouraged by the actual movement of the transcendental deduction to connect this origin, which is the *a priori* itself, back to a still more originary point that is the innate constitution of our cognitive power? The relation of epigenetic engendering between the *a priori* and *a posteriori* really does appear to be inevitably returned, or even reduced, to that which roots it *deep* down. In this manner, readings of Kant often focus more willingly on accounting for stratification than on determining a point of contact. And yet, it is precisely this contact point that must be located.

Localization and Surface

But where is the contact point? Where is the epicenter? How can epigenesis be located in the transcendental deduction?

Epigenesis takes place exactly at the articulation, which Kant terms an *opportunity*, between the presence of the categories as they "*lie ready*" in the understanding and their implementation in experience. We recall the opening paragraph of the Analytic of Concepts, in which the deductive process is announced as follows:

> We will therefore pursue the pure concepts into their first seeds [germs] and predispositions in the human understanding, where they lie ready, until with the opportunity of experience they are finally developed and exhibited in their clarity by the very same understanding, liberated from the empirical conditions attaching to them.[3]

The departure from epigenesis is the meeting place between pure concepts and experience, the trigger point in their relation. It is here, at this delicate juncture, that all the difficulties arise! We note that Kant distinguishes two moments: first, the development of pure concepts by experience; second, the possibility of presenting these concepts once they are "liberated" from experience.

Of course, on first sight the genetic inquiry is legitimized by the illu-mination of what these two moments appear to leave in the shadows, the mystery of the shared origin about which Kant says nothing, namely the status of the "germs" and "predispositions" that "lie ready" in the understanding and represent the embryonic state of the categories. In order to understand, first, the development of the cat-egories "with the opportunity" of experience, and then the purity of their manifestation, is it not necessary to examine the nature of their seed and to explore the ground in which they lie virtually ready? Isn't this ground the pre-transcendental ground where the transcendental takes root? Doesn't it refer back to an innateness prior to the *a priori*? As we shall see, the theme of germs and predispositions appears to constantly threaten epigenesis and its spontaneity, condemning it to be nothing but the paradoxical expressions of a hidden preformation-ism. This threat not only hangs over the *Critique of Pure Reason*, it is also present every time epigenesis appears in Kant's work in his writing about human races as much as in the biological discussions of the third *Critique*. Consequently, it spreads its shadow over "the idea of freedom as a power of absolute spontaneity."[4] Finally, it destines

38

all genetic interpretations to join the same vicious circle, despite their apparent divergence.

Indeed, since they do not situate the epicenter of categorial or practical spontaneity precisely, these interpretations either over- or under-emphasize the importance of the way germs and predispositions lie ready. They thereby accord experience an insufficient or an overly extensive role in the movement of transcendental epigenesis. The springing forth of transcendental epigenesis, which is thus always derived, is never located in a rigorous manner.

To avoid according too great a role to experience in categorial development amounts to postulating that this development occurs according to a preformed or predisposed plan. In that case, what happens to the logic and autonomy of epigenesis? Paradoxically, some readers support the thesis of a certain preformationism in Kant as the only way of saving epigenesis by protecting it from any empirical constitution. Alternatively, minimizing the role of the originary predispositions amounts to leaving too much latitude to experience and unsettling the purity of the transcendental. Faced with these impossibilities, we can only conclude that Kantian philosophy is incapable of reducing both innatism and the empiricism still hidden within it.

— 4 —

KANT'S "MINIMAL PREFORMATIONISM"

The "Pure" Readings of §27

The role accorded to experience is insufficient. We shall follow the "critical" track defined earlier as we explore this first orientation in the readings, bearing in mind that the critical approach includes interpretations justifying the idea of *a priori* epigenesis and seeking to protect it from any contradiction or risk of skepticism.

Günter Zöller's article "Kant on the Generation of Metaphysical Knowledge," published in 1988 in the volume of collected essays *Kant, Analysen – Probleme – Kritik*, is the most representative example of this approach. In this finely wrought study, Zöller identifies a "minimal preformationism"[1] in Kant. Although this is a common thesis, it is surprising and requires careful presentation.

Zöller's objective is to justify the legitimacy of the phrase "system of the epigenesis of pure reason" by defending this epigenesis from any risk of empirical contamination. Transcendental epigenesis develops "with the opportunity of experience" but does not receive any of its own structure from it. In order to understand Kant's analogy, it is therefore important to hold simultaneously the idea of a generative and productive spontaneity and the non-empirical nature of this generating. In Zöller's view, there is considerable risk of "falsely empiriciz[ing] the transcendental deduction of the categories"[2] by granting experience a role, however minimal, in the constitution of the objective reference.

The problem is that the idea of pure epigenesis is never as pure as when it stops being an epigenesis! Zöller's genetic reading inevitably produces the contradiction that in order to restrict epigenetic freedom so as to better protect it, epigenesis becomes preformation.

40

The transcendental thus appears as a stable form, closed to any changeability, the invariance of the categories is reaffirmed, and through a series of divisions and reductions of scope, spontaneity is reduced again to innateness.

Does this offer a better foundational assurance? Are rigidity and fixity the guarantors of stability? Do they rid us of the artificial nature of the origin, or do they aggravate it? Let's trace out the argument step by step.

Zöller's reading is based on three main points.

First, the genitive in the phrase "system of the epigenesis of pure reason" can only be an objective genitive ("*genitivus objectivus*"). It should be read as "epigenesis *by* pure reason"[3]: reason engenders its forms without forming itself in the process. By contrast, a subjective genitive would suggest that reason engenders itself through the generation of the categories, and that these categories are in some ways its germs and the seeds of the system. Thus, there would be an epigenesis of reason by itself. This possibility, which would imply that reason has a self-formative drive, is unacceptable inasmuch as Zöller claims that it grants far too much initiative to epigenetic spontaneity. This spontaneity must be limited to the products of reason, and even, more specifically, to those of the understanding. Once again, then, we find that epigenesis does not affect the structure of reason and the understanding.

The second main point, which is closely connected to the first, comes from the need to define very carefully the generative production relation between the *a priori* and the *a posteriori*. Zöller argues that no commentary of §27 has yet managed this task with sufficient care. In his view, the term "'epigenesis' has been unanimously taken to designate a relation of generative production between the *a priori* and the *a posteriori*"[4] without knowing what exactly is produced by this epigenesis. Is it the categories themselves, or simply the reference of the categories to objects? Zöller opts for the second solution. Let's not forget that the categories are found to "lie ready" in the understanding. The germs and predispositions hold them, ready to go. Not only does epigenesis not intervene at the level of the structure of the faculties, but it is not involved in the structure of the categories either. It is the relation of the categories to objects, not the categories themselves, or their logical "essence," that is subject to epigenesis. Brought back to its focus – innate germs and predispositions – epigenesis once again sees its impact potential diminished.

The third main point concerns the extent of Kant's preformationism: Zöller claims that it is constant throughout his work, in all his texts. In this way it supports not only the dynamic of §27, but also all the other occurrences of the motif of epigenesis, including those in the third *Critique* that come directly from biology. Zöller's project is to show that as early as 1764, Kant held a certain concept of epigenesis that was compatible with preformationism, and that while it certainly underwent "modifications," it nevertheless remained fundamentally the same throughout his work. "Minimal" preformationism thus also prevails in the *Critique of the Power of Judgment*. The genesis of the motif of epigenesis in Kant's work thus reveals the transcendental impossibility of transcendental epigenesis!

The "System of the Epigenesis of Pure Reason": The Objective Genitive Hypothesis

Let's return to the first of the three main points. Note 4275, which appears to have been written at the same time as the *Critique of Pure Reason*, opens the possibility of the two readings of the genitive in the phrase "system of the epigenesis of pure reason." Kant writes:

> Crusius explains the real principle of [pure] reason on the basis of the *systemate praeformationis* (from subjective *principiis*); *Locke*, on the basis of *influxu physico* like *Aristotle*; *Plato* and *Malebranche*, from *intuitu intellectuali*; we, on the basis of *epigenesis* and from the natural laws of reason.[5]

Again, we see that Kant privileges epigenesis over preformation, empirical genesis ("*influxu physico*"), or pure intellectual intuition. But there are two ways of understanding the Note. Zöller argues that "natural laws of reason," a phrase rarely used by Kant, can refer either to the nature of reason itself, or to the activity of the understanding – whose laws, we recall, are the same as the laws of nature. In the first instance, if we believe that the "natural laws of reason" are synonymous with "pure reason," then the phrase "system of the epigenesis of pure reason" can be read as a subjective genitive. Reason engenders itself.[6] If, alternatively, the "natural laws of reason" refer to the understanding, then epigenesis is concerned only with the relation between the laws of thought (categories, judgments, principles) and objects. In this case, it would be an objective genitive: epigenesis is concerned with the productivity of these laws, with what they engender. The difficulty now for the genetic inquiry is to succeed in identifying where epigenesis starts and what *exactly* it engenders. This brings us to the second idea: the specific determination of the generative relation between *a priori* and *a posteriori*.

The Reductive Division of the Source

We return to Kant's claim that pure concepts develop "with the opportunity" of experience. First, this means that these concepts would not develop without experience. They would exist ready formed in the minds of children and would have no need for the sensible manifold to be operational. Kant firmly rejects this hypothesis. Experience is the indispensable opportunity for the development of pure conceptual forms, as Zöller acknowledges: "[A]lthough experience does not constitute the origin of the categories, something about experience is nevertheless an essential factor in the transcendental deduction of the categories; for it is only with respect to possible experience that categories refer *a priori* to objects."[7]

The question then is how to recognize and limit the impact of this "essential factor" without "falsely empiriciz[ing]" the transcendental deduction. The area of epigenetic unfolding sits very precisely – as we recall, along with all the difficulty it presents – *between* the production of experience by pure concepts (inasmuch as they are its form or condition of possibility) and the "exhibition" or "development" of these concepts by experience. How do we measure the precise extent of this "development"?

Zöller responds that Kant "limits the function of empirical factors in the production of such *a priori* forms as the categories to that of 'occasioning causes'"[8] whose action must not be pushed too far. Besides, the critique of Locke developed in §13 of the Deduction warns against this temptation. Kant writes:

> [I]n the case of these concepts [the categories], as in the case of all cognition, we can search in experience, if not for the principle of their possibility, then for the occasional causes (*Gelegenheitursachen*) of their generation, where the impressions of the senses provide the first occasion for opening the entire power of cognition to them. [. . .] Such a tracing of the first endeavors of our power of cognition to ascend from individual perceptions to general concepts is without doubt of great utility, and the famous Locke is to be thanked for having first opened the way for this. Yet a *deduction* of the pure *a priori* concepts can never be achieved in this way; it does not lie down this path at all, for in regard to their future use, which should be entirely independent of experience, an entirely different birth certificate (*Geburtsbrief*) than that of ancestry from experiences must be produced (*Abstammung von Erfahrungen*).[9]

The transcendental deduction and psychological derivation thus have nothing in common. It is impossible to trace back from perceptions to pure concepts insofar as sense perception leaves no trace on thought that might subsequently give rise to a form of internal perception of the categories, a type of logical experience that would be the opportunity sought, the starting point of a derivation of the transcendental elements. Zöller emphasizes this point firmly: obviously epigenesis cannot result from occasional causes, and the discovery of categorial "content" is not of the order of a perception of thinking by itself. This conception would lead to a "physiology of human understanding," in other words, to a pure and simple psychologism.

Note 4275 is absolutely clear on this point. We recall that in it Kant distinguishes epigenesis first from preformationism (Crusius), then from dogmatic idealism that denies the role of experience (Plato/ Malebranche), and lastly from the empiricism that considers that concepts and judgments are founded on "impressions" (Aristotle/Locke). Epigenesis allows for the development of the transcendental, but this development cannot come from innatism, nor from a pure intellectual intuition, nor from experience.

Hence we again run up against the difficulty for which it seems that Zöller has but one solution. In order to protect both the idea of a presence triggered by experience and the idea of the purity of epigenesis, it is necessary to isolate the true site of epigenesis as strictly as possible, identifying and limiting its source very clearly in order to better restrict its playing field.

Rejecting "Empiricist" Readings

Zöller claims that however interpreters have apprehended the production relation, they have all accorded too extensive a role to experience. This is especially the case in readings by Judy Wubnig, A.C. Genova, and Herman Jan de Vleeschauwer. We shall spend some time considering these readings.

"Form of the materials" and "epistemological environment"

Zöller argues that in Judy Wubnig's article "The Epigenesis of Pure Reason," she makes the mistake of comparing the mind to a living organism and explaining the analogy in §27 by asserting that the categories form the relation to objects while themselves being subject to a formation process.[10] According to Wubnig, epigenesis is a "theory that living organisms have the ability to take in materials and reform them."[11] Thus, for example, "the cow has the ability to take in grass and water and to form flesh, blood, bone, milk, etc."[12] The animal "forms herself from the materials she takes in."[13] She adds: "Caspar Wolff and Johann Blumenbach, who were major proponents of the theory of epigenesis, emphasized that the living organism has the power to form materials in this way. Wolff called this the 'vis essentialis' and Blumenbach called it the 'formative drive' ('der Bildungstrieb' or 'nisus formativus')."[14]

In this interpretation, Kant treats the mind as analogous to a living organism since "it has the power to form materials (sensible intuitions) into objective experience, and the categories are the principles of the organization of these materials."[15] The mind would therefore be both formative and formed. Zöller calls this conception a "constructivist phenomenalism," a theory of the fabrication – facticity – that concurs with a "neo-empiricism" that is unacceptable within the framework of transcendental philosophy.[16]

In "Kant's Epigenesis of Pure Reason," A.C. Genova also undertakes an overly biologizing interpretation of the transcendental in which we shall see that he corroborates many of the points in the contemporary "skeptical argument." In contrast to Wubnig, Genova emphasizes the production of knowledge over the production of the "material" elements of the mind. He makes reference to post-Darwinism[17] – we'll return to the legitimacy of this move – and highlights the importance of adaptation in the growth process. He seeks to explain how the theory of epigenesis argues that the complex adult organism results from the gradual self-differentiation of a relatively simple embryo in an appropriate environment.[18] This approach emphasizes the idea of *adjustment*: the formative activity must develop in a favorable environment to which it adapts. By analogy with this adaptive economy, it is evident that once the categorial agreement has been produced, it also adapts to its environment (its "epistemological environment"[19]) and adjusts itself to experience via some reworking.

Genova anticipates in a very interesting manner the contemporary meaning of epigenetics as a set of non-genetic transformation mechanisms of the organism. He writes: "Biological epigenesis and transcendental idealism function in analogous ways in their respective contexts. [. . .] The epigenetic explanation functions as a synthetic principle of dynamic interaction by means of which external environmental factors and internal genetic potentialities are related [. . .]."[20] Similarly,

Kant's principle of self-consciousness serves as a principle of interaction between the activity of intelligence and the manifold of empirical data resulting in self-produced, progressive differentiations of objectivity. Its "epigenetic" products are objects of knowledge. Analogous to the development of a biological organism, our mental faculties develop under the influence of the epistemological "environment," i.e., our process of thinking, as stimulated by sensation, differentiates itself progressively.[21]

Again, Zöller is highly critical of this type of approach, in which Kant is supposed to have anticipated the perspective of neo-Darwinism by allowing the idea of environmental factors of the transcendental. Zöller argues that "the notion of knowledge's progressive self-differentiation cannot be claimed as a well-founded interpretation of transcendental epigenesis."[22] This excessive "biologization" can only alter the purity of *a priori* production and generation.

Original acquisition and derived acquisition

Zöller considers de Vleeschauwer's interpretation in his book *La Déduction transcendantale dans l'œuvre de Kant* to be more acceptable, even if ultimately no more convincing.[23] De Vleeschauwer sets out to illuminate the meaning of the analogy by referring to the distinction Kant draws between "original acquisition" and "derived acquisition" in *Response to Eberhard* (1790), discussed in the introduction.[24]

This distinction is borrowed from the legal field. In *The Doctrine of Right*, Kant defines original acquisition as taking possession of an object of choice that has never belonged to anyone. By contrast, derived acquisition is taking the possession of a good that previously belonged to someone. Kant emphasizes the fact that the *first* acquisition opens the history of a good (the history of future property), but that it is not itself "based [. . .] on history."[25] It is derived from pure "principles."[26] These "moments," he continues, are:

> 1. *Apprehension* of an object that belongs to no one [. . .]; 2. *Giving a sign* (*declaratio*) of my possession of this object and of my act of choice, to exclude everyone else from it; 3. *Appropriation* (*appropriatio*) as the act of a general will (in Idea) giving an external law through which everyone is bound to agree with my choice.[27]

The concept of original acquisition makes it possible to think the existence of an intermediary instance between something that will never be acquired, a sort of permanent property, without an appropriation process, and that which is acquired after a series of other acquisitions ("derived acquisition"). If this situation is transposed into the field of cognition, we can see that, like original acquisition, epigenesis is situated between an innate property and a reappropriation.

Epigenetic production is just that – a production that assumes an act of appropriation, namely the appropriation by the mind from exactly that which it produces – which is another definition of its spontaneity. This appropriation assumes a movement, an extension, and a time. And yet it is not derived. The mind is the first and only acquirer of its own product. De Vleeschauwer calls this type of epigenesis "*generatio originaria*."[28]

De Vleeschauwer connects this generation to its focus: for Kant there is certainly an innate ground to the faculty of knowledge, which relates to the constitution of the mind via the dual structure of receptivity and spontaneity. Acquisition occurs starting from this base that is innate, unknowable, and unintelligible in itself. The pure forms of cognition (pure intuitions, categories, and principles) are not contained in this base – otherwise it would be a matter of innatism or preformationism. But they relate to it as their condition of possibility. The playing field of epigenesis is thus situated between an innate ground and the constitution of the pure elements of cognition.

De Vleeschauwer goes on to explain that it would be wrong to think, however, that experience has no generating power in the production of *a priori* determinations. The production of the categories and the agreement with appearances is not only the objectification of their base or foundation. It contains something "more" than that which is contained in the focus. Experience *solicits* epigenetic unfolding and thus assumes an active role in it. The analogy with epigenesis makes it possible to "mark the fact that the original acquisition is made through the direct solicitation of experience. Consequently, this term evokes Kant's simultaneous opposition to empiricism and innatism."[29]

In Zöller's view, the unacceptable argument is the idea that experience plays a role in soliciting epigenesis, which appears to distance it from its focus. He posits that to attribute a truly generative function to experience (as if it in some sense *drew out* the categories, as if it called for their birth) amounts to "assimilat[ing] transcendental epigenesis to the illegitimate concept of an equivocal generation of *a priori* forms out of an *a posteriori* material."[30]

Some Reminders about Metaphysical Knowledge

How then can we identify and define the relationship of the *a priori* and the *a posteriori* in transcendental epigenesis? How can we avoid "falsely empiricizing" transcendental epigenesis?

As I have said, Zöller insists on the need to further circumscribe the source, to situate the focus more carefully, and to further limit the pure generating power.

To understand the analogy in §27, it is necessary to recall that transcendental philosophy is an "epistemology of metaphysical knowledge."[31] Indeed, Zöller proposes that we understand Kant's question regarding the foundation from the very specific demands of this epistemology. Metaphysical knowledge is unique in that it is "1) *a priori* as opposed to the *a posteriori* knowledge of the empirical sciences; 2) synthetic as opposed to the analytic knowledge of logic; and [. . .] 3) discursive as opposed to the intuitive knowledge of mathematics."[32]

What is the relation between this definition and the problem presented in §27? Unlike logic and mathematics, metaphysics, as *a priori* discursive knowledge, must understand the relation to the objects whose definitions it presents in and by itself.

> It is Kant's original insight, historically developed between the *Inaugural Dissertation* (1770) and the first edition of the *Critique of Pure Reason* (1781), that the two peculiarities of metaphysical knowledge, its *a priori origin* and its *a priori objective reference*, are intimately related and cannot be accounted for separately.[33]

Nevertheless, the articulation of these two constitutive features, the origin and the *a priori* reference, must be justified. Indeed, discursive knowledge is knowledge by concepts alone, which means that it is not related to any intuition. How then can it be proven that the *a priori* forms refer to experience? This is exactly what the transcendental deduction is intended to prove. But the deduction is split: Kant distinguishes between the "metaphysical" deduction and the strictly "transcendental" deduction. The split in the source starts here. In order to better situate the focus of epigenesis, Zöller will show that it appears in the development of only one of the "two" deductions, namely the Transcendental Deduction.

The Metaphysical Deduction and the
Transcendental Deduction

What are these two deductions? Kant explains: "In the *metaphysical deduction* the origin of the *a priori* categories in general was established through their complete coincidence with the universal logical functions of thinking; in the *transcendental deduction*, however, their possibility as *a priori* cognitions of objects of an intuition in general was exhibited (§20, §21)."[34] Zöller interprets this distinction as follows: the metaphysical deduction is about the problem of origin understood as the first base or focus; the question of the innateness and thus the impenetrable nature of the structure of our cognitive power. The transcendental deduction is, for its part, about the proof of the *a priori* reference of the categories to objects. "The unintelligibility of our cognitive constitution pertains directly only to the issue of *a priori* origin as addressed in a *metaphysical* deduction. The issue of the objective reference [the agreement of the categories to objects], the genuine concern of a *transcendental deduction*, is not directly affected by it."[35] Zöller even goes so far as to say that epigenesis is concerned only with the objective reference of the categories, not the categories themselves, whose origin would then be dealt with properly in the metaphysical deduction.

> It is this *a priori* reference of the categories to possible experience (experience considered in its principal conditions) that is disclosed in the transcendental deduction and figuratively represented in the phrase, "the epigenesis of pure reason." There is "epigenesis of pure reason" insofar as the understanding generates *a priori* knowledge concerning possible experience. This generation of non-empirical, metaphysical knowledge of possible experience comes about in what Kant considers the "first application" (B152) of the understanding to sensibility.[36]

Epigenesis is only about the agreement, the *Übereinstimmung*, and not, he repeats, about "the essence" of the categories.

The analogy of *generation* is therefore concerned not with the origin of the categories (which are not, strictly speaking, engendered), but rather with their objective reference only. In other words, there is no *epigenesis of the categories*, there is only an *epigenesis of the relation of the categories to objects*. I should add that the metaphysical deduction also covers the dual problem of the origin of the categories and the agreement of the categories with the objects; it reveals the dynamic relation between the two. But epigenesis, developed solely

49

in the transcendental deduction, deals only with the second problem. And this is supposed to prove that the transcendental is well and truly founded and that it exhibits no instability, nor any facticity. "Correlation" – the objective reference in this instance – is well rooted in a ground more ancient than itself, a legitimate ground that is also recognized in the metaphysical deduction.

Preformed Epigenesis

Zöller grants this ground, this innate focus, the role of a restrictive condition that leaves epigenesis very little initiative. The unfathomable nature of the foundational structure of our cognitive power limits *a priori* production. Epigenesis is autonomous, and yet it is not free. Epigenesis cannot do as it wishes.

Zöller argues that Kant cannot explain why we have these specific categories and them alone, nor why we have only these types of judgments. Indeed in §21 Kant writes:

> [F]or the peculiarity of our understanding, that it is able to bring about the unity of apperception *a priori* only by means of the categories and only through precisely this kind and number of them, a further ground may be offered just as little as one can be offered for why we have precisely these and no other functions for judgment or for why space and time are the sole forms of our possible intuition.[37]

There is, therefore, a first base, in the sense of a natural given without origin: the structure of our mind. Then there is a second natural given, from whence emerges an activity, the epigenetic production of the objective reference. The objective reference is a starting point for "theoretical self-determination." And yet it is destined neither to exhaust nor to transgress the first base. In other words, epigenesis can produce, but it cannot invent anything.

In §24 of the *Critique of Pure Reason*, Kant states:

> [S]ince in us a certain form of sensible intuition *a priori* is fundamental, which rests on the receptivity of the capacity for representation (sensibility), the understanding, as spontaneity, can determine the manifold of given representations in accord with the synthetic unity of apperception, and thus think *a priori* synthetic unity of the apperception of the manifold of *sensible intuition*, as the condition under which all objects of our (human) intuition must necessarily stand, through which then the categories, as mere forms of thought, acquire objective reality [. . .].[38]

Zöller draws two paradoxical conclusions from this passage. First, he notes that Kant asserts the power and autonomy of the spontaneity of the understanding. The production of the relation to objects should be understood as *auto-affection*. It results from the intrasubjective process by which the understanding self-determines. In other words, spontaneity affects itself, which corresponds to the production of a pure sensible manifold. Thus, the understanding "can determine the manifold of given representations in accord with the synthetic unity of apperception."[39]

But the passage also establishes a *limit* to this spontaneity, one that acts on the basis of the form of intuition that lies "in us," in other words, from the innate receptivity of our cognitive power. Thus there is both autonomy (engendering of the objective reference by the understanding) and restriction (our cognitive power, which obviously also includes spontaneity itself, is as it is, while the structure of auto-affection is restricted). There are both original acquisition and appropriation, but the process is *constrained* even within freedom. What is this called other than an originary *preformation*?

We then understand what authorizes Zöller, who follows this second approach, to speak of a "*minimal preformationism*" in Kant. The engendering takes place starting from a matrixial base that retains more than it gives:

> [A]lthough the *a priori* principles of experience are not actually pre-formed in the understanding, there are nevertheless principal limits to the generation of *a priori* knowledge, limits that are imposed not *qua* empirical facts but *a priori*. [. . .] [T]here is evidence for a minimal preformationism in Kant's concept of transcendental epigenesis.[40]

Again, we end up with a paradoxical conclusion. The phrase "system of the epigenesis of pure reason," understood according to the objective meaning of the genitive, concerns the origin of the objective reference alone and epigenesis is limited by the preformation of the innate stem of the *a priori*. The understanding is spontaneously productive of the agreement between objects and the categories *as they stand*. The agreement certainly *happens*, but this facticity is absolutely pure, without process.

> It is important to notice though that the facticity thus introduced into the epistemology of *a priori* knowledge is not an empirical one. [. . .] Although the categories as such [. . .] are simply *given a priori*, their necessary and universal reference to possible experience [. . .] is *made a priori*, namely it is generated through *a priori* theoretical

self-determination. The specific character of the generation process constituting the *a priori* objective reference of pure reason can be aptly determined as an "epigenesis of pure reason."[41]

Thus, preformationism, a key element in the skeptical argument, serves here to support the critical approach so as to save *a priori* epigenesis from any empiricist – in other words, again, skeptical – contamination.

— 5 —

GERMS, RACES, SEEDS

Zöller pursues his genetic inquiry by examining the sources of the Kantian concept of epigenesis and its evolution throughout his work. In making this, his third main point, he seeks to show that despite the modifications this concept undergoes up until its definitive version in the *Critique of the Power of Judgment*, it retains the preformationist influence to the end.

Four Main Exploratory Tracks

What was Kant's concept of epigenesis in 1781? What exactly did it involve? In asking these questions that are essential for understanding §27, Zöller proposes a genesis of Kantian epigenesis and concludes that preformationism is present throughout his work.

It is likely that until he discovered Blumenbach's theory of the formative drive (*Bildungstrieb*), Kant based his views on Wolff's *Theoria generationis*, even though he never makes any explicit reference to the text. There are no grounds for arguing unequivocally that he could have read Blumenbach's *Über den Bildungstrieb und das Zeugungsgeschäfte* (1780/1) before the *Critique of the Power of Judgment*, even though commentators think it probable that he was aware of it during the period between the two versions of the first *Critique* – as the review of Herder's *Ideas* seems to attest.[1] Consequently, it is difficult to know precisely which view of epigenesis §27 supports.

Fortunately, there is proof of the presence of epigenesis in Kant's texts prior to 1787. This proof is found in the posthumous work and lecture notes, which, despite the chronological uncertainty of their publication, offer precious clues. Notes 4104, 4275, 4446, 4851, and 4859 develop the idea of "intellectual epigenesis," another name for the transcendental epigenesis of the origin of the categories.[2] On the question of life, the 1763 text *The Only Possible Argument in Support of a Demonstration of the Existence of God* confirms that Kant was aware of the "epigenetic turn" that Maupertuis and Buffon introduced to biology.[3] The concept of epigenesis also appears in the works on the variability of the human species, a central problem that, from around 1775, led Kant to his interest in theories of generation. The main instances appear in three texts on the difference of the human races, the first of which precedes, and the second and third of which follow, the *Critique of Pure Reason: Of the Different Races of Human Beings* (1775); *Conjectural Beginning of Human History* (1786); and *On the Use of Teleological Principles in Philosophy* (1788). But, as we shall see, the most important text on this topic, on which Zöller focuses all of his attention, is Kant's 1785 two-part review of Herder's 1784 book, *Ideas for the Philosophy of History of Humanity*.[4]

There are four principal contexts where the concept of epigenesis is deployed: the origin of the categories; the discussion of Herder's "vital force"; the question of human races and their variability, starting from a single stem; and the exhibition of the "formative drive" at work in the living being, developed in the *Critique of the Power of Judgment*.

According to Zöller, a single idea traverses all of these contexts, unifying each occurrence of epigenesis, whether it dates from before or after the first *Critique*. In his view, this idea supports the thesis of Kantian preformationism: it is the constant affirmation of the existence of germs and original predispositions,[5] both of which limit the amplitude and power of epigenesis. We have just examined the extent of this motif in the Transcendental Analytic, which asserts the presence of the "germs" of the categories in the understanding.

One awkward fact is that in §81 of the *Critique of the Power of Judgment*, Kant does indeed identify epigenesis with a system of "generic preformation." He writes: "[T]he system of generatings as products is called the system of *epigenesis*. The latter can also be called the system of *generic preformation*, since the productive capacity of the progenitor is still preformed in accordance with the internally purposive predispositions that were imparted to its stock, and thus the specific form was preformed *virtualiter*."[6]

As we shall see, some commentators do not consider this "virtual preformation" to be the avowal of preformationism at all, and see in it no contradiction with Kant's declared epigenesist position. Yet the ambiguity of the expression must be acknowledged. Zöller certainly recognizes it. He reminds us that, according to their technical meaning, "[pre]dispositions (*Anlagen*) are opposed to germs (*Keime*)."[7] The "dispositions [predispositions]" are mere "wrappings" that unfold in a mechanical order, while the "germs" are the conditions of the development of new parts. In other words, predispositions make sense in an economy of preformation, while germs make sense in an economy of epigenesis. Yet it seems that Kant makes frequent use of the two without distinction.[8] While we have seen that he differentiates the *producta* (the life that develops through self-differentiation) from the *educta* (which are but the unfolding of a first form), he still blurs the line between the two because he does not always rigorously distinguish between them (this is also the case in the passage from the Transcendental Analytic analyzed above). For Zöller, this state of affairs, in the order of natural history, establishes the pre-eminence and essential nature of the first focus: are "productions" not determined as "eductions," if considered in terms of the undatable and unintelligible stem from which they originate? Doesn't this stem allow us to consider all germs as predispositions? And again, shouldn't epigenesis be understood, as it emerges, as a derived source that owes its strength to the subterranean and primary obscurity of the originary source?

As the innate base of *a priori* knowledge, this focus would then also be the sole stem of the human races, as well as the one that appears in the third *Critique* in the term "original organization," the first form, the inaccessible source of life that gives life its reason. Thus, in different places in his work, Kant is said to deploy many versions of a single limit. The challenge is therefore to understand how this limit keeps company with the otherwise explicit rejection of preformationism.

Kant to Herder: The Limits of the Formative Drive

I shall begin the examination of occurrences of epigenesis with the review of Herder's *Ideas*, a key element in this debate. Zöller argues that the review implicitly shows what must be viewed as Kant's "reservations" about epigenesis. It also makes it possible to illustrate the precise relation these reservations have to the transcendental in Kant's work as a whole.

In his review, Kant pays tribute to the achievement of Herder's text while firmly resisting the conception of "vital force" elaborated within it. This concept is directly inspired by Blumenbach's "formative drive." Indeed, Herder develops his own concept of *Bildung* (formative education) primarily with reference to Blumenbach's refutation of preformationism and defense of epigenesis.[9]

Kant does not mention Blumenbach in his review. Yet it is as if he were offering a first version of the analysis of the "formative drive" that he was to present in §81 of the *Critique of the Power of Judgment*. This version, like the one in the third *Critique*, presents an apparent attack on Herder's interpretation.

What is this "formative drive" then? Blumenbach explains as follows:

> In all living creatures, from man to maggot and down, from the cedar to the mold, there lies a specific, inborn, effective drive that acts throughout life to take on from the beginning its determinate form, then to maintain it; and if it be destroyed, where possible to repair it. A drive (or tendency or striving, by whatever term one calls it) that is as wholly distinct both from the general properties of the body in general, as from the other forces of the organized body in particular; the one seems to be the first cause of all generation, nutrition and reproduction, which, to fend off all misinterpretation and to distinguish it from the other forces of nature, I here give the name of the *Bildungstrieb* (*nisus formativus*).[10]

The "formative drive" is, then, the organic instinct that gives life its general configuration, allows it to conserve and take care of itself, as well as to reproduce and repair itself. Kant argues that Herder grants it too much force, a force that is independent of any internal predisposition or germ. He writes: "The author does not reckon with germs here but rather with an organic force, in plants as much as animals."[11] This drive without any origin other than its own spontaneity is then characterized by its total freedom in morphological improvisation. For Herder, this type of freedom defines the epigenetic drive exactly, at work in the constitution of natural forms. It is important to note that in contrast, until 1790, Kant maintained a definition of epigenesis as "generic preformation," a kind of supervised freedom.

Herder distinguishes two meanings of epigenesis: an old meaning and a contemporary meaning. It is important to mention that to complicate things still further, epigenesis was sometimes used to refer to a type of mechanical growth through the addition of new parts. To differentiate the new meaning from this previous alternate meaning, Herder calls contemporary epigenesis, as presented by Blumenbach, "genesis." Yet it is true that Herder does not view this "genesis" as proceeding from any "germ." He rejects preformationism entirely:

No eye has ever seen preformed germs. If one talks of an epigenesis, one does so inappropriately, as if the members grew on *from outside*. Rather, there is a formation (*genesis*), an effect of *internal forces*, for which nature has prepared a matter, that they are supposed to organize (*sich zubilden*), in which they are supposed to manifest themselves.[12]

Herder develops his own interpretation of the organic growth caused by "internal forces" that cannot be reduced to mechanical causes. Hence his rejection, following Blumenbach, of the idea of "germs," which, as we have seen, implies a "wrapping" lying in wait for its pure and simple unwrapping. The unlimited "genetic force" (formative force or epigenesis) is opposed, in its very freedom, on the one hand, to any logic of encasement and, on the other, to occasional-ism (equivocal generation).

Even as he agrees with Herder regarding the superiority of the epigenesist theory, Kant still considers it necessary to restrict the unfolding of the formative drive to a given number of forms of pos-sible life. In his review, Kant writes: "[W]ith this the reviewer fully concurs" with Herder, but "only with this reservation": the organ-izing cause is "limited by its nature only perhaps to a certain number and degree of differences."[13] Once these have been established, the formative force is "not further free to form yet another type under altered circumstances." Kant goes on to say we might very well "then call this natural vocation of the forming nature also 'germs' (*Keime*) or 'original predispositions' (*Anlagen*)." In his view, this does not amount to a return to preformationism. Nor is it "thereby regarding the former as primordially implanted machines and buds that unfold themselves only when occasioned [. . .], but merely as limitations, not further explicable, of a self-forming faculty, which latter we can just as little explain or make comprehensible."[14]

In other words, Kant does not consider the formative force to be protean. The repertoire of the formation of forms is limited. And while the terms that describe this limitation – germs and original pre-dispositions – are identical to those used by the opposing camp, they do not have the same meaning or the same function. For the propo-nents of preformationism, they express predetermination, the content of the embryonic envelope that will simply unfold. For the critical philosopher, they refer to the natural boundaries of organic growth, the register of types that the formative drive cannot transgress. They are the limits that this force "imposes on itself."

Epigenesis and Anthropological Variety

After presenting Herder's theory of epigenesis at length in the first part of the review, in the second part, Kant returns to the concept of "formative drive" and its ability to explain biological adaptability to the variety of external circumstances. Kant addresses this key question in his texts on the races and "the climatic difference of human beings."[15]

Herder considers the "formative drive" to be the principle of anthropological variety, the diversity of the races and types of humans. Kant agrees with him on this point but questions Herder's conception of the relation between fixity and contextual variability of the drive. For Herder, the "force" is able to modify itself indefinitely depending on climate, thereby adapting itself to any context. Kant explains that Herder "assumes as its cause a principle of life, which appropriately modifies *itself* internally in accordance with differences of the external circumstances."[16] Hence Herder's formative drive is not only unlimited in its creative resource, it is also capable of transforming itself by adapting to circumstances. This is the point that Kant takes issue with, for mutability too must have its limits!

Let us return to the passage cited earlier. Kant says that in this "force" he cannot but see "limitations, not further explicable, of a self-forming faculty, which latter we can just as little explain or make comprehensible." Yet again these limitations are the "germs" and "original predispositions" that constrain the variability of the type and prevent it from transforming so as to become monstrous or degenerated. Whatever the circumstances, the type of species, especially the human species, remains the same! Kant reacts very strongly against what he views as a sign of an "insupportable hylozoism."[17] The "formative drive" with its unbridled freedom, as conceived by Herder, appears to come from an idea of "radical spontaneity in matter itself."[18] Kant is intransigent when it comes to the fact that *the formative drive is not, in itself, its own origin.* He states this firmly:

> [T]he unity of the organic force, which, as self-forming in regard to the manifoldness of all organic creatures, and later in accordance with the difference of these organs working through them in different ways, is supposed to constitute the entire distinctiveness of its many genera and species – this is an idea that lies entirely outside the field of the observational doctrine of nature and belongs merely to speculative philosophy: but even there, if it were to find reception, it would wreak great devastation among the accepted concepts.[19]

The consequence of the inaccessibility of the source – a source that can only have the status of a question – appears to be that, as John Zammito writes, "even epigenesis implied preformation: at the origin there had to be some 'inscrutable' (transcendent) endowment, and with it, in his [Kant's] view, some determinate restriction in the species variation. Thereafter, the organized principles within the natural world could proceed on adaptive (mechanical) lines."[20]

We always return to the same idea: the genesis of epigenesis leads back to a stem that resists it. The formative drive – spontaneity spontaneously restrained – is limited at the source.

On Human Races

In his texts on human races, Kant examines the organic archetypes that lead to the production of intraspecific varieties. Here too we find the idea that the development of organized beings comes from "germs" and "predispositions" that are realized and differentiated through the combining of male and female seeds. Epigenesis thus describes the spontaneous unfolding of the organizing forces at work in this combining. But the content of this unfolding appears to be present already as a predisposition inherent to the generative power (*Zeugungskraft*), which restricts the fate of occasional developments depending on circumstance. The functional preordination of germs and predispositions depending on specific type cannot be transgressed: the contingent developments that are varieties and organic variations are restricted both in number and in quality.

The 1776–7 text *Of the Different Races of Human Beings* presents the idea of a stem common to the species, which differentiate by "subspecies," "strains," and "varieties." All of these are without doubt the fruit of "germs" or "natural [pre]dispositions,"[21] that prevent "modifications" from reproducing themselves. Kant writes:

> [W]hat is supposed to propagate itself must have laid previously in the generative power as antecedently determined to an occasional unfolding in accordance with the circumstances in which the creature can find itself and in which it is supposed to persistently preserve itself. For the animal must not be subject to a foreign intrusion into the generative power, which would be capable of gradually removing the creature from its original and essential destiny and of producing true degenerations that would perpetuate themselves.[22]

In 1785, Kant repeated his support for the argument of the unique stem:

[I]n the germs of *a single first phylum*, so that the latter would be suitable for the gradual population of the different regions of the world, can it be comprehended why, once these predispositions developed on occasion and accordingly also in different ways, different classes of human beings had to arise, which subsequently also had to contribute to their determinate character necessarily to the generation with each other class, because this specific character belonged to the possibility of its own existence, thus also to the possibility of propagating its own kind, and was derived from the necessary first predisposition in the phyletic species.[23]

Later, in *On the Use of Teleological Principles in Philosophy* (1788), we encounter the idea of variation according to an end, which again restricts the extension of the intraspecies mutability. Kant writes:

[N]ature has to be viewed not as forming in complete freedom but as only developing and as predetermined with respect to those varieties through original [pre]dispositions, just as is the case with the racial characters. For in the variety too, there is to be found purposiveness and corresponding suitability, which cannot be the work of chance.[24]

Lastly:

I myself derive all organization from *organic beings* (through generation) and all later forms [. . . from] *original predispositions*, which were to be found in the organization of its phylum. Such development can often be seen in the transplanting of plants. How this phylum itself *came about*, this problem lies entirely beyond the limits of all physics possible to human beings.[25]

The limitation on the variability of the original dispositions contained in the stem (focus or hypocenter) may then be understood as the equivalent, in the field of anthropology, of the limitation of the production of pure forms in the field of knowledge. In both instances, epigenesis is restricted and restrained by a preformationism that prevents uncontrolled proliferation of morphological deviations. The refusal to grant too great a role to experience in intellectual epigenesis can be interpreted, by analogy with the critique of Herder's vital force, as an unwillingness to consider the transcendental not only as a formative power (of the categories) but also as a malleable instance, susceptible to self-transformation, to varying in its productions according to circumstance and the consequences of its development.

"Intellectual" Epigenesis

It is directly in line with the arguments exposed in the Herder review that Zöller is able to return to the problem of the categorial epigenesis and conclude that Kant's position is unchanging.

But what are the antecedents for an epigenesis of the categories? In Kant it is prefigured first by the notion of "psychological" epigenesis, and then by that of "intellectual" epigenesis. Zöller writes: "An examination of Kant's *Reflexionen zur Metaphysik* [*Notes on Metaphysics*], compiled from marginal notes and commentaries on his copy in use of Baumgarten's *Metaphysica* and from loose leaves of varying provenance, reveals two distinct applications of the term 'epigenesis' for the presentation of metaphysical problems and their suggested solutions."[26]

The first "application" emerges with the commentary on Baumgarten's meditations on the "*origo animae humanae*" – origin of the human soul – in rational psychology. In order to describe the material psychological principle according to which the souls of children are engendered by and from those of their parents, Kant uses the phrase "*epigenesis psychologica.*" In the same way that in biology, epigenesis refers to the entirely separate production of a new being, psychological epigenesis describes the fact that new souls result from reproduction. Kant did not return to this argument, yet it already contains an essential element: the idea of combining a generic model with the independence of the offspring that come of it.

The second application is concerned precisely with the origin of "transcendental" concepts. In at least four Notes, epigenesis is no longer presented as "*epigenesis psychologica*" but instead as "*epigenesis intellectualis.*" The latter term refers to the emergence of a type of knowledge that has its source in finite understanding and is not derived from divine or intuitive understanding.[27] We have already mentioned Note 4275, in which Kant situates epigenesis between the three positions of preformationism (Crusius), empiricism (Aristotle/Locke), and intellectual intuition (Plato/Malebranche).[28] In Note 4851, he reconsiders the question of determining "whether [pure] concepts are mere *educta* or *producta* [...] (*producta* either through physical (empirical) influence or through the consciousness of the formal constitution of our sensibility and understanding on the occasion of experience, hence *producta a priori*, not *a posteriori*.)"[29] In the same way, in Note 4859, he wonders about the possibility of the "origin of transcendental concepts [...] through intellectual epigenesis (*per epigenesin intellectualem*)"[30] – a process of discursive engendering in contrast to the process of intellectual intuition. The response is clearly in the affirmative. Intellectual epigenesis is certainly an *a priori* production, one that is spontaneous, but it nevertheless cannot be cut off from its seed, which is buried so deep that it is only the echo or outer showing of them.

Of course, cognition is entirely produced, proceeding from a generative, dynamic synthesis. It is in no way the copy of a pre-existing order and appears instead far more as a production of itself and as the forms of the objects themselves. Indeed, metaphysical knowledge consists in the anticipation of the formal *a priori* characteristics that will be exhibited by the objects of experience. Nevertheless, just as there are a limited number of variations in the human species and in living species in general, the repertoire of categories is limited in its germinating prefiguration. The agreement with the objects of experience is never modified either. Zöller thus implies that in some senses Kant adds to his use of epigenesis a "critique of epigenetic reason" in order to limit the claims of the formative force in both the biological and the transcendental fields. The genetic inquiry leads epigenesis back to the invariability of its focus.

The *Critique of the Power of Judgment*

Finally, what about the *Critique of the Power of Judgment*? It appears that there are no remaining difficulties for understanding the phrase "generic preformation" from §81: it means that "the productive capacity of the progenitor is still preformed in accordance with the internally purposive predispositions that were imparted to its stock, and thus the specific form was preformed *virtualiter*."[31] The same principle is at work here.

It is the whole design of the specific form that is preformed. Epigenesis, be it intellectual, anthropological, or biological, thus always appears to be the development of pre-existing entities. In §81, as noted in chapter 2 above, Kant states: "No one has done more for the proof of this theory of epigenesis as well as the establishment of the proper principles of its application, partly by limiting an excessively presumptuous use of it, than Privy Councilor Blumenbach."[32] Now, according to Zöller, the end of the sentence ("presumptuous use") is a reference to Herder. "An excessively presumptuous use" of the theory of epigenesis would, in fact, be Herder's use of it in the *Philosophy of the History of Humanity*. We have seen that according to Kant this use bears the mark of hylozoism, rightly or wrongly. And it is precisely this hylozoism that is so strongly rejected in the final lines of the paragraph: "For he [Blumenbach] rightly declares it to be contrary to reason that raw matter should originally have formed itself in accordance with mechanical laws, that life should have arisen from the nature of the lifeless, and that matter should have been able to assemble itself into the form of a self-preserving purposiveness by itself."[33]

Blumenbach distinguishes the "formative drive" from the other vital forces, but especially, as we have seen, from any *physical* force of the body in general. Kant does not fail to remind us of this: "He [Blumenbach] begins all physical explanation of these formations with organized matter."[34]

Thus, Kant asserts that the "formative drive" cannot be reduced to a "merely mechanical formative force," as Herder's anarchic vital force appears, ultimately and paradoxically, to be. Indeed, this force that is capable of everything is a force without reason. A mad mechanism. An uncontrolled automaton. Nevertheless – and in this lies the challenge – Kant declares that in opposition to Herder's interpretation, we must assume that a mechanical force originally limits the formative drive and thereby protects it from the mechanism, preventing its possible degeneration into an unchained motive power. Kant writes:

> [Blumenbach] leaves natural mechanism an indeterminable but at the same time also unmistakable role under this inscrutable *principle* of an original organization, on account of which he calls the faculty in the matter in an organized body (in distinction from the merely mechanical *formative force* that is present in all matter) a *formative drive* (standing, as it were, under the guidance and direction of that former principle).[35]

Life thus borrows from the mechanism so as to avoid becoming mechanical. This is the problem at the source. In any case, it is the same problem that Zöller faces. In biological order, the original organization plays a role similar to that of an innate bedrock, which is the constitution of our cognitive power. The focus refers to some unfathomable mechanical principle. The difference between this "mechanism" and Herder's hylozoism is that it serves life by restricting its inventive abilities, rather than giving free rein to its monstrosity. Zöller insists that Kant's concern is to emphasize as much as possible the limits of a self-forming vital force.[36] The analogy of the growth of an organic body and the growth of knowledge is based on the same idea of constrained productivity.

A "Maximal" Preformationism?

John Zammito is even more explicit in the conclusions he draws. Arguing that the language in the first edition of the *Critique of Pure Reason* is "unequivocally [. . .] *preformationist*"[37] in its analogies, he claims that throughout his work, Kant is quite simply unclear when it comes to epigenesis. Referring to the same texts as Zöller, he argues that the idea of *a priori* epigenesis is contradictory and ultimately indefensible. Understood literally, rather than serving it, pure epigenesis could do nothing but ruin the transcendental edifice: "Epigenesis incites a fundamental erosion of Kant's boundary between the constitutive and the regulative, between the transcendental and the empirical: a naturalism beyond anything Kant could countenance."[38]

According to this view, Kant never really supported epigenetic theory. Beginning with a reading of §27, Zammito insists again:

> My contention will be that neither before nor after this now somewhat famous analogy was Kant entirely comfortable with the idea. Indeed, I argue that Kant proved resolutely hostile to the idea in both published and unpublished sources from his first mention of it in the 1760s until as late as 1787, making the comment at B167 all the more perplexing. Further, I argue that in the immediately ensuing years leading up to the publication of the *Critique of Judgment* in 1790, and in particular in relation to Johann Friedrich Blumenbach, Kant remained more ambivalent than has frequently been contended. It is not altogether clear that Kant and Blumenbach really understood the full implications of their respective positions and consequently may well have overestimated the convergence of their views.[39]

The critical legitimacy of the analogy in §27 must therefore be proven against the analogy! Once again, the only way to save Kant from skepticism is to have him accept something skeptical: preformationism, for example, which, as we have seen, is an expression of skepticism. Epigenesis could then be renamed preformation so as to be granted the right to critical philosophy.

Yet how can we not think of Kant's attack in §27 against the skeptical argument of pre-established harmony according to which "the categories were neither *self-thought a priori* first principles of our knowledge nor drawn from experience, but were rather subjective predispositions for thinking, implanted in us along with our existence [. . .]"?[40] Doesn't pre-established harmony, "a kind of *preformation-system* of pure reason," amount to destroying the *necessity* of the pure elements of knowledge? Against this "system," Kant also writes that the "decisive" objection is "that in such a case the categories would lack the necessity that is essential to their concept."[41] Indeed, if the categories were based only "on a subjective necessity, arbitrarily implanted in us," they, along with the order of nature of which they are the form, would be entirely contingent.

But, however minimal, however atheist it might be to emphasize Kant's preformationism – as do Zöller and Zammito – is this not to claim, one way or another, the *contingency of transcendental necessity*? Isn't drawing from the germs of a more ancient past than spontaneity a paradoxical manner of relinquishing this necessity?

— 6 —

THE "NEO-SKEPTICAL" THESIS AND
ITS EVOLUTION

Genova's argument, which Zöller read too hastily and judged too severely, comes to mind again at this point. Genova argues that to imprison Kant in preformationism is to hold him captive to an unacknowledged theological prejudice. He writes:

> Without a clear understanding of the role of epigenesis as an organizing principle of Kant's transcendental arguments, it is all too easy to construe Kant's theory of knowledge as a sophisticated version of the preformationist alternative. What is typically done is to treat the preformation hypothesis as unacceptable to Kant because of its dependence on theological presuppositions and its association with philosophers like Leibniz [. . .]. But then, Kant's critics, paradoxically enough, often proceed to interpret his epistemology precisely in terms of a working model which is isomorphic with the logical structure of the preformationist theory but devoid of the overt, theological content.[1]

To take Kant for a preformationist is to attribute to him arguments that he rejects explicitly, notably the "implantation" of the categories of thought in us by God. This is a clear misinterpretation, which, in Genova's view, completely misses the point of §27.

Yet is the neo-Darwinian reading of Kant that Genova develops in his article capable of reconciling the two terms "epigenesis" and "transcendental," whose contiguity appears to be increasingly difficult to justify? Does substituting an evolutionary and adaptive dynamic for preformationist fixity offer a more satisfying approach to the problem?

Who's a Skeptic? Role Reversal in §27

It would be a difficult argument to make. Contrary to what Genova claims, neo-Darwinism is not compatible with transcendental idealism. This is what the second reading track reveals, structured as it is around the notion that the transcendental is nothing but a front whose purpose is quite simply to mask innatism. If it is true that the agreement between the categories and the objects of experience is the product of epigenesis – which is to say, well and truly a birth – then this epigenesis must be cut off from any relation to the transcendental, despite what Kant claims. The agreement, which has nothing to do with an *a priori* structure, is formed via adaptation and evolution. Again, Kant would have described this thesis as skeptical. But who's the most skeptical? If contingency presides in some way over the agreement of the forms of thought and their objects, wouldn't it be better to say it openly, rather than trying to conceal the shaky and factitious nature of the transcendental? Have we not just seen that Kant doomed his most faithful readers to borrow from skepticism (by having recourse to preformationism) in his attempt to save the purity of the source? The time has come to then ask: what is an authentically skeptical – anti-transcendental – take on the transcendental?

This is what I intend to examine now by analyzing the adaptive views of the constitution of rationality. It is a matter of seeing whether this new genesis – for again it is a matter of genetic readings – avoids the aporia of the previous reading.

Bouveresse Analyzes Kant's Innatism

In his interpretation of §27 of the *Critique of Pure Reason*, Jacques Bouveresse insists that there is no way that the idea of epigenesis is possible in a transcendental economy.[2] Rather, epigenesis undermines the transcendental from within by revealing the *a priori* as an innate cognitive arrangement.

Kant is certainly a skeptic. Hegel always said so, and analytic philosophers confirmed it on other grounds. Moreover, there is indeed an element of preformation in critical philosophy; whether it affects the first focus, the hypocenter – the origin of the *a priori* – or whether it coincides with the *a priori* itself is of little importance. The circularity of the *a priori* and the transcendental, which is as impossible to prove as to found, is only an object of logical belief since the Kantian rejection of pre-established harmony is based on another type of pre-established harmony: the assumed harmony between this belief and reality. However reluctantly, previous attempts to identify the reasons for Kant's preformationism all produce the same result: in Kant, necessity always proceeds from arbitrariness. Things are as they are; the *a priori* exists – this one cannot but believe.

Bouveresse writes:

> The goal of the transcendental arguments is [. . .] to supply "not only reasons but also good reasons for the defence of some of our most central instinctive beliefs," such as, for example, our belief in a causal order among appearances that exist outside of experience. [. . .] Clearly the price of this is idealism, which seemed excessive and unacceptable to many philosophers and scientists since the Kantian solution apparently obliges us to accept that transcendental arguments reveal nothing about the nature of the objects of our experience to us *a priori*, except in so far as this *a priori* cognition [. . .] is first and foremost knowledge of a contribution made by the mind and not by the objects themselves.[3]

However much this type of "belief" references the germs and predispositions on which it is based, it will never succeed in its attempt to pass as being objectively necessary that which is no more than a presupposition.

Let us return to the supposed "skeptic" that Kant calls upon in §27, the "preformationist," who is perhaps none other than his own mirror image. What would the "true" skeptic say in response to the argument developed in this paragraph? Bouveresse demonstrates indisputably his point that true skepticism has nothing to do with preformationism. Rather, and this is precisely the problem, it shares an epigenesist conception of the truth. The positions attributed to the critic and the skeptic in §27 are thus reversed. Kant defends a position that he cannot support (epigenesis) and rejects one that he actually supports (preformation).

From that point on, epigenesis belongs to the skeptical, a-transcendental reality, of which it is simultaneously the image and the process. In having recourse to epigenesis in §27, Kant can be said to have handed over the weapon of his own destruction.

From Pre-Established Harmony to Gradual Harmonization

What does this mean? Bouveresse demonstrates that what Kant calls Hume's "preformationist" position was actually already laying the ground for a position – developed in the late nineteenth century and later radicalized with the appearance of epigenetics – that reflected a biological evolution of thought. Far from serving preformationism, the so-called Humean thesis of "pre-established harmony" was the forerunner of the thesis of a *"gradual harmonization"* of the categories and objects of experience, the idea of a continuous epigenetic development as a result of their agreement. This thesis, which Bouveresse terms "neo-skeptical," thus leads us from Hume to the theory of evolution. Bouveresse explains his approach as follows: "Having examined the Kantian argument, I shall consider a classic type of 'skeptical' solution (according to the Kantian criterion), based on the theory of evolution [. . .], which at a certain time enjoyed considerable support among some theorists who were both declared supporters of Darwin and determined adversaries of the unknowable thing in itself."[4] What does this "solution" mean for our problem?

Another Version of the Source, Another Genesis of Epigenesis

Bouveresse begins by presenting the content of §27 and recalling the three options identified by Kant. He starts by returning to the initial problem:

> [T]o the question of how the agreement we observe is achieved between the spontaneity of cognition, on the one hand, and what might be called the concurrent spontaneity of the appearances, on the other, that nothing, at first sight, obliges it to align with the former, Kant responds that this agreement is made simultaneously possible and necessary by the fact that the appearances, as objects of a possible experience, draw their formal possibility from the understanding itself and are thereby constitutively obliged to submit themselves to its rules.[5]

This agreement can only be thought of as necessary, in other words, *a priori*. For Kant, any point of view other than that of transcendental idealism must be a skeptical viewpoint. The three analogies then follow: equivocal generation, preformationism or innatism, and epigenesis. From the point of view of epigenesis: "the categories of the understanding contain the principles of the possibility of experience"; they contain them by producing them. The only way to ward off skepticism is to admit that "without understanding there would not be any nature at all, i.e. synthetic unity of the manifold of appearances in accordance with rules."[6]

Indeed, "the understanding is itself the source of the laws of nature."[7] However, to avoid concluding that the understanding would project simple subjective proprieties onto the real, Kant calls on the epigenesis argument. The *a priori* is not a predisposition of the mind implanted in us in an arbitrary manner. If the unity of nature is necessary, it is because the agreement of categories with objects is produced spontaneously and depends on nothing other than itself.

Bouveresse argues that the problem is that "many philosophers and scientists" never accepted this argument, which was deemed mystifying. For them, whether or not the understanding is spontaneous, *a priori* simply means innate. Whatever he may say, the necessity that Kant calls the "necessity of nature" or the "necessity of the agreement between the categories and the objects" is only, and can only be, the result of a transfer of innate proprieties of the mind onto the phenomenal real. Kant's demonstration is anything but epigenesist. If one wishes to explain the origin of the agreement, then why not accept again a gradual harmonization rather than a mysterious *a priori* synthesis (pre-established harmony!) between the categories and objects? Bouveresse explains:

> Instead of a harmony established once and for all at the origin, between the laws that govern the functioning of the mind and those that govern the functioning of the laws of nature, we could apparently [. . .] imagine a gradual harmonization made possible and explained by the mechanisms of biological evolution, and that ultimately leads to the correspondence that we observe between the categories of thought and objects. We might say that, in some senses, under the influence of these same laws of nature that we are trying to know, in the end, a being was created whose constitution is adapted to the laws in question.[8]

The subject of cognition would then not be the producer, but rather the product of evolution.

This is Peirce's conception, for instance. For him, the *a priori* actually marks the impossibility of going back to the origin of the agreement between the mind and objects. What Kant calls the "spontaneity of the understanding" is in fact the paradoxical expression of a prohibition against accessing the source or against having a retroactive perspective on the origin of the agreement. Countering Kant, it is incumbent on us to insist that this agreement can only proceed from a natural tendency and result in an evolution. In the "Principles of Philosophy," Peirce states:

> It is certain that the only hope of retroductive reasoning ever reaching the truth is that there may be some natural tendency toward an agreement between the ideas which suggest themselves to the human mind and those which are concerned in the laws of nature.[9]

70

Later he continues:

> In examining the reasonings of those physicists who gave to modern
> science the initial propulsion which has insured its healthful life ever
> since, we are struck with the great, though not absolutely decisive,
> weight they allowed to instinctive judgments. Galileo appeals to *il lume
> naturale* at the most critical stages of his reasoning. Kepler, Gilbert,
> and Harvey – not to speak of Copernicus – substantially rely upon an
> inward power, not sufficient to reach the truth by itself, but yet sup-
> plying an essential factor to the influences carrying their minds to the
> truth.[10]

"Instinct" and the "natural tendency" to agreement thus wrote – more
surely than the *a priori* – the subtext of the Copernican revolution!

The synthesis between categories and objects of experience, far
from proceeding from an improbable spontaneity, thus appears
instead as the "result of a long evolution that Darwinian theory
allows us to explain."[11] This is an evolution that renders possible a
progressive adaptation of our mind to objects. The so-called "pure"
forms of cognition and thought are in fact biological adapters: the
only thing that is true is that which the mind can assimilate at any
given moment. This harmonization, which develops constantly, "is
probably always in process."[12] Again we see that the "neo-skeptical"
argument *steals epigenesis from critical philosophy*.

Against "Nativism": Helmholtz and Boltzmann

Arguing against Kant, Bouveresse states, "[T]he possibility of a
Darwinian interpretation of everything that may give the impression
of being innate or *a priori* in cognition [will] be used systematically
later on."[13] An entire intellectual tradition, from Charles Sanders
Peirce to Ludwig Boltzmann, via Hermann von Helmholtz and Robert
Musil, develops the adaptive argument and prepares the ground for
the contemporary thesis of brain epigenesis, in other words, the shift
from epigenesis as traditionally understood to epigenetics.

It is particularly interesting to see physicists such as Helmholtz and
Boltzmann defend the Darwinian point of view and accept an adaptability of both the laws of physics and the laws of the mind. Helmholtz
is a great defender of evolutionary harmonization. Bouveresse writes:
"When Helmholtz criticizes authors who believe in a pre-established
harmony, or, worse yet, an identity between nature and the mind,
he targets first and foremost the tendency to explain production [of

the agreement] by innate mechanisms, whose origin remains entirely mysterious."[14]

Helmholtz argues that the form of our perception of objects is not innate, but rather acquired (*acquisitio derivativa*!), and that it results from an interaction, produced in course of the learning process, between the perceiving subject and objects. In his 1869 lecture "Über das Ziel und die Fortschritte der Naturwissenschaft" ("On the Goal and Progress of the Natural Sciences"), he praises the great resource of Darwinian theory that offers him an entirely new interpretation of "organic purposiveness" (*organische Zweckmässigkeit*) and emphasizes the absence of an origin and goal in evolution, in other words, highlighting the absence of final causes. Adaptation – the adaptation of our mind to particular objects – thus proceeds from a strict, meaningless mechanism.[15]

Moreover, Boltzmann considers that the laws of the mind are merely *inherited* habits of thought. To view them as *a priori* is therefore erroneous.

> Our innate laws of thought are indeed the prerequisite for complex experience, but they were not so for the simplest living beings. There they developed slowly, but simple experiences were enough to generate them. This explains why they contain synthetic judgments that were acquired by our ancestors but are for us innate and therefore *a priori*, from which it follows that these laws are powerfully compelling but not that they are infallible.[16]

Our synthetic judgments, inherited from gradual acquisition, are thus not *a priori* initially, but have become so. The *a priori* would thus be produced by experience. The laws of thought, like the form of objects themselves, would result from the evolutionary process that certainly grants them some stability, but not unconditional truth. We do have *a priori* cognitions, but *a priori* has an entirely different meaning here from in Kant's work:

> It is entirely certain that we have *a priori* representations. According to Darwinian theory, on the grounds of which I base myself, it is also equally clear. Some concepts were acquired by our ancestors; little by little their knowledge was transmitted to their heirs; and eventually it came down to us.[17]

The conclusion is without possibility of appeal: the *a priori* is the result of becoming. Over time, that which was the object of a process of conquest and learning for our ancestors was reduced to a form that is transmitted but that can also change in response to new environmental demands.

72

Consequently, mathematical and logical truths are not immutable. Bouveresse writes: "After all, even in the case of logic itself, we could bequeath our distant descendants very different principles to those that we have received from our ancestors and that they would consider as innate, even though they are the result of a modification that was gradually acquired."[18] The mechanisms, habits of thought, concepts, or behavioral aptitudes, all the acquisitions that come from specific learning, are not definitive and cannot give rise to any immutable certainty. There is no *a priori* necessity insofar as the *a priori* is an acquisition – and so resists any transcendental approach.[19]

Retrospectively, doesn't the Kantian recourse to epigenesis act as a means of destroying exactly that which it intended to deduce? It appears that the circle is drawing close around two incompatible positions. Either one wishes to defend the possibility of an *a priori* epigenesis, but this attempt paradoxically leads to a justification of preformationism. Or one defends an epigenesist conception of the truth and the agreement of the categories with the objects, but at the same time the *a priori* and its necessity are discharged. At that point, an intermediary position, such as the one taken by Genova, appears to be a dead end. How, indeed, can we simultaneously maintain the purity of epigenesis and the adaptability of the transcendental to the "environment" of its development? We recall that Genova tried to reconcile the Kantian point of view of a production of the categories and their relation to objects with the Darwinian theory that he describes as "neo-epigenesist." He asserts that "Darwin, in effect, performed a neo-epigenetic synthesis which turned on the subtle interrelation between external, environmental factors and internal, genetic variability."[20] It would then be possible to see the transcendental prefiguration of this type of synthesis in the Kantian conception of cognitive faculties that develop like a biological organism.

Clearly, neither the Kantians nor the anti-Kantians can really accept this sort of compromise. Apparently there is no intermediary solution between predetermination and evolution, which undermines the argument in §27 and the very idea of spontaneity, in other words, the notion of a pure source. Indeed, according to Boltzmann, if the forms of cognition "are given *a priori*, then there is no longer any need for an examination of the sources, it is indeed no longer possible to talk about it anymore under these conditions; but in practice this is no advantage whatsoever, for how can we know if they are correct or not if they are given to us *a priori*?" How can we know, among the laws of nature, "which of the *a priori* judgments are correct and which are mere prejudices that we find in our mind and that we must extricate?"[21]

Through a strange effect of a posteriori response, the skeptic's argument swallows up the Kantian position. What remains, then, of a "system of the epigenesis of pure reason" when the a priori and innateness are assimilated to one another? We do understand that it is the defense of the a priori that passes for a preformationist position. The "pure" elements of knowledge become contingent implants. The a priori appears as a denial of epigenesis. Whoever is unwilling to accept the evolutionary nature of cognition is therefore of necessity a supporter of innatism.

Transcendental Idealism Disappears from the Debate: Frege versus Darwin

Strangely, transcendental idealism disappears from the debate that Bouveresse stages. We might quite legitimately have expected that ultimately he would return to Kant at the end of the article to develop, if only to even better criticize, the "neo-Kantian" argument that might contradict cognitive neo-Darwinism. And yet, the extreme conclusion that Bouveresse reaches is as follows: the most effective opposition to the neo-skeptical thesis can no longer be a Kantian-style opposition. Ultimately, it is Gottlob Frege, not Kant, who is called upon to figure as the adversary of neo-skepticism – Frege, whose position is entirely distinct from Kant's. The eclipse of transcendental epigenesis is confirmed: on the one hand, it is entirely confiscated by the neo-skeptical thesis; on the other, it is no longer even mentioned in the counter-argument. Kant cannot defend himself and is quite simply excluded from the discussion.

Frege's response to skepticism does not involve the reaffirmation of a pure engendering of the objective reference of the categories. And this is simply because in his work it is no longer a question of engendering at all! It appears that at this point there remains only one type of argument to oppose the skeptical thesis: the dogmatism of absolute truth.

What does this amount to? Frege develops a virulent critique of mental evolutionism. Bouveresse writes: "At a time when the theory of evolution was already widely accepted and had begun to be used to resolve several traditional problems in the theory of cognition, Frege reacted with characteristic distrust against the tendency – which he viewed as disastrous – to introduce evolutionary-type considerations into all fields, including that of logic."[22] Frege in fact asserted that "in the sense in which we speak of natural laws, psychological, mathematical, or logical laws, it is, strictly speaking impossible for laws to change at all."[23] He states:

> A proposition may be thought, and again it may be true; let us never confuse these two things. We must remind ourselves, it seems, that a proposition no more ceases to be true when I cease to think of it than the sun ceases to exist when I shut my eyes. Otherwise, in proving Pythagoras' theorem we should be reduced to allowing for the phosphorous content of the human brain; and astronomers would hesitate to draw any conclusions about the distant past, for fear of being charged with anachronism, with reckoning twice two as four regardless of the fact that our idea of number is a product of evolution and has a history behind it. It might be doubted whether by that time it had progressed so far.[24]

Laws are true without any reference to our cognitive power, and this intrinsic validity also guarantees the agreement with objects. It is true that our cognitive power may well register changes, and may even have a history, but this in no way affects the objective truth of laws. This is the case in all universal instances and "entirely independently of the reference to space and time."[25] We may, by all means, accept that thought "occurs differently now than it did three thousand years ago,"[26] but this transformation in no way affects the validity of laws:

> [T]he validity of the laws of nature is subordinated to the achievement of various conditions, which are or are not entirely mentioned in the statement of the laws, or which, if they are indicated, are so in a manner that allows a certain indetermination to subsist, such that it is always possible to discover at any given moment that it is necessary to add further details or additional restrictions in order to be able to continue to assert the universal validity of the law.[27]

But this law is not relativized at all, which protects its independence in relation to experience.

And to what do we attribute the possible changes that make up the history of the mind? Frege says that it is important not to confuse "holding-true" (*Fürwahrhalten*) – the relation of the subject knowing the truth – and "being true" (*Wahr*) itself. To say that the true evolves would be to suffer from this confusion:

> '2 times 2 is 4' is true, and will continue to be so even if, as a result of Darwinian evolution, human beings were come to assert that 2 times 2 is 5. Every truth is eternal and independent of being thought by anyone, and of the psychological make-up of anyone thinking it.[28]

It is therefore clear that for Frege, transcendental idealism, which is guilty of psychologism since it confuses "being true" and "holding-true," objective truth and subjective truth, ultimately joins – once again – the skeptic's camp. All recourse to a knowing subject in the search for the origin of truth in fact leads to psychologism and relativism.

It seems that one might retort that a transcendental approach to truth includes a constitutive reference in regard to the subject of cognition, but that this does not necessarily coincide with the "human," empirical, or psychological subject. But still, the Kantian distinction between the empirical and the transcendental subject does not convince Frege: "[I]t is unlikely that Frege would have managed to draw a real difference between the fact of making truth depend on the acts of an empirical subject and the fact of relating it to the constitutive activities of transcendental subjectivity."[29] Here again, any reference to subjectivity, whatever the concept might be, remains a figure of "holding-true" for Frege, and for this reason cannot have the value of an origin. The transcendental philosopher is condemned to "attempting to escape his own skin," in other words, to watching himself think and thereby falsely equating truth and the subjective recognition of truth.[30]

Kant is never again given a chance to speak in this debate. Bouveresse insists repeatedly that Frege's position does not coincide with the critical position: "[D]espite the use Frege occasionally makes of Kantian terms and concepts, he should rather [. . .] be viewed as a dogmatic realist."[31] In fact,

> the Kantian solution apparently forces us to accept that transcendental arguments do not reveal anything to us about the nature of the objects of experience *a priori*, except insofar as this cognition that we gain *a priori* is above all a contribution made by the mind and not by the objects themselves.[32]

Kant confirms that "laws exist just as little in the appearances, but rather exist only relative to the subject in which the appearances inhere, insofar as it has understanding, as appearances do not exist in themselves, but only relative to the same being, insofar as it has senses."[33] For Kant, to assume the absolute validity of laws would amount to considering that these laws are "in" appearances and to thereby simultaneously eluding the problem of the origin of the agreement between the categories and the objects of experience.

In counterpoint, Frege asserts that an epigenesis of reason can be nothing but a psychogenesis. So again, transcendental idealism is simply the adventure of "holding-true." With this position we are clearly returning to dogmatism pure and simple. The conflict between skepticism and dogmatism not only does not cease, but definitively swallows the transcendental and, with it, the analogy in §27.

In the end, what is Frege really criticizing, which Kant would not have been entirely able to warn us of, by countering simply with the weak force of "holding-true"? Isn't it the equating of reason with an organ? What does the neo-skeptical thesis actually claim? If the agreement between categories and objects is the result of biological adaptation, if the *a priori* and the transcendental disappear to give way to a gradual harmonization of reason and the real, then it is possible to consider reason as a biological given. Without transcendental structures, isn't reason quite simply a brain? Wouldn't the genesis of epigenesis then be confounded with brain development itself?

FROM EPIGENESIS TO EPIGENETICS

This last conclusion is all the more powerful given that contemporary mental evolutionism, or mental Darwinism, puts the concept of brain epigenesis to work and thus presents itself as the most contemporary version of the neo-skeptical thesis.

Mental or neural Darwinism is based on a theory known as the *epigenesis of neuronal networks by selective stabilization of synapses.* It is striking that even in this theory it is again a matter of describing the agreement process between cognitive categories and the objects of experience. However, in mental Darwinism, epigenesis sheds its role as analogy and appears instead as a physiological reality. The systematic alignment of cognitive structures and the constitution of mental objects develop through epigenesis on the basis of a natural, biologically determined dynamic.

In what respect is neural Darwinism a radicalization of the neo-skeptical argument, and to what extent does it cut epigenesis off still further from its transcendental moorings? How does it construe the relation between the focus and epicenter of the agreement? And how do we measure the distance that separates it from the Kantian position?

Defining Epigenetics

Let's start by explaining that the contemporary understanding of epigenesis draws on the meaning of "epigenetics," to which it is closely linked. The neologism "epigenetics" was created in 1940 by British biologist Conrad Waddington. The noun "epigenetics" refers to the branch of molecular biology that studies relations between genes and the individual features they produce, that is, the relation between genotype and phenotype. Reflecting with hindsight on the creation of this term, in 1968 Waddington commented: "Some years ago [. . .] I introduced the word 'epigenetics,' derived from the Aristotelian word 'epigenesis', which had more or less passed into disuse, as a suitable name for the branch of biology which studies the causal interactions between genes and their products which bring the phenotype into being."[1] The adjective "epigenetic" thus refers to everything to do with this interaction and is concerned with the mechanisms of expression and transcription of the genetic code.

These mechanisms are largely determinant for the activation or inhibition of genes in the process of constituting the phenotype. Take, for example, cellular differentiation. In 1935, in his acceptance speech for the Nobel Prize, Thomas Morgan was already asking: "[I]f the characters of the individual are determined by the genes, then why are not all the cells of the body exactly alike?"[2] How can the difference between a neuron and a hepatic cell, for example, be explained, given that their starting point is one and the same, since all the cells of a single organism share an identical genetic heritage? Differentiated cellular development depends on the selective use of certain genes via activation and silencing. Epigenetic mechanisms structure the self-differentiation of the living being.

One essential aspect of the meaning of "traditional" epigenesis is thus also found in contemporary "epigenetics." It is still a matter of defining ontogenesis, or individual development, as an autonomous, self-formed, and formative growth, also known as "epigenetic history."

The prefix *"epi"* is illuminated in an entirely remarkable manner at this point since epigenetics studies the mechanisms that modify the function of genes by activating or deactivating them. *Insofar as these modifications never alter the DNA sequence itself, epigenetics is said to work on the "surface" (epi) of the molecule.*

So what kinds of changes take place on the "surface"? Three main epigenetic actors are currently known: RNA, the nucleosome, and the methylation of DNA. The function of RNA as messenger and transmitter of information between DNA and proteins situated outside the cell is familiar. It has a major role, particularly since the discovery of RNA interference. The nucleosome is a structure that represents the first level of compression of DNA in the cell's nucleus. By controlling the accessibility of the double strand of DNA, it is directly involved in the regulation of nuclear processes such as the transcription, regulation, or repairing of DNA. It is formed from four histones (proteins) and is the basic unit of the chromatin (the chromosome substance) for eukaryotes.[3] Modifications and variations in these histones impact the degree of openness or closure of the chromatin. The third epigenetic mechanism is the methylation of DNA. DNA has four nucleobases: thymine, adenine, guanine, and cytosine. The methylation of DNA modifies these bases and also plays a key role in the activation and inactivation of genes.[4]

To be Done, Once and for All, with "Everything's Genetic"

Again, changes implemented by epigenetic factors do not affect the DNA sequence. While epigenetics has a wide field of action, it does not have any impact on the code. It is striking that the complex relation between the genetic and the epigenetic – a relation that is one of the fundamental questions of contemporary biology – is a renewed version of the debate between preformationism and epigenesis that gave rise to just as many polemics. In the second half of the twentieth century, the concept of "program" dominated genetics. This phenomenon was often described as the symptom of a "resurgence of preformation-ism."[5] But the idea of a program is precisely that which is in question today as a result of the importance of epigenetic factors in debates on heredity. In his "critique of the notion of genetic program," Changeux even proposes that we "relinquish" it, just like the transcendental![6]

This new orientation in the "logic of life" derives largely from the results of the sequencing of the human genome. On February 15, 2001, the American scientific journal *Nature* published the virtually complete sequence of the three billion bases of this genome.[7] The result was surprising: the human genome is made up of only 30,000 genes, in other words, just 13,000 more than *Drosophila* (commonly known as fruit flies). Furthermore, it appears that genes make up only 5 percent of the genome. Assembled in bunches and clusters, they are separated by vast expanses of so-called "gene deserts," made up of "junk" or "repetitive" – that is, non-coding – DNA. According to studies, this "non-coding" DNA accounts for a quarter or a third of the totality of the genome. Consequently, within chromosomes there are long DNA sequences which, according to current understanding, do not appear to match genes and cannot be given any particular function.[8] The sequencing of the genome did not, therefore, offer the expected revelations.

Nor did the sequencing of the genome show the all-powerful effect of genetic determinism; instead, it indicated its weakening. In his book eloquently entitled *La Fin du "tout génétique"? Vers de nouveaux paradigmes en biologie*, Henri Atlan notes the challenge to the "genetic paradigm." He writes: "The idea that 'everything is genetic' is starting to be seriously unsettled."[9] More recently, he wrote:

> During the last forty or fifty years, the classical ideal that seeks to explain very complex observations by reducing them to laws or simple mechanisms appeared to have been attained in biology thanks to the discovery of the genetic code and its universality. This was truly an extraordinary discovery that ought to have led to the invariable law underlying all biological processes. As such, a genetic reductionism crowned with success appeared to be in sight and it was assumed that the achievement of the sequencing of the human genome would conform to this expectation. In fact, the completion of this project showed that everything was not written in DNA sequences, even at the molecular and cellular level.[10]

From that point on, a new model was established, "which renews interest in molecules that vector information that is not reducible to the information contained in the DNA structures alone." Atlan subsequently wrote:

> [T]he idea that the totality or essential aspects of the development and functioning of living organisms is determined by a genetic program tends to be gradually replaced by a more complex model that is based on notions of interaction, reciprocal effects between the genetic, whose central role is not denied, and the epigenetic, whose importance we are gradually discovering.[11]

We have thus entered the biological "post-genomic" era.[12] François Jacob had already anticipated this when he wrote:

> [T]he genetic programme is not rigidly laid down. Very often it only sets the limits of action by environment, or merely gives the organism the ability to react, the power to acquire some extra information which is not inborn. Phenomena such as regeneration or modifications produced in the individual by environment certainly indicate some degree of flexibility in the expression of the programme.[13]

This "flexibility" is precisely the object of epigenetics today.

The Importance of Environment

Epigenetic modifications have the particularity of being inheritable from one generation of a cell to the next. Unlike genetic heredity, this heredity is reversible. Nevertheless, it causes increased complexity in the evolutionary process. Let me explain this point. Epigenetic modifications depend on two types of causes: *internal and structural*, on the one hand, and *environmental*, on the other. First, it is a matter of the physical and chemical mechanisms described earlier (RNA, nucleosome, methylation). Secondly, epigenetics also supplies genetic material with a means of reacting to the evolution of environmental conditions. For example, while plants do not have a nervous system, they have the ability to memorize seasonal changes at the cellular level.[14] Among animals, reactions to environmental conditions are even greater. Laboratory studies of consanguine mice have recently shown that a change of diet has an influence on offspring. The fur color of the young – brown, yellow, or dappled gray – depends strictly on this change. When pregnant females are given certain food supplements,[15] the majority of their young develop brown fur. The young mice born of the control mice that did not receive these supplements have yellow or dappled fur. There is, therefore, a transmissible memory of changes linked to environment. Many geneticists now think that the behavior of genes can thus be modified by life experiences.[16]

Let's return to our initial question. I said that the debate between preformationism and epigenetism has shifted and now occurs between genetic determinism and epigenetic shaping. The fundamental question of the biology of development is to determine whether genes contain all the information necessary for the formation of the embryo and the adult organism. An increasing number of scientists support the idea that, more than a program that simply unfolds (the thesis held by biologists from 1970 to 1990), "it is the system constituted by the organism and its environment that in fact develops."[17]

The quarrels between the two parties (genetic/epigenetic) are reminiscent of the debates that raged during Kant's era.[18] Despite it all, contemporary epigenetics seems not to serve the Kantian thesis insofar as it does appear to present a greater contradiction with the idea of *a priori* epigenesis! An important element in epigenetic factors in fact derives from the environment, the outside, and, as we shall see with brain epigenesis, learning, the milieu, habit, in a word, experience. The definition of phenotypical malleability proposed by the American biologist Mary-Jane West-Eberhard is eloquent in this respect. She says that it is a matter of the "ability of an organism to react to an environmental input with a change in form, state, movement, or rate of activity."[19] The *a posteriori* thus plays an essential role in the "formative drive" of epigenetics!

"Neural Darwinism" and Brain Epigenesis

The example of brain epigenesis appears to confirm these conclusions once and for all. In *Neuronal Man*, Jean-Pierre Changeux revealed to the general public for the first time the theory initially presented in 1976 in an article entitled "A Theory of Epigenesis of Neuronal Networks by Selective Stabilization of Synapses," which was the result of his collaboration with Philippe Courrèges and Antoine Danchin.[20] A later version of this theory appeared under the title: "Selective Stabilization of Developing Synapses as a Mechanism for the Specification of Neural Networks."[21]

To speak of mental or neural Darwinism might initially appear contradictory. Indeed, for Darwin, epigenesis, as a theory of individual development, was relegated and subordinated to the concept of the evolution of the species. Yet contemporary epigenetics reintroduces precisely the development of the individual into the heart of evolution, opening a new theoretical space called "evo-devo" – "evolutionary developmental biology." Philosopher of biology Thomas Pradeu confirms this innovation when he writes: "There is a virtual consensus that in the years to come evo-devo will be one of the most dynamic fields of biology and one of the most fascinating objects for the philosophy of biology."[22]

The genetics' claim that development does not influence the passage from the genotype to the phenotype is no longer tenable today. For this reason, it is now impossible to separate embryology, developmental biology, and evolutionary biology. Without going into the lively debates that this new understanding of evolutionism provokes, I should mention that the adaptive factors of organisms other than natural selection are now recognized as playing a prime role in evolutionary processes. The evolutionary dynamic is enriched by the contribution of epigenetics.[23]

Synaptic Mechanisms

Let us return to synaptic epigenesis. During the life of the fetus, most of the 100 billion neurons at work in the brain are formed, as are the innumerable synaptic connections that link them. Under the influence of experiences lived *in utero* and later on during the first years of life, many of these so-called "irrelevant" or "redundant" connections are eliminated, while others are consolidated. This is the work of epigenesis by selection–stabilization. This process does not only take place during the "critical" periods of development, for throughout life the brain undergoes synaptic modifications imposed on it by experience.

In fact, brain development continues long after birth and depends to a large extent on environmental and cultural factors. As Changeux constantly reminds us, the theory of epigenesis by synaptic stabilization is thus the *opposite of innatism*. This results in a widened definition of epigenesis: epigenesis now concerns everything "that is not preformed." As Changeux also points out, we observe "an evolutionary paradox" that marks the discontinuity between brain complexity and genetic complexity, with brain complexity being far greater than genetic complexity.[24] This discontinuity, or non-linear evolution, between the increasing complexity of brain organization, on the one hand, and the apparent invariability of the DNA content in the cellular nucleus at the level of living beings, on the other, prevents us from calling on innatism or any other version of preformationism. Here again the brain has its own life and development, which do not depend entirely on genetic information. Neurobiologists agree that "the brain is more than a reflection of our genes."[25]

Selection Levels

How do epigenetic brain mechanisms function? During the development of the nervous system, the networks' activity leads either to stabilization or to the elimination of the synapses of which they are formed. Among all the possible neuronal pathways that exist between two areas of the brain, the most efficient will be chosen and consolidated with a view to subsequent solicitations.

Cognitive organization is constituted of several levels. The most concrete and elementary is the perceptive level; the most abstract is the symbolic level. These levels are distributed hierarchically in the neuronal architecture. From the elementary circuits of the spinal cord, brain stem, and ganglions to the frontal cortex, everything combines to form "the neural architecture of reason."[26] At their highest level, the neuronal "assemblies" or "populations" code cognitive operations ("population coding").

At each level of brain organization, "matter" elements combine, like Darwinian variations, to engender the "forms" at the next level. Some of these forms are then stabilized after being selected on the basis of their functional efficacy. Hence, "the function feeds back

84

into the [matter–form] transition."[27] Mental representations are thus elaborated on the basis of the operations of the selection–stabilization pairing.

The Example of Mathematics

The theory of brain epigenesis by synaptic selection and stabilization makes no mention of *a priori* data in the constitution of mental objects and their agreement with cognitive structures. The eliminativist cognitive model substitutes the idea of a gradual, biologically determined agreement for the notion of a transcendental agreement of the categories with objects. Mathematical truths are the products of this type of adaptation. In *Conversations on Mind, Matter, and Mathematics*, a collection of conversations with mathematician Alain Connes, Changeux states that mathematical objects are indeed "coded in the brain as forms,"[28] but that they have a material existence and show themselves to "correspond to physical states"[29] perfectly. It is these "states" that are subject to evolutionary processes. Existence, reality, even the truth of mathematics, are "*a posteriori* results of evolution."[30]

It is clear that this position quite naturally prolongs the oldest evolutionist thesis analyzed by Bouveresse. Against Frege and Husserl, Changeux defends a cognitive psychologism according to which the reality of mathematical objects and logical idealities is the reality of mental states and processes, which, again, exist materially in the brain. "Mental representations – memory objects – are coded in the brain as forms in the Gestalt sense, and stored in the neurons and synapses, despite significant variability in synaptic efficacy."[31] Mathematical axiomatization, which is also defined as a brain process, is only possible on the basis of this materiality of forms.

Mathematical representations are selected according to a contingent evolutionary process. They constitute mathematical objects as "cultural objects, [. . .] public representations of mental objects of a particular type that are produced in the brains of mathematicians and are propagated from one brain to another [. . .]."[32] From this it follows that according to Changeux there can be no mathematical ontology: mathematical truth is in fact the result of an aleatory process that only becomes necessary through the action of selection. Thus, "the science of 'why?' isn't theology, it's evolutionary biology. And the 'why?' of the existence of mathematics has as much to do with the evolution of our knowledge acquisition apparatus – our brain – as it does with the evolution of mathematical objects themselves."[33]

The brain, whose embryogenesis and development are subject to the dynamic of stabilization by elimination, can therefore be defined as a biological machine produced by evolution. The agreement of the "forms" and mental objects, whether they are "pure" mathematical objects or the objects of experience in general, could not therefore be constituted *before* this dynamic. According to Changeux, there is nothing in brain organization that might correspond to the "transcendental" one way or another. The economy of rationality concurs entirely with the dynamic of brain epigenesis.

Edelman's Theory of Systems of Recognition

It might be objected that there are less reductive, less hard-wired versions of neural Darwinism. On these grounds, American neurobiologist Gerald Edelman argues simultaneously for the theory of brain epigenesis by synaptic selection and stabilization and the existence of *a priori* structures of cognition. The epistemology that Edelman proposes also assumes the epigenetic constitution of all cognitive processes from the elementary biochemical and cellular level up to the appearance of consciousness. This is the "theory of neuronal group selection" (TNGS). This theory nevertheless allows for the existence of "value-categor[ies]."[34] But is the vision of epigenesis that underlies it compatible with that of Kant?

In *Bright Air, Brilliant Fire: On the Matter of the Mind*, Edelman explains that synaptic selection is a dual process that operates both at the "topobiological" level and at the level of "recognition systems."

The first selection operates within a cellular mass that contains possible structural variants. Selected structures are formed by elimination. The nerve cells project a series of extensions that stimulate target cells. When the signal for an extension fails to correlate with the target, these "fascicles" retract or disappear. Successful correlations form the basis of neuronal maps. This is the "epigenetic drama." In this drama, Edelman explains,

> [S]heets of nerve cells in the developing brain form a neighborhood. Neighbors in that neighborhood exchange signals as they are linked [. . .]. They send processes out in a profuse fashion, sometimes bunched together in bundles called fascicles. When they reach other neighborhoods and sheets they stimulate target cells

and in this way they form connections. Others retract and the emitting cells pass on.

Finally, as growth and selection operate, a mapped neural structure with a function may form. The number of cells being made, dying, and becoming incorporated is huge. The entire situation is a dynamic one, depending on signals, genes, proteins, cell movement, division, and death, all interacting at many levels.[35]

The second level of selection, that of "recognition systems", implements a so-called "degeneration property." This time the selection impacts the neural maps that result from selective elimination. The systems are eliminated by "degeneration" or consolidated in response to their "reaction" to exogenous solicitation. If the adaptive response is not viable, the system degenerates. Edelman develops the example of vision, but considers that the brain as a whole is a system of recognition that encompasses all the particular systems.[36]

At this second level it is essentially the behavior of the individual that causes the reinforcement or weakening of the diverse populations of synapses involved in neural maps. Behaviors also play a primary role in the formation of a secondary repertoire of neural groups. As a general rule, experience is an essential factor in synaptic selection, which modulates and modifies networks and circuits.

However, Edelman emphasizes one key point: in the brain, everything does not take place *a posteriori*. Thus, for example, the systems of recognition form themselves *a priori*, and not after or according to the forms they recognize. The units of recognition are certainly selected *a posteriori*, but the arrangement from which they derive forms itself. This is the reason why Edelman believes that the existence of *a priori* categories is compatible with neurophysiological properties. As he says, "[T]he brain carries out a process of conceptual 'self-categorization.'"[37] This system of categories ("value-category system") then responds to the solicitations and signals coming from the outside world. Phenomenal experience results from this interaction between concepts and objects. It "arises from the correlation by a conceptual memory of a set of ongoing perceptual categorizations"[38] and thus depends on pre-existing structures.

It is readily apparent, however, that what Edelman calls *a priori*, and that which relates to the antecedence of the structural units of recognition on the forms or objects recognized, clearly does not coincide with the Kantian *a priori*. Although, unlike Changeux – and this is a considerable difference – Edelman accepts a certain functional autonomy of the structures of recognition ("self-categorization"), it is still dependent on adjustments and is therefore not entirely spontaneous.

Let's return to the discussion about the initial status of the categories in the understanding. The categories develop "with the opportunity" of experience, but (at least according to Zöller) it cannot be said that they later undergo a series of eliminations and transformations by reaction. On first sight it appears impossible to identify in Kant's work a process of adjustment of the categories to objects and a system of response of objects to the categories. This is why neural or mental Darwinism, even in its moderate form, contradicts the critical position and once again deprives it of ownership of epigenesis. The biologization of the transcendental appears to need to destroy it irrevocably, which presupposes that the agreement of the categories with the objects cannot be thought outside the dynamic of adaptability, which itself is subject to variability. Edelman concludes: "[M]ind, which arose from material systems and yet can serve goals and purposes, is nevertheless a product of historical processes and of value-based constraints related to evolution."[39]

From Methylation to Hermeneutics

But is it so easy to dismiss Kant from the debate? After these two chapters devoted to neo-evolutionism and mental Darwinism, let us return, in closing, to the relation between genetics and epigenetics. It is striking to see that scientists often describe the work of epigenetics metaphorically as improvisation, practical or artistic elaboration, creative spontaneity, in a word, as if, against genetic determinism, epigenetics related to the register of interpretative freedom.

The most common image used to describe the work of epigenetics is indeed *interpretation*. Thus, Thomas Jenuwein, director of the Department of Immunobiology at the Max Planck Institute, describes epigenetics in these terms:

> The difference between genetics and epigenetics can probably be compared to the difference between writing and reading a book. Once a book is written, the text (the genes or DNA: stored information) will be the same in all the copies distributed to the interested audience. However, each individual reader of a given book may interpret the story differently, with varying emotions and projections as they continue to unfold the chapters. In a very similar manner, epigenetics would allow different interpretations of a fixed template (the book or genetic code) and result in different readings, dependent upon the variable conditions under which the template is interrogated.[40]

In order to figure the relations between the genetic and the epigenetic, other scientists, such as Eva Jablonka and Marion Lamb, have recourse to the metaphor of the impact of music and its instrumental performance.[41] The image of interpretation, whether textual or musical, evokes the style, individual fashioning, and endless possibilities for reading or playing in every instance. The use of this image does seem to indicate the opening of a hermeneutic dimension in the heart of the biological. It is as if the phenotypical event were in some senses an epigenetic version of the program. As if a space opened between them that calls for *critical* exploration. If epigenetic factors encompass physical mechanisms as much as environmental and social influences, then how, in the constitution of phenotypical individuality, could this be anything but the formation of a singularity that transcends strict determinism and places epigenesis and the development of all living beings in an intermediary space between *biology* and *history*? Following the metaphors used by scientists themselves, shouldn't we go beyond the strict epistemological field to return to philosophy and claim the importance of epigenetics for thinking, and not just for cognition?

And what if these remarks led us to reconsider the power of the transcendental, to reclaim it not as invariance and logical predisposition (as Zöller does, for example), but rather as hermeneutic latitude, the power of *meaning*, opened in the heart of the biological?

These questions bring us back to the critical reading track and to its second line of understanding the transcendental as a *historico-critical dimension of rationality* that accompanies objectivity as its necessary shadow. This is a dimension that clearly cannot be assimilated by the "neo-skeptical" thesis, a dimension that resists it.

— 8 —

FROM CODE TO BOOK

Our question now turns back on itself. What if, in the end, with his phrase "system of the epigenesis of pure reason," Kant was thinking less about the objective process of engendering the relation between categories and objects than about the way that the subject explains herself in this process? What if epigenesis referred precisely to the point of emergence of auto-affected, interpreting subjectivity, starting from the unfathomable source of its genetic program – the innate background of the *a priori*? And what if we came to see something like the constitution of a transcendental "phenotype" of the thinking subject at work in Kant?

The Problem of History

What does this other aspect of the first reading track offer? I began by analyzing the attempt to reduce the role of experience in transcendental epigenesis as much as possible. Now, on the same track but differently, it is a matter of exploring a certain formation of subjectivity, starting from the question of interpretation, while simultaneously introducing historical becoming into the *a priori*.

In his article, Zöller himself in fact, almost surreptitiously, opens a path other than that of "minimal preformationism." He says that the epigenesis analogy *also* has a hermeneutic dimension in the transcendental deduction. What does he mean by this? The transcendental deduction is entrusted with a dual mission. It must explain and legitimize the objective reference of the categories by showing that the agreement proceeds from none other than itself and not from any decree or intrinsic property of the objects of knowledge. But it must

90

also account for the position and reaction of the subject of cognition in regard to the spontaneity of its own thinking – a spontaneity which, in a sense, does not proceed from its own initiative.

Thus, the transcendental deduction necessarily includes a dimension of "figurative self-interpretation."[1] This relates first to the way in which transcendental philosophy, through recourse to biological analogies, explains itself to itself. We must not forget that in the Deduction Kant is justifying himself to his detractors. But this self-interpretation is also, of course, more generally, the act of any subject inasmuch as the subject appropriates the generating power of the understanding, takes ownership of it, and thus becomes *its* subject. The problem of the origin of the agreement between categories and objects is necessarily compounded by another problem: the question of the structure of auto-affection through which the subject receives its own spontaneity.

Epigenesis not only serves, therefore, to describe the *a priori* production of the agreement between the categories and objects through an analogy; it also allows the subject to figure themself.

This structure touches on that which distinguishes the critical position entirely from the skeptical position in the eyes of Kant's readers, whose turn it is now to speak. The skeptical position, especially in its contemporary version, says absolutely nothing about the self-interpretative aspect of the constitution of rationality. The subject's explanation and reception of the ability to self-determine, the arrangement whereby the subject appropriates spontaneity, which also corresponds to the process of a formation by epigenesis, are a set of operations that mental, or neuronal, evolutionism does not acknowledge.

Even though, as we have just seen, the metaphor of textual hermeneutics or musical interpretation is the figure that epigenetics explicitly foregrounds, no extensive study seeks to determine what it is in this figure that exceeds the strictly biological register to engage in a *critical* relation of the thinking individual to themself. Those who argue in favor of brain epigenesis by synaptic stabilization never ask, for instance, what type of representation the subject has of this structure, what type of "consciousness" the subject has of their brain, how they might in some way take possession of it.[2] For them, this type of question is a purely egological refinement without a sensible or real correlate, one that simply harkens back to the old mind/brain distinction.

This lack of acknowledgment also results from apparently opposed dogmatic positions, such as Frege's view, analyzed earlier, which associates the idea of an affection of the subject through their own spontaneity with a pure and simple mode of "holding-true" that is foreign to the intrinsic validity of truth.

And yet, if there is a posterity and specificity to the critical position, do they not derive from an affirmation of the absolutely necessary nature of the subjective appropriation of the *a priori* forms of cognition and thought for the constitution of truth?

To take transcendental idealism for psychologism, or for a pure and simple theory of the subject, to oppose it to an absolute objectivity of truth, is to ignore the immense question hidden in this appropriation. Likewise, for the skeptical argument regarding an evolution of truth; a gradual adaptation of the subject of cognition to objects; and a biological adjustment of agreement. There is no mention whatsoever of the epistemological status of the subjective dimension – mental, neuronal, or spiritual – of this agreement. Yet the transcendental is perhaps no more than the form of the question: how does the subject become the principle of their act, of the originally acquired spontaneous agreement between categories and objects of experience? The founding value of the transcendental, which salvages its necessity, would then derive from the validity and efficacy of the act by which the subject authorizes themself to be who they are.

Now, one might ask, how does this alter the meaning of epigenesis? Confronted with this new understanding, what does the biological meaning of this term become? And how does the supposed "minimal preformationism" that epigenesis is said to conceal deal with a hermeneutic of spontaneity?

Epigenesis and Teleology

To answer these questions, it is important to start by emphasizing that the expression "minimal preformationism" is not suitable or acceptable for any of the three *Critiques*. This is the case even within the framework of the third *Critique*, despite the fact that, as we have seen, it associates epigenesis with "generic preformation." As François Duchesneau demonstrates, from the mid-1770s, Kant developed a theory of "generic preformation that is *compatible* with the implications of epigenesis."[3] It is certainly true that Kant "links the organized development to germs (*Keime*) and predispositions (*Anlagen*) which are realized in the organic combination of male and female seeds."[4] It is also true that everything occurs "as if nature had included in its archetypes of living organizations a variety of arrangements for

92

development preadapted to the external conditions of life in which individuals are called upon to reproduce,"[5] in other words, *limited* varieties, which must respond to some preordination. We recall that Kant recognized this: "[W]hat is supposed to propagate itself must have laid previously in the generative power (*Zeugungskraft*) as antecedently determined to an occasional unfolding in accordance with the circumstances."[6]

We must therefore acknowledge the existence of a preordination of epigenetic powers that restricts the variety of types of organization. However, preordination does not mean predetermination; rather it implies "organizing project."[7] "Generic preformation" does not mean traditional preformation; it is the other name of a structural schema capable of integrating varieties, that is, a *system*.

Zöller clearly accepts that germs and predispositions are irreducible to any causal mechanistic nature, but he never focuses on the specificity of the Kantian concept of teleology, which grounds the structural unity of the organism. It is important to recall the famous statement in §65 of the *Critique of the Power of Judgment* that says "its parts [of the organism] be combined into a whole by being reciprocally the cause and effect of their form."[8] This unity – the synthetic links between the parts – is the only mode in which we can conceptualize a totality.

Preordination, then, is structure, that is, self-organization. Of course, the archetype of this structure remains unknown to us. Kant emphasizes again the "inscrutable principle of an original organization."[9] But Blumenbach's *Bildungstrieb* makes it possible to reconcile the outline of the whole of a structural unit and the gradual development of self-organization. Thus, "it is necessary to have recourse to a concept of a self-structuring formative force (*sich bildende Kraft*) that actualizes its own model in the realization, conservation, and reproduction of an integrated organic form."[10]

The limiting of types of individuals capable of self-organizing thus does not represent an essential limit to the formative drive; rather it appears as its condition of possibility. *It is the idea of a living being that would not self-organize that is excluded by the structure of "generic preformation."* Any type of vital unity other than the organic unit is inconceivable. The relation of mutuality and reciprocity between the parts forms the circularity that is "preordained." Germs and predispositions are the necessary preliminaries for self-organization, not the outlines of preformed living beings.

By tracing back the line of thought that leads from Wolff's *vis essentialis* to Blumenbach's *Bildungstrieb*, it is possible to claim that what is at stake in the theory of epigenesis is the idea of a "force capable of prefiguring the structural and functional organization to be established, a force that incarnates a sort of immanent plan and that realizes it by adapting to external and internal circumstances that affect organic development."[11] Thus there is no hiatus between plan and epigenesis. Here again, the synthesis of the two is organization.

The question recurs: what then can we say, by analogy, about a possible transcendental *Bildungstrieb*? Is it the same distance from the originary focus of the constitution of the cognitive power to the spontaneity of the understanding as the distance Kant establishes between the unfathomable principle of an original organization and the organizing spontaneity of the living being? In other words, is it possible to retrospectively conceive of the categories as organized beings, and their agreement with the objects of experience as the essential form of this self-organization?

One might well think so. The linchpin of the analogy is the idea of system, which returns again in the "system of the epigenesis of pure reason." Starting with the "determining spontaneity of the transcendental self, [the categories] produce an integrated forming, an 'organization' of the appearances apprehended under the general conditions of sensibility and thus they found the objective representation of things of nature."[12] This organizing production consequently coincides with the formation of the productive subject itself. Thus, bringing together transcendental epigenesis and self-organization not only opens up a perspective on the generation of the objective reference, it also makes it possible to describe the dimension of *subjectivation* referred to earlier and to outline the parallel between the self-structuring capacity of the formative force (*sich bildende Kraft*) and the epigenesis of the subject through the act of receiving its own spontaneity.

We are starting to understand transcendental epigenesis now as the *adventure of subjectivity*, an adventure that contemporary epigenetics glimpses, but does not think.

"Life and History Are Fields Not of Explanation, But Rather of Interpretation"[13]

Adventure. Long before the epigenetic revolution, this is the word Gérard Lebrun used when he interpreted the phrase "system of the epigenesis of pure reason" in *Kant et la fin de la métaphysique*. His reading tends towards a convergence of *categorial epigenesis*, *biological epigenesis*, and *practical autonomy*.

94

While it remains the original concern, the genetic concern changes direction here. If it is not possible to plumb the focus from whence epigenesis derives, if each time the inquiry runs up against the inaccessible nature of the root, then perhaps this very inaccessibility should be considered the root, perhaps this lack of origin is the origin, and perhaps it is here that one must start as from a focus. Lebrun writes: "[A] stem that is impenetrable for our reason is a limit that we establish rather than a natural beginning."[14] In other words, that which is not of our doing is also the starting point of a decision. We are the ones who "establish" the limit. But this "we" must begin itself, constitute itself, *make* itself. The inaccessibility of the source thus frees up a facticity that, far from being artificial – a pure fabrication or pure state of affairs – is confounded with the movement of a *becoming*: "Thanks to the Kantian 'deduction' of epigenesis, a new concept, *becoming*, starts to make its way."[15]

This becoming is the meeting point between the epigenesis of the subject of cognition, the autonomy of the practical subject, and the creativity of life. This, then, is how "the meeting between Kant and Blumenbach supersedes the history of biological concepts"[16] and how, contrary to what various reductionist positions claim, epigenesis is a concept that is situated precisely at the intersection of cognition, freedom, and life. This intersection marks the emergence of history. Indeed, the "inaccessible nature of the origin" appears as this "theoretical interruption" where, later on, "Cournot will make himself engender history."[17]

Let's return to biology for a moment. It is certainly true that in Kant living forms are dependent on an originary potential that restricts their unfolding. It is likewise also true that "the 'plastic faculty' [or formative drive] is not endowed with all the possibilities. [. . .] There would be no specificity of the living being without a limitation of its structures."[18] However, once again, in this view there is no borrowing from preformationism – not even minimally. Lebrun adds, "Certainly life does not invent any way, nor from any thing; but the fact that it respects the specific model does not prevent it from also being the invention of forms (as embryology, since F. G. Wolff, is beginning to demonstrate)."[19] The life plan is "the very example of the plasticity of life,"[20] which protects the formative force from both the chaos of equivocal generation and the programmatic rigidity of predestination. Epigenesis imposes its logic against all inexplicable animation (the magic of equivocal generation), as well as against all preformation. The inaccessible nature of original organization is the sign of a linking of life and thought not to the underground mystery of their source, but rather to what frees them from it:

> [T]he importance granted to history is the consequence of this infinite receding of the origin and of the recognized impossibility of ever determining the laws (or designs) intertwined in it. The fate of an embryo as a species is written nowhere: within the "generic preformation" (of the model that the organic creation no longer transgresses today), their becoming is an adventure.[21]

This is to say that between the unknowable nature of the principle of original organization (the source of self-organization = X) and self-organization itself lies a gap from which proceeds epigenesis with its specific temporality: "Kant restores the role of time against preformationism" by defining epigenesis as an "improvisation [. . .] that generates order." A temporal order that is "oriented, but not determined."[22] This view prefigures contemporary epigenetics!

In *On the Use of Teleological Principles in Philosophy*, Kant himself recognizes that he would willingly use the word "history" to describe such a becoming, if this word, "taken to mean the same as the Greek *historia* (narrative, description)," had not "been in use too much and too long for us easily to tolerate that it be granted another meaning which can designate the investigation of origin in nature."[23] Kant thus tries to avoid the risk of confusing "history" and "natural history." In this admission, we nonetheless see that history is called upon negatively at this point of the analysis "in the wake of the vital force (*Lebenskraft*)" and epigenesis, to counter any preformationism, however minimal.[24]

By now widening the problem to the whole of transcendental philosophy, Lebrun argues that it is possible to introduce becoming into the *a priori* synthesis. And indeed, the three *Critiques* are structured by the same problem: the existence of a second source, which means that the source does not grasp itself at the source, but in what it produces, in what, starting from it, takes form and develops by differentiating itself. To explain §27 by holding on to the spontaneity of the understanding without taking its after-effects into account – the pure production of the subject through self-interpretation – amounts to amputating one of the essential dimensions from the motif of transcendental epigenesis, namely the appropriation of the origin as the subject's self-formation.

In the second *Critique*, Kant demonstrates that the coincidence between the source of objectivity and subjective arising is the specificity of practical spontaneity. The *Critique of Practical Reason* also explicitly abandons all innatism and all preformationism when it brings to light the engendering point – epigenesis – for the objective reference of practical causality. A single *a priori* generative link is at work within thought and freedom. In the Transcendental Deduction of the *Critique of Practical Reason*, Kant returns to the discussion with Hume about "pre-established harmony." He says that Hume would again deprive causality of all objective necessity, this time in the practical field:

> If, with Hume, I had removed the objective reality from the concept of causality in its theoretical use not only with regard to things in themselves (the suprasensible) but also with regard to objects of the senses, then the concept would have lost all signification and, as a theoretically impossible concept, would have been declared entirely unusable; and since one also can make no use of nothing, the practical use of a *theoretically null* concept would have been entirely absurd.[25]

As already posited in §27 of the first *Critique*, to establish both the theoretical and practical validity of causality thus requires proof that its origin is not an innate predisposition. Returning to the link between the two works in the Dialectic of Pure Practical Reason, Kant states:

> By these reminders the reader of the critique of pure speculative reason will completely convince himself how extremely necessary, how profitable for theology and morality, was that laborious *deduction* of the categories. For if one posits the categories in pure understanding, only that deduction can keep one from considering them, with *Plato*, to be innate and from basing on them extravagant pretensions of theories of the suprasensible [. . .].[26]

There is, therefore, a *"relation of equality"* between speculative and practical reason, which is the epigenetic source of the objective validity of the categories.[27]

Epigenesis thus loses any connection to preformation and innateness definitively. A real morphological inventiveness of the transcendental must be recognized. Not in the sense that it would be possible to invent any category whatsoever, but in the sense in which this very restriction engages the subject in the invention of themself.

"Between disorder and deliberation, there is a third way,"[28] writes Lebrun. Between the chaos of equivocal generation and the divine decree of preformation lies the space of just such an invention.

What invention? Lebrun also expands on the book metaphor:

> Would not a traveler have lost his mind, writes Leibniz in the *Theodicy*, if, arriving at an uninhabited land and finding books and clocks there,

he thought he had found himself in a land "where the books write themselves"? Consequently, he concludes, "there is a moral certainty that it is Providence that governs things." Kantian purposiveness and epigenesis refuse this alternative between insanity and piety: life is this land where books do not write themselves, but nor are they written under dictation there.[29]

The land where books do not write themselves, but where they are not mere copies of an original text either, is the land where the only writing possible resides: previously oriented, but without being programmed. A writing that, even as it develops itself from a structural outline, is not predestined. An interpretation.

The spontaneity of the understanding cannot reach itself substantially, and it is precisely due to this that it is impossible to think it as predetermined or pregiven. This is also why explanation and comprehension yield to exegesis. Lebrun then veers off towards a dimension of the problem of categorial epigenesis that distances it from strictly biological and epistemological lines to open up the problem of *meaning*, or, rather, meaning as an absence of preformed meaning. There is an epigenesis of reason because the *a priori* has no meaning. Rationality engenders itself – invents its forms – out of this necessary lack.

On this point, Lebrun calls on §666 of the *Will to Power*, in which Nietzsche writes, "'Nothing has any meaning' – this melancholy sentence means 'All meaning lies in intention, and if intention is altogether lacking, then meaning is altogether lacking, too.'"[30] The interest in associating the formative vital force and the formative transcendental force ultimately consists in the revelation of the fundamentally senseless nature of the origin. Categorial spontaneity does not respond to an intention any more than does the life stem. Again, critique thus slips away from the problem of cognition to the question of interpretation, and from the problem of interpretation to the question of history.

History exists precisely because meaning is not given. History thus appears as the subtext of critique. Foucault demonstrated this magisterially. The identification between the opening of interpretation and the beginning of history signals a certain age or certain moment in reading Kant. According to this reading, meaning constructs itself, engenders itself – through epigenesis – it *becomes* what it is, starting from a blank.

Epigenesis is thus the origin born of the lack of origin, the lack of meaning of the origin, the spontaneity of its silence. And if this origin is indeed the place where history is engendered, then it is possible to

assert that the agreement of the categories with the objects is a historical meeting.

At this point in the analysis, we see that the questioning of the
existence of a Kantian preformationism does not, for all that, lead
to an eclipse of the transcendental or its disappearance in favor of an
evolutionary and adaptive biological schema. If the analysis leads to
taking the living being and the formative drive into account, it does
not lead to the reduction of reason to brain epigenesis and appears to
cut short the presumed instability of its founding validity. It is clear
that, from one metaphor of the book to the next, from the image
of reading employed by Jenuwein to the image of writing called on
here, the question of *meaning* changes the game. This question eludes
proponents of mental Darwinism entirely. More generally, no biologist examines the relation between genetics and epigenetics in terms
of meaning.[31] Yet isn't meaning what makes it possible to reassert the
resistance of the transcendental to its biologization?

IRREDUCIBLE FOUCAULT

What Is Enlightenment?

With the encounter between transcendental philosophy and history, we arrive at a turning point on the critical reading track when we discover the place towards which Foucault – in the brief but unbelievably rich "What Is Enlightenment?" – displaces the *a priori* by deliberately opening the structure of the transcendental to transformation. Adopting an entirely different approach to the perspectives of neo-Darwinism, mental evolutionism, or brain epigenesis, in a line of continuity with Kant and never against him, Foucault asserts that there is an *experimental* modifiability of the transcendental structure. What are the consequences for the relation between categories and objects? How is our understanding of the expression "system of the epigenesis of pure reason" refreshed by this approach?

There are several versions of this text in French, spread over a period of twenty years – proof that the relation of the transcendental to change is a key question for Foucault, one that he develops throughout his work. The first version, from 1965, is called "What Is Critique?"[1] Two other versions appeared in 1984 under the definitive title "What Is Enlightenment?"[2]

Foucault's text clearly echoes Kant's earlier text with the same title – "Was ist Aufklärung?" (What Is Enlightenment?) – published in 1784 in the *Berlinische Monatschrift*.[3] In December 1784, the Berlin periodical ran a competition in which it asked its readers this question and promised to publish the best response. Kant was the prize winner. Two hundred years later, Foucault repeats the exercise, asking:

Let us imagine that the *Berlinische Monatschrift* still exists and that it is asking its readers the question: What is modern philosophy? Perhaps we could respond with an echo: modern philosophy is the philosophy that is attempting to answer the question raised so imprudently two centuries ago: *Was ist Aufklärung?*[4]

By reiterating the question, Foucault simultaneously repeats and displaces the argument. The guiding ideas in Kant's text are still just as powerful and relevant today. However, it is important to radicalize them by asserting no less than the *historicity of the transcendental*. How can such a reading be justified? Foucault argues that in his text, Kant reveals the determining nature of the notion of the *present* in philosophy for the first time. Kant takes the question "What is Enlightenment?" to mean "what is happening to thought today?"[5] It not only signals the relevance of an idea but also constitutes the present as the condition of possibility of philosophy. Since thought always arises at a given moment, its very modernity is constitutive of its object. From this, Foucault concludes that there is most certainly a contextuality of the transcendental, which is linked not only to the factuality of its emergence here and now but also to the form that thought gives this factuality. From this perspective, the other name for this contextual formation is categorial epigenesis.

In the decision to bring to light the intimate relation between critique and history, Foucault's interpretation is certainly one of the most profound and audacious readings ever proposed. While the motif of epigenesis is not explicitly present in it, nonetheless, everything seems destined to illuminate and explain it.

Foucault demonstrates that in the 1784 text Kant himself asserts the possibility of linking the question of the agreement between categories and objects to the question of the transformation of a natural subject, a subject "as he is,"[6] as a subject of truth.[7] The relation of the subject to objects is possible only on the basis of this transformation. The modification of the subject – which can be called its epigenesis – occurs at the foundation of this "critical ontology of ourselves"[8] that Foucault suggests is another name for Kantian philosophy. The transcendental structures of rationality thus coincide with the rules for the constitution of the subject, its relation to objects, and thus, in a sense, to objects themselves.

For Kant, the critique of reason is necessarily dependent on a moment, an age of rationality – one which marks the Enlightenment specifically. In this context, the word "historical" has a different status than in other texts by Kant. It refers to the question of the passage, transition, and decisive moment of the entry into rationality. The "historical" transformation of the subject into the subject of truth is both a *chronological process* and a *biological development*. This transformation is actually defined as the departure from a state of immaturity. The motif of epigenesis is read here in the two senses, both biological and temporal, the passage from minority to majority, a differentiated development, the prelude to a second birth. "Kant indicates right away that the 'way out' that characterizes Enlightenment is a process that releases us from the status of 'immaturity.'"[9] Foucault adds: "The critique is, in a sense, the handbook of reason that has grown up in Enlightenment; and, conversely, the Enlightenment is the age of the critique."[10] This intrication of reason and age again situates epigenesis at the articulation point of the rational and the physiological, giving history the dimension of a process of growth here and transcending the simple paradigm of events.

The Elaboration of the Subject and Access to Truth: Prelude to Agreement

The idea that access to truth requires a transformation of the subject is central to Foucault and appears in different texts and lectures from the period 1980–5. This motif, which is considered in *The Hermeneutics of the Subject* in particular, describes epigenesis precisely as a process during which the subject becomes truly autonomous and "capable of truth."[11] This becoming is central to Kant's text, as Foucault writes: "From the very first paragraph, he [Kant] notes that man himself is responsible for his immature status. Thus it has to be supposed that he will be able to escape from it only by a change that he himself will bring about in himself."[12]

The joint reading of the *Critique of Pure Reason* and "What Is Enlightenment?" allows us to assert that here again the problem of the agreement of the categories to objects is not separable from the problem of the way in which the subject makes themself a subject, that is, becomes the subject of the relation. Since the subject cannot account for their own spontaneity, it is received and must be appropriated. This need for the appropriation of self is confounded with the entry into rationality and "majority" that implies the use of enlightenment as the "principle of a critique and a permanent creation of ourselves in our autonomy."[13]

The subject of truth is both "element and actor"[14] in the transcendental economy. The subject is an "element" insofar as they are preceded by the *a priori* necessity of the synthesis that they absolutely do not determine; the subject is an "actor" because they must self-interpret, deduce, this position. During this hermeneutic, the subject assumes themself as "the one who speaks as a thinker."[15] On the horizon of this epigenesis of rational responsibility lies the belonging of the subject to "a certain *us*."[16] This "us" thus becomes the primary question. To identify the "us" in its singularity and historical moment is a fundamental task that is constitutive of critical philosophy. Foucault writes, "No philosopher can go without examining his own participation in this *us* which is becoming the object of the philosopher's own reflection."[17]

Contrary to appearances, this type of questioning does not reduce transcendental idealism solely to an inquiry by subjectivity into itself. Rather, within a reflection on "us," transcendental philosophy explores the interval between subject and object that is the space of its own deployment and that situates the transcendental deduction at the crossroads of what is neither absolutely objective nor entirely subjective. This space, a site of self-interpretation and meaning, breaks with the vision of a neutral, atemporal, and ahistorical encounter of subject and object. Each time, this type of encounter is enabled by certain material conditions that engage truth in its adventure.

Indeed, to become a subject capable of truth is to understand that the agreement of our categories to objects depends also on the way in which we recognize ourselves as subjects. The "forms of rationality" are inseparable from the "ways of doing things"[18] that "define objects," and thus reveal, behind "questions of general import," contexts and historically singular identities.[19]

The historical understanding of the transcendental opens up the practical dimension of the problem. The question raised by the way in which the subject receives and in return interprets their own spontaneity manages only to establish the perfect convertibility of spontaneity and autonomy one within the other. The theoretical epigenesis of the subject corresponds to the theme of progress in the practical domain. In that context, the difference between preformation and epigenesis becomes the difference between obedience to the authority of the other and the assertion of "an instruction that one gives oneself" – an instruction that Kant summarizes in the form of the Enlightenment dictum, "*Aude sapere*: 'dare to know,' 'have the courage, the audacity, to know.'"[20]

In the development of the child, the passage from minority to majority is figured by another stage: learning to walk. Having the courage and audacity to know is having the ability to walk alone.

103

Enlightenment is the human being's emergence from his self-incurred minority. Minority is inability to make use of one's own understanding without direction from another. [. . .] It is so comfortable to be a minor! If I have a book that understands for me, a spiritual advisor who has a conscience for me, a doctor who decides upon a regimen for me, and so forth, I need not trouble myself at all.[21]

There follows the image of walking:

Precepts and formulas, those mechanical instruments of a rational use, or rather misuse, of his natural endowments, are the ball and chain of an everlasting minority. And anyone who did throw them off would still make only an uncertain leap over even the narrowest ditch, since he would not be accustomed to free movement of this kind. Hence there are only a few who have succeeded, by their own cultivation of their spirit, in extricating themselves from minority and yet walking confidently.[22]

This need for maturation, self-differentiation, and the development of the subject's autonomy authorizes Foucault to see Kant's article as a text that "is located in a sense at the crossroads of critical reflection and reflection on history,"[23] and to argue that it is certainly not a "minor" text. By defining the urgency of the revolutionary moment in thought and by defining the Enlightenment as the historical decision to find a "way out," an "exit" from tradition and authority, Kant inscribes, for the first time, the question of philosophical time in critical philosophy itself. The present is the meeting point between structural permanence and the historical specificity of the transcendental structure. An epicenter. The *day*, today, thus marks the date and moment in the *a priori*. Foucault writes:

It is in the reflection on "today" as difference in history and as motive for a particular philosophical task that the novelty of this text appears to me to lie. And, by looking at it in this way, it seems to me we may recognize a point of departure: the outline of what one might call the attitude of modernity.[24]

The epigenetic malleability of thought already expresses the imperative for the self-transformation of modern humans that Foucault sees at work in Baudelaire, whom he claims prolongs and realizes the Kantian definition of the Enlightenment:

Modern man, for Baudelaire, is not the man who goes off to discover himself, his secrets and his hidden truth; he is the man who tries to invent himself. This modernity does not "liberate man in his own being"; it compels him to face the task of producing himself.[25]

104

Genealogy and Archeology

Foucault's analysis is especially interesting insofar as it appears to break decisively with the genetic inquiry against Kant himself that his readers undertake to bring him back to the source, to the "focus" of the transcendental. Initially the revelation of the historical dimension of the transcendental is a turn back towards a new sort of origin, which, as we know, Foucault first called *genealogy* then *archeology*. Genealogy and archeology are not the same as the reconstitution of a genesis. Rather, they attempt to locate the rational, starting from a failure of essential foundation, one which, far from appearing as a lack or fault, instead characterizes the structure of all foundation in general. As Foucault writes in his article "Nietzsche, Genealogy, History," "If the genealogist refuses to extend his faith in metaphysics, if he listens to history," what does he learn? "He finds that there is 'something altogether different' behind things: not a timeless and essential secret, but the secret that they have no essence."[26]

Clearly, it is possible to read this article alongside "What Is Enlightenment?" Indeed, both texts again present the idea that the absence of a foundation is a resource, not a lack. Moreover, it is perhaps the resource of absence that defines the transcendental. In the article on Nietzsche, Foucault emphasizes the difference between the German terms *Ursprung, Herkunft*, and *Entstehung*, all of which refer to origin. While *Ursprung* refers to origin in the sense of foundation, which here I have named focus, *Herkunft* and *Entstehung* refer rather to the provenance and arising that *start* from the absence of foundation. It is thus these two terms that "are more exact than *Ursprung* in recording the true objective of genealogy."[27] Contrary to all expectations, it is a matter of thinking the origin, starting from that which *did not* "impos[e] a predetermined form on all its vicissitudes."[28] It seems that finally here we have found exposed the motif of the epicenter and the "surface," defined as "the inscribed surface of events."[29]

Genealogy, which appears as the specifically Foucauldian version of epigenesis, thus proceeds starting from a divided origin, a network of forces, disparate instances of "an unstable assemblage of faults, fissures, and heterogeneous layers."[30] This uneven and discontinuous formation also refers to an understanding of *Entstehung* as "arising" at the surface, as a source that reveals no secret or underground focus: "*Entstehung* designates *emergence*, the moment of arising. It stands as the principle and the singular law of an apparition."[31] Appearance

105

without a hidden structure. Thus, genealogy "is not the erecting of foundations: on the contrary, it disturbs what was previously considered immobile; it fragments what was thought unified; it shows the heterogeneity of what was imagined consistent with itself."[32]

The End of the Order of Genetic Derivation?

But will we really manage a satisfactory determination of what an epigenetic transcendental might be, one that would allow us to return to our initial problem and situate the categorial agreement as it should be, proceeding in fact from a foundation to the surface? Is the transcendental itself, genealogically and archeologically reread and redeveloped, really freed from the inquiry into its genesis?

In a sense, it seems that this is the case. The great singularity of Foucault's reading derives from the upheaval to which it subjects the agreement of categories with experience. Indeed, it is no longer, we understand, a matter of thinking the concordance of transcendental structures and objects, but rather one of asserting the possibility of constituting the transcendental itself as an object of experience. The end of "What Is Enlightenment?" certainly unearths the conditions of possibility of an *experimental philosophy*:

> [T]his historico-critical attitude must also be an experimental one. I mean that this work done at the limits of ourselves must, on the one hand, open up a realm of historical inquiry and, on the other, put itself to the test of reality, of contemporary reality, both to grasp the points where the change is possible and desirable, and to determine the precise form this change should take.[33]

The archeo-genealogical critique "will separate out, from the contingency that has made us what we are, the possibility of no longer being, doing, or thinking what we are, do, or think."[34] Foucault explains that, henceforth, "criticism is no longer going to be practiced in the search for formal structures with universal value, but rather as a historical investigation into the events that have led us to constitute ourselves and to recognize ourselves as subjects of what we are doing, thinking, saying."[35] There would therefore be no more essential difference between the idea of formal structure and that of historical metamorphosis.

Still, does Foucault manage to bring to light a true historico-critical malleability of the transcendental?

The Two *A Priori*

It's far more complicated. In reality, and by contrast, a new *rigidity* of the transcendental comes of Foucault's claim regarding its transformability. Let me explain. Foucault's relation to the transcendental is not as clear and unambiguous as implied above. Indeed, in other texts prior to "What Is Enlightenment?" but that were never subsequently refuted, Foucault simultaneously retains and rejects the need to allow for a transcendental framework for thinking. On the one hand, he recognizes that there is no knowledge without "a play of form that anticipates all contents insofar as they have already rendered them possible."[36] These forms, "anterior to all explicit acts, to all concrete manipulations, to all given contents," establish "the unity of a science defined by a system of formal requisites and a world defined as the horizon of all possible experiences."[37] On the other hand, he rejects this necessity, as can be seen very clearly, for example, in a 1972 interview in which he says: "In all my work I strive [. . .] to avoid any reference to [the] transcendental as a condition for possibility for any knowledge."[38]

The categories and other so-called "pure" structures are tributaries of discursive formations and are "molded by a great many distinct regimes."[39] So, contrary to what he says in "What Is Enlightenment?," Foucault also states that the transcendental and history reject each other. From the time of *The Archaeology of Knowledge* (1969), he came to distinguish two *a priori*, the "formal *a priori*" and the "historical *a priori*." The formal *a priori* retains its definition as condition of possibility, while the historical *a priori* makes it possible to account for the transformation of objects of discourse and discourse itself, and consequently also their formal framework. Foucault writes that by "historical *a priori*, what I mean [. . .] is an *a priori* that is not a condition of validity for judgments, but a condition of reality for statements."[40] Later he continues:

[T]he reason for using this rather barbarous term [historical *a priori*] is that this *a priori* must take account of statements in their dispersion, in all the flaws opened up by their non-coherence, in their overlapping and mutual replacement, in their simultaneity, which is not unifiable, and in their succession, which is not deductible; in short, it has to take account of the fact that discourse has not only a meaning or a truth, but a history [. . .].[41]

There is, therefore, not as much unity between the transcendental structure, with its timeless purity, and the historical dissemination of its effects as Foucault himself asks us to believe.

It is certainly necessary to acknowledge a reciprocal action for rules and facts that destines the "agreement" between categories and objects of experience to be, in some ways, a constant decision, in the present. A permanent negotiating point must be acknowledged between the formal *a priori*, "whose jurisdiction extends without contingence,"[42] and the historical *a priori*.

At the same time, there is also a separation between form and history in Foucault. He recognizes this very early on: "The formal *a priori* and the historical *a priori* neither belong to the same level nor share the same nature: if they intersect, it is because they occupy two different dimensions."[43] Foucault versus Foucault! If the split of the *a priori* should not be envisaged as a frank rupture, a mysterious "syncopation," or a mere "play of intermittent forms"[44] – as if the formal *a priori* were "additionally" endowed with a history – then a rift must be seen between them, a difference in level, in short, a lack of coincidence.

The problem posed by this cut between the two *a priori* derives from the fact that it remains unexplained and inexplicable. Above all, it introduces a new hierarchy, with one of the two *a priori* becoming more "fundamental" than the other depending on the context – all of which surreptitiously reinscribes the possibility of genesis and dismantles the epicentric structure of discourse that we thought had finally been acknowledged.

Foucault, too, does in fact appear to relinquish the transcendental from the start by dividing it. We can't really say that "What Is Enlightenment?," which was written fifteen years after *The Archaeology of Knowledge*, really corrects and modifies his conclusions. Actually, in "What Is Enlightenment?", Foucault ultimately declares that the "new" criticism, "genealogical in its design and archeological in its method," is "not transcendental."[45] But it is not the mere return of the skeptic's circle that is the most astonishing here. What is most surprising is that what may appear to be a hesitation, an opposing position, in Foucault's uncertainty with regard to the transcendental paradoxically produced the dominant definition of the transcendental in twentieth-century continental philosophy.

The Transcendental as a Residuum

Let me explain. Foucault says that he does everything to "avoid" having recourse to the transcendental. That he "historicize[s it] to the utmost." That the two levels of the *a priori* – the formal and the historical – are discontinuous and impossible to adjust. But then, in the 1972 interview cited above, he adds:

> When I say that I strive to avoid it, I don't mean that I am sure of succeeding. [. . .] I try to historicize to the utmost to leave as little space as possible to the transcendental. I cannot exclude the possibility that one day I will have to confront an irreducible *residuum* which will be, in fact, the transcendental.[46]

In the last resort, having considered the possibilities of experimenting with, historicizing, or avoiding the transcendental, Foucault ultimately proposes a minimal definition that jams the cogs as they move towards a break. The transcendental is defined as a residuum, that is, as something that it is impossible to evacuate entirely. While Foucault's critical position questions the value of universality and the necessity of the conditions of possibility of cognition and thinking in Kant's work, and while it breaks the continuity between formal and historical structures, it still retains the *irreducible* nature of the transcendental. A *residual definition itself* on which continental philosophers would generally agree. The transcendental could lose the technical meaning it has in Kant, it could even lose its status of formal structure, of logical anteriority: it is what *resists*, what cannot be reduced. Again, this irreducibility is the other name for meaning. In the end, the difference between criticism and skepticism lies in the support of "critical" philosophers – that is, actually the majority of continental philosophers – for the residual existence of meaning as that which does not allow itself to be assimilated to any empirical determination, especially biological determinations. Of course, we have seen that the mind leaving its state of minority is presented as a maturation. All the same, this question of age and growth does not imply any organic definition of the mind. Biology without body. Body without organs.

But after all, what's the problem? Why would we not be satisfied with this definition of the transcendental as irreducible? Quite simply because the assertion of the irreducibility of meaning is merely postulated, never deduced. What do we call irreducible? Who could ever answer? And what exactly is irreducible since Foucault says, moreover, that any formal structure is subject to different modes of historical and experimental transformation? We'll never know. The residuum has no reason. Hence the "irreducible" appears as the new aspect of a presupposed, *preformed* instance that contradicts the economy of transformability in which it is supposed to be inscribed. The entire development of "What Is Enlightenment?" regarding the present and history is accompanied by the assertion of the irreducible's character as being outside of time. By definition, irreducibility cannot change; it *remains* what it is; it forms a bar of principled resistance that does not develop, does not differentiate itself, an identitarian rock without formation that resists all experimentation and presides over all the historical occurrences of its subjects, of its "us." In this sense, it is incompatible with the whole idea of epigenesis.

— 10 —

TIME IN QUESTION

Stem and Root

At this point, where the aporia appears in its most extreme form, we might ask why we have waited so long before allowing Heidegger to speak, why he has been left hanging since the introduction to this book. Wouldn't Heidegger have helped us immediately settle the question of the instability of the transcendental and thereby escape all these dead ends?

Heidegger completely adjourns all hesitation in regard to the nature and role of the transcendental. First in *Being and Time* and then in *Kant and the Problem of Metaphysics*, he shows that what Kant called "transcendental" cannot be anything but the form of time. Not present time, nor a simple historical now, but an original time that depends on no particular age, not even the age of Enlightenment. I might have saved myself considerable effort by establishing from the start that if there is a possible mobility or transformability of the transcendental, revealed by the figure of epigenesis, then this is originally equated with what Heidegger calls the "temporalization of time." Only this understanding of the transcendental as primordial temporality makes it possible to describe it simultaneously, without any contradiction or dissociation, as both structure *and* movement. As antecedence *and* deployment. As before *and* after. In a word, as *a priori epigenesis*. This understanding of the transcendental also modifies its definition as an "irreducible" dimension that, paradoxically, detemporalizes it. And if, for Heidegger, time itself may be called irreducible, this irreducibility is engaged in the ecstatic process to which it refers, a moving and fluid process that rips it out of all fixity.

It is important at this point not to confuse the temporal mobility of the transcendental with ordinary instability. If Heidegger does indeed claim that there is a lack of a bedrock for the transcendental, this lack is certainly not the result of its temporal nature, but instead results from the fact that Kant denies this temporal aspect in the second edition of the *Critique of Pure Reason*. This instability is not therefore an essential instability but rather the instability of a disavowal. It is linked not to time, but rather to the negation of time – a negation that Foucault failed to notice. Kant "shrank back" from the view, developed in 1781, of a transcendental that – because it is temporal, because it is linked to time itself – is without rigidity and has no essence except outside of itself. Instability derives only from questioning this view, which leads to a reduction in the role of the transcendental imagination and explains the now shaky character of synthesis.

Had I followed the arguments of *Kant and the Problem of Metaphysics* from the start, I would therefore have been able to demonstrate swiftly that behind the debate between preformation and epigenesis hides a more fundamental question, namely the question of the temporal meaning of the *a priori*, which indicates an antecedence, a "before" of a very particular sort, and which, far from lacking in stability, is none other than the true meaning of the Kantian laying of the ground for the origin.

Readings of Kant that are not attentive to this meaning are marked by the stamp of the disequilibrium that they either condemn or attempt to ward off. If no attention is paid to the ontological-temporal sense – in other words, for Heidegger, the "metaphysical" sense of the transcendental – then in every case the question of the origin is reduced to the "vulgarity" of a beginning, whether it be that of a preformation, a historical "now," or even a biological determination, as so many versions of the same ambiguity.

Taking Stock

From the start, it is indeed the question of time that, explicitly or not, orients all the readings of Kant analyzed up to this point. As a whole, they express a symptomatic indecision between "before" and "after." The interpretations by Zöller and Zammito are the most representative examples of the "before" approach. We recall that, according to them, despite what he says, Kant does not advocate epigenesis and was never able to "come to terms with the implications for his analogy between epigenesis and transcendental philosophy."[1]

112

According to both Zöller and Zammito, if one does not know how to read the analogy in §27, it can only give rise to "a fundamental erosion of Kant's boundary between the constitutive and the regulative, between the transcendental and the empirical."[2] We must therefore conclude that when he appears to be a supporter of epigenesis, Kant does not really think what he says or say what he thinks. The agreement between categories and objects is certainly not innate, but the epigenetic analogy, to contradict innatism, introduces no less to it than the idea of an embryonic development and formation that do not match the definition of the transcendental. The only way to escape the paradox thus occurs via recourse to preformationism: everything must be decided *before*. The "after" is nothing but the unfolding of this antecedence – the "*germ*" or the "original predisposition" of the *a priori*.

By contrast, taking their cue from the "evolutionary" skeptical argument, those who support the "after" declare that there is no *a priori*: time and development follow the same line. The epigenesis of reason – in reality the epigenesis of the brain – has no identity other than that which results from evolution, visible after the fact, and that is, moreover, both modifiable and unpredictable. Time is the time of adaptation, and its product is the agreement of the categories with objects. The transcendental then dissolves in the movement of its adjustment to the real. Everything is postponed until tomorrow.

As we have seen, between this "before" and "after," Foucault attempts to bring to light a historical "present" that actualizes the form of the transcendental and situates it exactly between the preliminary structure and the subsequent transformation. Despite it all, this "between two" is not one, since Foucault does not manage to articulate the terms and in fact emphasizes their discontinuity. The transcendental is assimilated to the paradoxically *atemporal* form of the "irreducible."

The figure of epigenesis thus seems to be fated to provoke this oscillation between the *a priori* and the *a posteriori*, before and after, in Kant's text – an oscillation between structural fixity and historical-adaptive transformation that is the flagrant marker of the instability of the transcendental. And so this figure fails to find its place. It causes a series of apparently uncontrollable logical-temporal collisions. The result is a fundamental indecision in regard to the definition of reason: is it the development of the brain or the ultimately atemporal irreducibility of critique?

By emphasizing this oscillation, this fragmentation, we can ask Heidegger, *now*, what he thinks of these approaches. For him, none of them would have been sufficient to resolve the question. Epigenesis is often related to time without time being rigorously thought and without illuminating the supposed disequilibrium – the irreducible disequilibrium, to play on the phrase – of the transcendental structure.

Schematism and Objectivity

Heidegger shows that the true problem presented by *a priori* agreement of our categories to the objects of experience, of their synthetic connection to their objective validity, is *authentic* time.[3] Without mentioning epigenesis, Heidegger nevertheless speaks about the *a priori* "formation" of the categories, stating that: "In the question concerning the possible use of the categories, their particular essence itself first becomes a problem. These concepts present us with the question of their 'formation' in general (*Diese Begriffe stellen vor die Frage nach die Möglichkeit ihrer 'Bildung' überhaupt*)."[4]

Yet the question of this formation cannot be understood from the Deduction alone. The mistake of many previous readings is that of limiting themselves to this sole framework. The production or epigenesis of the categories, as well as their agreement with objects, occurs not as a present, now, or historical moment, but rather in the operation of the *schematism*. "In the Transcendental Schematism the categories are formed first of all as categories,"[5] writes Heidegger. The question of epigenesis cannot therefore be understood and resolved except by taking into account the essential role of the schematism. In the Deduction, the synthesis, and the fundamental role that the productive imagination plays in it, must first be exposed in order for the idea of a pure development of *a priori* forms to subsequently find its concreteness.

In the Deduction of the first edition of the *Critique of Pure Reason*, Kant demonstrates that the imagination plays the role of a middle term between the understanding and intuition. Indeed, it produces the first "scene," the "pure look (*reiner Anblick*)," that makes any objective encounter possible *a priori*. Thinking and objectivity agree with each other from the start in this scene. "This unique possibility of having a certain *look* shows itself in itself to be nothing other than always just time and the temporal."[6] Imagination opens the "horizon" prior to the encounter, time itself, a "pure look" on "what is offered." But we must go further, reading beyond the Deduction.

Indeed, further on, Kant asserts the necessity, for this look, of concretely elaborating, of being "formable (*bildbar*) in a variety of

114

ways."[7] As we have seen, the look is not innate, nor is it "established." The opening that it is has yet to occur, to order the modes of grasping and the rules of connection of objects determined by the categorial agreement according to a "now," a "before," and an "after". Epigenesis thus truly takes off in the passage from the initial pure look to the multiple images that are the schemata, specific determinations that render categories homogeneous with objects. "The pure look of time must exhibit four possibilities of formability as 'time-series, time-content, time-order, and time-inclusiveness.'"[8] The schemata objectivize agreement, bringing it to maturity in a sense without ever threatening to introduce experience into the *a priori*, and conversely without ever fixing it in an antecedence without development or future. Thanks to a sort of *a posteriori* of and in the *a priori* itself, "[the schemata] articulate the unique pure possibility of having a certain look into a variety of pure images."[9] In this way, they form a contact surface between the first horizon and objectification that founds the validity of the agreement. A series of images spring up at the epicenter, orienting the transcendental to the object.

The agreement, "preliminary letting-stand-again which turns-our-attention-towards,"[10] is indeed the structure's coming out of itself towards the form of the world. When Kant states that this agreement is not innate, but rather is produced *a priori*, he is doing far more than adopting a position against innatism or Hume. He is also doing more than refuting the idea of a possible contingency of the laws of nature or the founding principles of science. He is, in fact, developing the philosophical question of the origin in an entirely new manner. Heidegger maintains that the initial project of the *Critique of Pure Reason* is the "attempt to point out an origin for pure thinking in the transcendental power of the imagination, and therewith for theoretical reason in general."[11] All questions of origin – what is innate? what is originarily acquired? – are derived from the perspective of that which precedes them all ontologically: how does the time of the origin come to the mind, and does it coincide with it? Heidegger writes that in Kant: "Time and the 'I think' no longer stand incompatibly and incomparably at odds; they are the same."[12]

It is *a priori* that at the origin, the origin can be nothing but an image. Not the image of something, nor even the image of itself, but a pure image, the first image of all – which opens its horizon to thinking and, thereby, through a series of schemata, to the world. Rationality thus draws its source from the iconic form – neither categorial nor sensible – of such a scene. Time is the inaugural poïetic of reason.

The pure image (of) time thus appears as the absolute antecedence that the schemata serve to differentiate, pluralize, and regulate. In this pure image, the three ecstasies (past, present, future) are equiprimordial. "Before" and "after" are contemporaries there. Thus, there is no contradiction in envisaging their coexistence and reversibility at this level. Taken into account from this perspective, the idea of *a priori* epigenesis loses its contradictory character. It is inscribed in this first moment where the past is always at the same time to come, or tomorrow, reciprocally, always comes before today.

Thus, and once again, for Kant, "the laying of the ground for metaphysics grows upon the ground of time."[13] Absolutely no instability of the transcendental structure ensues from this, there is no lack of solidity whatsoever, and there is no skeptical wandering secretly inscribed in the heart of the *a priori*. Instead, what appears is "the essential unity of ontological knowledge."[14] In Kant, the meaning of the pure image coincides with the question of being.

The Second Edition

Or at least this is what would happen unless a counterforce appears to threaten to unsettle this foundation and unity, despite it all! According to Heidegger, this is precisely what happens in the second edition of the *Critique of Pure Reason*. In it, the Kantian breakthrough in the direction of primordial temporality is covered over. This dual move of concealment and unconcealment explains the ambiguity of the status of the transcendental, which closes almost immediately to its own dimension of opening.

In the second edition, the assimilation of the transcendental and primordial temporality disappears as a result of the relegation of the productive imagination to a subaltern role. The understanding becomes the nourishing ground of objectivity and truth through its spontaneity alone. Heidegger writes:

> However, because the transcendental power of imagination, on the grounds of its indissoluble, original structure, opens up the possibility of the laying of a ground for ontological knowledge, and thereby for metaphysics, then for this reason the first edition remains closer to the innermost thrust of the problematic of a laying of the ground for metaphysics. With reference to this most central question of the whole work, therefore, it [the first edition] deserves a fundamental priority over the second. All reinterpretation (*Umdeutung*) of the pure power of the imagination as a function of pure thinking [. . .] misunderstands its specific essence.[15]

116

The henceforth definitive lack of an intermediary between the understanding and intuition causes the instability and precarious nature of the foundation. One essential term is lacking: the image. All that is left are logical acts that do not give time and that are no longer inscribed on a horizon. There is no longer any first ground. What remains is the spontaneity of the understanding, which is unjustifiable when it is not accompanied by the spontaneity of the productive imagination.

The figure of epigenesis – which appears only in the second edition – would then be viewed by Heidegger simultaneously as *witness* and *erasure* of the temporalization of the transcendental. As generative production, epigenesis reveals the inscription of time in thinking. But it can also be read as resistance to this very inscription. Indeed, for Heidegger, the time of epigenesis, borrowed from biology, would then be the very expression of vulgar time, derived from nature and life, which only shows once again a bit more of the loss of the status of the pure image. The way in which the formation of categorial agreement is presented in the second edition suffers the consequences of the amputation of the synthesis: without imagination, time is no longer anything but objective time. As an image, epigenesis does remain a product of the imagination, but of an impoverished imagination and, there again, entirely detemporalized. Embryonic development is henceforth its only horizon.

What We Might Have Understood

Heidegger would thus have enabled us to understand why most interpretations of Kant go round in circles because they do not consider epigenesis as an ontological symptom: sometimes it is a sign of time, at others a sign of the concealment of time, or a hybrid mix of primordial temporality and leveled-down temporality. Deprived of this searching look, these interpretations themselves also suffer from the same ambiguity and remain undecided regarding the ontological status of the transcendental. Whether they subsequently decide to situate the transcendental, to actualize it, or to relinquish it – ultimately, all amounts to the same.

Once again, transcendental epigenesis is indeed brought back by one side to the problem of auto-affection (Zöller), to a certain power of invention and *a priori* improvisation (Lebrun), in a word, to temporalization. Foucault's claim that there cannot be any *a priori* without history, nor any transcendental without a present, is clearly an attempt to take into account the temporality of the transcendental.

Nevertheless, Heidegger would certainly have asked whether the time of "minimal preformationism" defined by Zöller – this prior time – was, truly, time. If so, wouldn't it unfold ecstatically, rather than remaining fixed to its prior or antecedent dimension, without any future, without development or formation? By dint of seeking to dispel the contamination of the transcendental by experience, it is deprived of posterity. We might therefore fear that "the before" that Zöller defends might also be nothing but a moment of leveled-down time. As for Foucault, what does he call "history" then? What is the nature of the separation that he introduces between the historical *a priori* and the formal *a priori*? Is this separation itself temporal, or does it appear, rather, devoid of any ontological status, detemporalized once again like the irreducibility that supports it? By what grace can it then be given in a "present"?

As for the skeptical track, it has allowed us to explore the dynamic of epigenesis as the evolution and gradual adaptation of thinking to its objects. This examination has opened up a confrontation between modern epigenesis and contemporary epigenetics and has led to an exploration of the equating of reason and the brain. Now, this type of equating also proceeds, in its own way, from a reflection on time. From the first moment of embryonic life, the brain prepares the synchronization of bodily movements. And this synchronization, as the motor program for planning of postures, constitutes the primitive notion of time and thus appears as the basis of the temporal form of consciousness. This first form is indispensable for the emergence of the categories. As Edelman argues, "[C]ategorization depends on smooth gestures and postures as much as it does on sensory sheets."[16] In fact, the "smooth movements" of postures are first categorized by perception, then logically redeveloped to give rise to categorization and conceptuality, strictly speaking.[17] The rejection of any transcendental dimension in the genesis of rationality is thus also based on a determinate concept of temporality.

Obviously, Heidegger would have objected that temporality can never derive from a natural given, nor from its redevelopment by consciousness. The psychological genesis of time is not time. The "biologizing" interpretation thus only takes into account derived time and entirely lacks the ontological reach of epigenesis. This is why it fails to understand what the transcendental dimension of thinking can mean.

It would then have been simple, rapid, and effective to systematically follow the two tracks of critical and skeptical readings back to the internal articulation of temporality as Heidegger explains it – an ontological ambiguity between authentic temporality and vulgar

118

time. The motif of epigenesis in §27 could have been illuminated right from the start from this articulation, and analyzed as its symptom.

Why Didn't I Take Heidegger's Lead?

If I did not do so, it is because it is not certain that Heidegger, who is no doubt the deepest of all of Kant's readers, himself escapes the genetic reading, even if he argues that he never had recourse to the concept of genesis. It is not certain that the difference between the two times – primordial and leveled-down – is not a new hierarchy, once again introducing a slope that situates the source as an overlook. Nor is it certain, finally, that this inequality is not the secret reason for the disappearance of the question of time.

— 11 —

NO AGREEMENT

Before I demonstrate this, I should pause to allow Meillassoux to intervene. According to Meillassoux, Heidegger remains prisoner to the conception of time that he criticizes in every instance. Heidegger's time is no more "authentic" than the time of metaphysics. Indeed, without exception, all the correlationist philosophers – Heidegger included – who start from the principle of the agreement or synthesis between thought and objects as the indisputable origin of truth end up missing precisely the first time, what one might call the primitive time of the "ancestral." They fail to situate the very antecedence of the origin, its past, how exactly it comes "before."

Meillassoux explains that starting from correlation in effect amounts to always starting from a now, a present, in order to *subsequently* make projections towards the past or future, in a "countersensi-cal temporality."[1] The correlationist proceeds "from the present to the past, following a logical order, rather than from the past to the present, following a chronological order."[2] The term *a priori* should not mislead us. In Kant, "before" is a logical present, the present of the agreement between thought and objectivity. It is this primacy of the logical over the chronological that has remained unshaken since then. The Heideggerian determination of transcendence, which grants the value of an origin, an ontological precondition, to the encounter between thought and the world, still signals this obedience. Thus we note "Heidegger's strict observance of the correlationist 'two-step.'"[3] For him, "there is a deeper level of temporality, within which what came before the relation-to-the-world is itself but a modality of that relation-to-the-world."[4] This temporality, which starts from the corre-lational present, is a "becoming – in which what came before no longer comes before, and what comes after no longer comes after [. . .]."[5]

120

The correlationist never takes into account the past understood as that which is prior to the relation, prior to life, and hence also indifferent to our existence, as well as to the fact of being thought. The transcendental is thus not the other name of time, as Heidegger claims, but instead is precisely that which inverts its course and, as such, denies it. No concept of time can be authentic in a philosophy that starts from synthesis as the primordial fact and thus accomplishes "a retrojection of the past on the basis of the present."[6] The main question "after Kant and since Kant" is thus not, as Heidegger argues, "what is the foundation of metaphysics?" but rather "which is the proper correlate?"[7] And this implies knowing how to determine the correlate: is it a pre-established harmony, a preformed whole, an instance of epigenetic development? Is it a production of transcendental imagination? While responses vary, the question is always the same. In the end, it is still and always in starting from the correlational *present* that the transcendental is questioned, critiqued, or deconstructed – and that we fail to relinquish it.

The discourses that could have, or should have, developed the post-critical succession of philosophy (destruction, deconstruction, genealogy or archeology) did not do so because they themselves were versions of correlationism. Correlationism is thus seen to encompass all philosophers from Kant to the present day. The list Meillassoux draws up is impressive: Schelling, Hegel, Schopenhauer, Nietzsche, Bergson, Heidegger, Wittgenstein, Deleuze . . . Correlationist metaphysics

> may select from among various forms of subjectivity, but it is invariably characterized by the fact that it hypostatizes some mental, sentient, or vital term [of course, this evokes the brain]: representation in the Leibnizian monad; Schelling's Nature, or the objective subject-object; Hegelian Mind; Schopenhauer's Will; the Will [. . .] to Power in Nietzsche, perception loaded with memory in Bergson; Deleuze's Life, etc. [. . .]. Nothing can be unless it is some form of relation-to-the-world.[8]

Return to §27:
The Impotence of the Transcendental Deduction

And so it turns out that in fact the direction that Kantian critique gave to the history of philosophy – including the destruction of metaphysics – is not impassible, as it was thought to be. The questioning of the primordial nature of correlation plunges us once again deep into the heart of the Deduction, to the same place as that of our problem, the "agreement" between thought and appearances, and, as a consequence, the legitimization of "the application of the categories to experience."[9] None of the readings of Kant discussed up to this point, including the anti-Kantian ones, question the fact that all truth, all objectivity, all stability, result entirely from the "agreement" between thought and objects, whether this agreement be declared logically transformable, biologically malleable, historically becoming, or ontologically ecstatic. Contemporary epigenetics itself does not for a moment question this state of affairs. Even derived, the agreement between brain and the external world remains the starting point of rationality.

Meillassoux argues that so long as the causal order of the world is examined in the light of the relation between the categories and experience, so long as this causal order constitutes the basis of any inquiry into the necessity of the laws of nature and the regularity of the world, the skeptical thesis and the critical thesis can but amount to the same. The vicious circle that traps all the previous approaches – which end up appearing identical even though they are opposed most of the time – is produced by the insufficiencies of a shared starting point.

It is the principle of the agreement that is problematic, not its modality. According to Meillassoux, it is in fact never possible to justify the agreement other than factually. We saw this at the start: the agreement is observed and cannot be deduced. The dimension of self-interpretation which, in Kant, consists in the reception and appropriation by the subject of its own spontaneity only serves to fill in the gap of the absent proof. The fact that the agreement proceeds from the dynamic of an epigenesis, from the logic of a genesis, or from the fixity of a preformation, whether situated at the epicenter or in the underground depths of the focus, changes absolutely nothing. The contingency that the transcendental can never dispel, which thereby escapes it and demands a total conceptual re-elaboration, is the contingency revealed by its own facticity.

The categorial agreement and the necessity that ought to flow from it can thus never be deduced in any case: they "can only be described, not founded."[10] The existence of a formative transcendental force remains a derived problem in this regard. Whether or not the transcendental is transformable is of little importance. It will never be plastic enough to explode its correlational origin.

We must face the facts: the transcendental is contingent. The problem is that it is not contingent the way Foucault says it is. Its contingency cannot be assimilated to its possible historical mutability, to the changing nature of its structures, to the factual and circumstantial genealogy of the *a priori* that might hide behind a supposed ahistoricity. Still more remarkable, the contingency analyzed here is not the contingency of the skeptics either.

Hume beyond Himself

Let us return briefly to Hume, the principal adversary addressed in §27. The "problem of Hume," which is at the core of the transcendental deduction, cannot be resolved by Kant, but nor is it resolved by Hume either. Its treatment can therefore be neither critical nor skeptical. Meillassoux asks:

> What is this problem? In its traditional version it can be formulated as follows: is it possible to demonstrate that the same effects will always follow from the same causes *ceteris paribus*, i.e. all other things being equal? In other words, can one establish that in identical circumstances, future successions of appearances will always be identical to previous successions? The question raised by Hume concerns our capacity to prove that the laws of physics will remain tomorrow what they are today, or still yet to demonstrate the necessity of the causal connection.[11]

Why must this problem be "reformulated" after Hume *and* after Kant? The answer is as follows: although Hume asserts that reason is incapable of proving causal necessity, he never for one minute questions this necessity itself. Hume and Kant thus "share a common assumption." Neither of them

> ever calls into question *the truth of the causal necessity.* [. . .] [T]he question is never whether causal necessity actually exists or not but rather whether or not it is possible to furnish a reason for its necessity. [. . .] Hume [. . .] never really doubts causal necessity – he merely doubts our capacity to ground the latter through reasoning. [. . .] [P]hysical processes are indeed possessed of ultimate necessity. And it is precisely because Hume concedes this that he can characterize his own position as *skeptical* – for to be a skeptic is to concede that reason is incapable of providing a basis for our adherence to a necessity we assume to be real.[12]

He goes on to write:

> [T]he skeptical position is the most paradoxical, for on the one hand it seeks to show how the principle of reason is incapable of founding its

ontological pretensions, yet on the other, it continues to believe in the necessity – the real, physical necessity – that this principle has *injected* into the world.[13]

The thesis of "pre-established harmony," *as* the thesis of a "system of the epigenesis of pure reason," thus starts from the indubitable nature of agreement.

As for the "neo-skeptical" argument that determines the truth of the adaptive processes of the mind and defends mental Darwinism, it certainly questions any notion of an *a priori*, but it also remains attached to the correlational structure. Evolutionists may well assert the contingent nature of truth, but this contingency does not put into question the process of joint development of mind and nature. A *posteriori* synthesis it may be, but agreement it is nonetheless.

It is therefore no surprise to see again the constant circularity of the critical and skeptical positions. They both recognize the indubitable nature of causal necessity and the agreement of categories with objects – whether the agreement be *a priori* or empirically derived. The pair of opposites that they form is thus not really one and offers thought nothing but a false alternative.

The Wholly Other World

Since correlation is the acknowledgment of a contingency that it cannot hide, let's put aside correlation to think through contingency. A radical contingency that is so radical that it becomes absolutely necessary as a result. This type of contingency leads thinking to recognize another origin of truth. Until now, we have only examined one type of possible transformation: the content of laws, according to the hypothesis of an adaptive changeability (mental evolutionism) or historical changeability (Foucauldian critique) of the agreement of the mind with objects. We have not yet envisaged the possibility that change may concern the synthetic structure itself, the first co-implication of subject and object.

Now, so long as correlation is not in question, the transcendental is safe. Its experimental becoming or evolutionary fluidification can always be invoked. So long as these hypotheses do not touch the subject–object relation, nothing changes. At the same time, because this permanence is paradoxically unstable, shaky due to its facticity, the correlational structure cannot protect itself against what it is nevertheless supposed to prevent: the thesis of another possible world. A

124

world in which it would not exist. Reading Meillassoux, it becomes apparent that the only real, serious possibility of a changeability of the transcendental would be the one implied by the revelation of its nature as a screen, and, consequently also, its real ability to disappear.

That the world could change, that it could become wholly other, absolutely other, without synthesis or agreement, is indeed the hypothesis that criticism completely rejects. And yet, as a result of its inability to show the reason for this rejection – the necessary nature of *a priori* synthesis and the causal connections between appearances – critical philosophy is a negative avowal of recognition of that which it disavows. Once again, the transcendental origin fails to self-deduce. Hence, it self-destructs.

Clearly this is not to aim at a "fault" in the Kantian argument, but rather to denounce a presupposition and to assert that whatever the origin and type of validity it confers upon it, the correlational structure can only ever reveal its precariousness. There is nothing but contingency. Better yet, "contingency *alone* is necessary."[14] We might as well accept then that "from now on, we will use the term 'factuality' to describe the speculative essence of *facticity*,"[15] in other words, the absoluteness of contingency. We also might as well accept that, contrary to what Kant claims in his refutation of Hume, the world can change form. Again, this does not mean that the transcendental may or may not modify, vary, evolve, but that it does not exist at all. The order of things "could actually *change at any moment*" and exceeds our "categories," on which it does not depend.[16]

> And indeed, one unavoidable consequence of the principle of factuality is that it asserts the actual contingency of the laws of nature. If we are seriously maintaining that everything *seems* to us to have no reason to be the way it is, *is* actually devoid of any necessary reason to be the way it is, and could actually change for no reason, then we must seriously maintain that the laws of nature could change [. . .] for no cause or reason whatsoever.[17]

I repeat that despite what we might initially think, this statement does not amount to the "classical" skeptical thesis. It is not to simply return to Hume by developing at new expense a critique of transcendental idealism based on the ultimately unsurpassable nature of the arguments developed in the *Treatise* and the *Enquiry*.

As we have seen, for Hume only a pre-established harmony between our understanding and the laws of the nature can explain the validity of our adherence – and it never amounts to anything more than a belief – to the principle according to which the same causes always engender the same effects, starting from the stability of nature and the possibility of physics. Yet, once again, Hume is not up to solving his own problem. He is not the one who can respond *a posteriori* to Kant, which makes the possibility of physics one of the fundamental questions of the *Critique of Pure Reason*.[18] Paragraph 27 emphasizes the fact that the Humean presupposition of pre-established harmony is incapable of demonstrating the solidity and stability of causal connections. According to Kant, the relation of our pure concepts to the objects of experience proceeds from an *a priori* necessity recognized by consciousness, upon which representations are based. Cinnabar must *always* be red and heavy in order to be constituted as an object for my representation. Indeed, for Kant,

> the very idea of consciousness and experience requires a structuring of representation capable of making our world into something other than a purely arbitrary sequence of disconnected impressions. This is the central thesis of the so-called "objective" deduction of the categories, the aim of which is to legitimate the application of the categories to experience (the categories being understood as those universal connections presupposed by physics in particular).[19]

Against Kant, Hume would have had nothing but his concept of chance as defense. But Meillassoux argues that chance is not the expression of radical contingency. While chance is commonly associated with the traditional concept of contingency, it is linked to the calculation of odds and probabilities. Yet the probabilistic conception of contingency – the famous example of the billiard balls – conceals absolute contingency. This is why Meillassoux invites us to rigorously distinguish absolute contingency from chance.[20] Indeed, "the effectuation of [chance] already presupposes a pre-existing set of laws."[21] In this sense, it does not question the order of the world, but rather confirms it in its own way.

> This is precisely what the example of the dice-throw shows: an aleatory sequence can only be generated on condition that the dice preserve their structure from one throw to the next, and that the laws allowing the throw to be carried out not change from one cast to the next. If from one throw to the next the dice imploded, or became flat or spherical, multiplied its sides by a thousand [. . .] then there would be no aleatory sequence, and it would be impossible to establish a calculus of probabilities. Thus chance always presupposes some form of physical invariance – far from permitting us to think the contingency of physical laws, chance itself is nothing other than a certain type of physical law – one that is "indeterministic."[22]

126

To take on the task of countering Kant's "necessitarian" argument solely with Hume's arguments, by claiming that "the continuing existence of our world can in fact be explained by chance alone,"[23] would not therefore have the scope on which it depends and would not allow the definitive relinquishing of the transcendental without reprieve. Chance, as we have just seen, does not impinge on the necessity of the laws of physics.

In other words, chance is never sufficiently chancy to put into question the concept of possibilities. Probabilities are possibilities. Chance in no way unsettles the stability of the concepts of the possible and the necessary. Rather, it presupposes them. Thus, the assimilation of contingency to chance, which allows for the calculus of probabilities,

> assumes that there does indeed exist a totality of non-contradictory conceivable possibilities. [...] It is necessary to assume that a set of possible worlds [...] is actually conceivable, if not intuitable [...]. Thus, probabilistic reasoning is conceivable on condition that it be possible to conceive a totality of cases within which one can then calculate frequencies by determining the ratio of the number of favourable cases to the number of possible cases. [...] Aleatory reasoning – which is to say, the very idea of chance insofar as the latter is subject to a calculus of frequency – presupposes the notion of numerical totality.[24]

This kind of idea of totality bears witness precisely to the adhesion of "skeptical" thought – the one that ventures into the game, throws the dice, or the billiard ball – to causal necessity. There is a whole set of possibilities. All the possibilities are possible, except the disappearance of possibility as the totality of possibilities.

It is therefore necessary to take Hume's problem beyond Kant, of course, but also beyond Hume himself, in order to look for the solution in a certain type of mathematical reasoning. According to Meillassoux, another thought of possibility is found in the notion of "transfinite," "progressively elaborated during the first half of the twentieth century on the basis of Cantor's work, [and which consists in] its unencompassable pluralization of infinite quantities."[25] The mathematical impossibility of totalizing possibilities frees up the way to a concept of contingency that is perfectly distinct from that of chance, a concept that requires a break with the logic of calculating probabilities and the random reasoning that is traditionally assigned to the topic of the contingent. The "transfinite," more infinite than infinity, reveals the invalidity of any attempt to totalize the possible under the name of the infinite. "*The (quantifiable) totality of the thinkable is unthinkable.*"[26]

Radical contingency must be thought well and truly as the possibility of a world "devoid of *any* physical necessity," without this possibility being probable or therefore quantifiable in any way.[27] An *irrecoverable* contingency therefore. Without an idea, if, following Kant, one is willing to define an idea as a totality of conditions. Radical contingency cannot give rise to any positive knowledge of the possible insofar as the possible that it is will perhaps never come to pass. To separate the possible from all totality – from all the possibles (Hume) and from all the conditions of possibility (Kant) – is the work of the philosophy to come, which marks its rediscovered affinity with mathematics.

Indeed, the relation between philosophy and science must be reconsidered in depth. This question is more urgent than ever. This relation can no longer depend on a critique of pure reason and assumes a renewed access to the absolute understood as the reality of a world devoid of all anthropological priority – including when this priority is hidden behind a deconstruction of what belongs to the human. Relinquishing the transcendental involves a far more radical move than the mere assertion of its biological or historical modifiability. It is no longer a matter of questioning the relation between the *a priori* and the *a posteriori*, between categories and appearances, but of thinking a world foreign to experience, to *our* experience. A possibility that even the destruction of metaphysics never envisaged. In the end,

we must grasp how the ultimate absence of reason, which we will refer to as "unreason," is an absolute ontological property, and not the mark of the finitude of our knowledge [. . .]. The failure of the principle of reason follows, quite simply, from the *falsity* (and even from the absolute falsity) of such a principle – for the truth is that there is no reason for anything to be or to remain thus and so rather than otherwise, and this applies as much to the laws that govern the world as to the things of the world. Everything could actually collapse: from trees to stars, from stars to laws, from physical laws to logical laws; and this not by virtue of some superior law whereby everything is destined to perish, but by virtue of the absence of any superior law capable of preserving anything, no matter what, from perishing.[28]

If everything can ultimately collapse, then why didn't I follow Meillassoux earlier as well? Isn't the answer to my original questions contained in *After Finitude*, in a manner that is even more radical than Heidegger?

— 12 —

THE DEAD END

Between Censure and License

Kant would no doubt have been amused to hear that two hundred and fifty years after the publication of the *Critique of Pure Reason* there are claims that the question of the agreement between categories and objects bars the way to scientific and philosophical truth. That the concept of *a priori* synthesis diverts the deep meaning of the Copernican Revolution by subjectivizing that which in reality is a decentering outside of all subjectivity.[1] That this error in orientation, or this set-up, this "catastrophe," ultimately brought about the defeat of speculative thinking. That one day someone argued that it was necessary to reformulate the question of how "a mathematized science of nature is possible". . .[2]

Yet, these statements must be taken seriously insofar as they reveal the profound transformation that continental philosophy is currently undergoing. Meillassoux's intervention bursts the abscess that has gradually formed around Kantianism and brings into broad daylight the symptomatic hesitation that the status of the transcendental continues to elicit.

I have deliberately sought to amass points of view, accumulate conclusions, juxtapose readings of §27, and present ways of understanding the transcendental, beginning with its supposed lack of foundation, so as to highlight the doubt whose acuteness is aggravated in contemporary thought. The transcendental: ought we to save it or deconstruct it, transform it or derive it, temporalize it or destroy it? As we have seen, more often than not, the moves to conserve and relinquish the transcendental overlap.

129

The question of how we should understand *a priori* epigenesis led me to present and evaluate theoretical interventions with serious consequences. Kant is not just any philosopher since, as I noted, he acts as the guarantor of the identity of continental or "European" philosophy. Doesn't this philosophy, whose visibility and institutional power are constantly shrinking all over the world, owe its specificity precisely to his claim that something like the transcendental exists? Something that Kant presents as the form of thought and whose theoretical and practical reality exist for thought alone? Undoubtably, adherence or opposition to the transcendental, more than any other criteria, marks the fracture line between the continental and analytic traditions, that is, between two ways of understanding rationality.

As I have tried to show, the problem is that acceptance of the transcendental, far from being univocal, is often already, in itself, an opposition to it. Any post-Kantian attempt to save the transcendental always turns out to be, one way or another, an attack on it. Indeed, as the critical track in the readings of §27 allowed us to demonstrate, Kant's heirs are forever divided between two views of the transcendental: the *hyper*-normative and the *hypo*-normative.

According to the *hyper*-normative view, the transcendental represents a sort of censure that absolutely prohibits any mixing with experience, and consequently all becoming and all transformation of logical forms. Assertions about Kant's preformationism, for example, proceed from just such a conception, from a policed, or even policing, transcendental, which causes its representatives to constantly purify their readings of critical philosophy.

According to the logic of the second, *hypo*-normative view, the transcendental is certainly a constraint – of form and structure – but, paradoxically, this is synonymous with freedom. In fact, it is supposed to guarantee the autonomy of thinking from all determinisms or reductionisms. The transcendental is defined then as irreducibility, pure symbolic latitude. This "freedom," this irreducibility, is what Ricœur, for instance, defends against Changeux when, as we saw in the introduction, he invokes the impossibility of assimilating the activities of thinking to brain processes. In this case, the transcendental becomes a safety barrier whose paradoxical value lies in its license: an exemption from defining *exactly* what in thinking cannot come from simple material determinations, especially biological ones, and that prevents this kind of assimilation. The transcendental appears simply as that which resists embodiment *in principle*. These minimal definitions give rise to the term's veritable polysemia. As I have just explained, in the twentieth century "transcendental" was

130

replaced by "irreducible," but it was also replaced by "structural," "quasi-transcendental". . .[3] Anything is possible so long as the transcendental *resists* its complete materialization, so long as it continues to designate that indefinable space of non-determinism.

Today, this constant ambiguity, or even contradiction, in views of the transcendental – as policing or permissive – is clear as day. It is no longer possible to conceal it under the supposedly unsurpassable name of Kantianism. On the one hand, because the censure is being lifted, it turns out that it is possible to break the lock of the transcendental and to reach into its ancestral past without, however, regressing to the pre-critical stage. On the other hand, the permissiveness of the transcendental comes to an end. Once again, materialism seeks to make itself heard.[4] The border between "thought" and cerebrality, for instance, is becoming increasingly difficult to define. To maintain its existence whatever the cost in the name of anti-reductionism is associated more often than not with a reactive and reactionary position that has run out of explanations.

The problem is that of knowing what philosophy might become if it forgoes the transcendental entirely. What happens if it *truly* "relinquishes" the transcendental? We still have no idea since the new theoretical orientations that are emerging fail to outline clearly the contours of a definitively post-Kantian landscape for continental philosophy. There is veritable disarray within Kantianism as it survives the destruction of metaphysics, the claims of speculative realism, and the early babbling of a philosophy of the brain that has not managed to free itself from the narrow cognitivism in which it is hopelessly ensnared. Before showing how Kant alone can still guide us – including towards an exit from Kantianism – let's put Heidegger, Meillassoux, and the neurobiologists into conversation. We shall also see how all the readings of §27 and the discussions of epigenesis ultimately bring us back to time, radical contingency, and the biologization of reason – and how they all rush headlong into the dead end.

Heidegger to Meillassoux: What Finitude?

Dating and mathematics

Inasmuch as it ended with a question, or more exactly the expression of a doubt, my examination of Heidegger's reading of Kant in *Kant and the Problem of Metaphysics* remained unresolved. I asked whether defining the transcendental as primordial temporality enables us to bring together the different readings of the critical track and to propose a satisfactory understanding of *a priori* epigenesis. Or, then again, is the Heideggerian difference between primordial and derived, authentic and inauthentic, just another way to do away with time?

In an apparent detour, let us imagine how Heidegger might have responded to Meillassoux. No doubt he would have relegated the argument developed in *After Finitude* to a poorly handled defense of vulgar time, caught between the dating of different "nows" (their "ancestral" character fails to mask their traditional determination) and the persistent, barely disguised, expression of a metaphysics of eternity. The dual support for the privilege of leveled-down time would have inspired some doubt about the move to "post-Kantianism" for which the work is supposed to prepare the way.

How, indeed, are we to respond to these "numbers" dating events "anterior to the advent of life as consciousness" that Meillassoux proposes in the name of fossil time: "date of the origin of the universe (13.5 billion years ago), the date of the accretion of the earth (4.45 billion years ago), the date of the origin of life on earth (3.5 billion years ago), the date of the origin of humankind (*Homo habilis*, 2 million years ago)"?[5] Far from being the marks of a dislocation of "that which is given in the present,"[6] are they not simply expressions of the present of succession, intact, unrecognized, and unquestioned?

For Heidegger, to dismiss the ontological question of the *opening* (*Erschlossenheit*) of truth by associating it roughly with correlationism is a move whose tremendous naïvety he would have flagged. Not thinking the opening leaves no other option than to situate oneself quite simply in "a domain of truth that has already been opened," and thus to lack originality in every sense of the term.[7] This domain "that has already been opened" is the one that Heidegger frequently associates with modern "science," with its presuppositions (read lack of foundation) about "that which shows itself to be possible and necessarily correct"[8] and which obscure the question of the *provenance* of truth. And as just such a provenance, the ontological economy of the opening goes far beyond the simple encounter of subject and object or the frame of "correlation."

Heidegger would therefore have criticized Meillassoux for his misconception of anteriority, whether *or not* it is originarily co-implicated in the existence of Dasein. On this point, Heidegger remains adamant to the end: that anteriority and posteriority are originarily held together in a structure, in other words, in a *synthesis*, does not imply that this synthesis is necessarily related to a psyche, a subject or an "I think." As Kant is the first to show, synthesis is a neutral event, anonymous, authorless.

132

It is not enough to refer to the fact that some statements by "empirical science" relate to "events anterior to the advent of life as well as consciousness," when such events "consist in the dating of 'objects' that are sometimes older than any form of life on earth,"[9] to reach the idea of an ancientness outside of correlation. Again, all dating assumes an originary synthesis without which figures such as "13.5 billion years ago" or "4.45 billion years ago" can have no meaning and place in what Aristotle described as the before and after.

It is not by chance that Aristotle is mentioned here. Heidegger would certainly have drawn attention to the error that comes of the constant confusion between *correlation* and *articulation* in *After Finitude*, a confusion that the reading of Aristotle prohibits specifically. A confusion between articulation – the neutral synthesis that holds together the moments of time – and correlation – the synthesis that holds together subjectivity (or *psychè*) and time. The fact that the two syntheses are themselves linked does not mean that they are reducible to one another. What the play of their engagement reveals is that dating is never intrinsically mathematical.

Let us recall the famous definition of time in Book IV of *Physics*: "For this is what time is: a number of change in respect of before and after."[10] Time allows us to distinguish before and after as we establish the distance from point A to point B on a trajectory, for example. It is thus clearly "a type of number." The challenge of passage 219b 2–9 is that of knowing how to interpret "number."[11] As Rémi Brague comments in his admirable analysis of *Physics*, Book IV, "[T]his passage is unintelligible if we do not see" that what is referred to here by the word number (*arithmos*) "is not what we habitually understand by the concept of number."[12]

The term *arithmos* also has a *pre-arithmetic* meaning, in which it refers to a structure, an assembly. In this sense, it is very close to *harmonia*. Thus, *arithmos* refers less to a number than to a structure organized by numbers. Brague continues by explaining that this is why it is better instead to translate it as "articulation." He therefore proposes the following translation of passage 219b: "This is what time is, the before and after articulation of movement." *Arithmos* is hence not what enables counting, but rather what a collection must have to be a collection. Not an aggregate, but again, rather, an order and a structure of conjuncture ("like pearls on a necklace"). That which is numbered in time is thus articulation, in other words, the difference and juncture of the before and the after.[13]

The fact that there is movement, and therefore time, in the soul does not mean that time is essentially psychic.[14] Certainly, the adjoining of the before and the after *matches* the correlation between time and *psychè*. But this point of synthesis between two syntheses allows us to ask Meillassoux a question *a posteriori*. He says that only the "absolutizing"[15] reach of mathematics makes it possible to access the concept of non-human time, one that is not dependent on our relation to the world. But the problem raised by Aristotle's very specific usage of "number" in Book IV of *Physics* is that the numbering of time reveals the non-mathematicity of number. And this is true even when one "takes counting techniques seriously."[16] That is to say that antecedence, the fundamental structure of the before and after, should be understood as that which Heidegger, in "Anaximander's Saying," calls the originary "usage (*Brauch*)" of the moments of time with one another.[17] There is clearly a deep affinity between usage in its original sense of "holding together," as conceived by Aristotle, and Kantian synthesis – an affinity that Derrida brought to light extensively in his seminal text "*Ousia* and *Grammè*."[18]

In reality, time is "four-dimensional." Its "fourth" dimension is actually that of the articulation that holds its moments originarily united and "holds them apart thus opened and so holds them toward one another in the nearness by which the three dimensions remain near one another."[19] Remarkably, writes Heidegger on the same page, we owe this idea of the proximity – "nearing", "nearness" – of moments of time to Kant himself, who uses the old word "nearhood" (*Nahheit*).[20] Heidegger could have shown that epigenesis *also* depicts this same proximity, through the type of organized unity it refers to and assumes.

In its own way, the figure of epigenesis has the same effectiveness as the Aristotelian image of pearls on a necklace. It is the sensible presentation of an articulation. Unlike preformation or equivocal generation, it assumes the co-implication of *all* the moments of time, without granting any privilege to either the past or the sudden emergence of a present. It is entirely possible to read epigenesis as a figure in this movement – "*Reichen*," which, as Heidegger writes in *On Time and Being*, means the "mutually giving to one another of future, past and present."[21] A synthetic approach, which, once again, does not begin with correlation. It is not, therefore, legitimate to equate synthesis and correlation.

As we have seen, Meillassoux claims that in the correlationist logic the "past" always means a past *for the present* of thinking. He writes:

Consider the following ancestral statement: "Event Y occurred x number of years before the emergence of humans." The correlationist

134

philosopher will in no way intervene in the content of this statement: he
will not contest the claim that it is in fact event Y that occurred, nor will
he contest the dating of this event. No – he will simply add – perhaps
only to himself, but add it he will – [. . .]: event Y occurred x number of
years before the emergence of humans – *for humans* [. . .].[22]

And so, contrary to what Meillassoux's remarks suggest, the elucidation of the structure of the before and after is precisely what makes
it possible to identify right from the outset the independence – which
Heidegger also calls "freedom" – of time in relation to thinking. *On
Time and Being* states this clearly: "[W]hat do they [the moments
of time] offer to one another? Nothing other than themselves –
which means: [. . .] there opens up what we call time-space."[23] This
"opening up of time-space" is free of the presence of any subject. It
has nothing to do either with the calculation of years and does not
mean, as it continues to do in Meillassoux, "the distance between
two now-points of calculated time, such as we have in mind when
we note, for instance: this or that occurred within a time-span of fifty
years [we could say several millions of years]."[24]

Heidegger would most certainly have pointed to the ontological
ambiguity of the term "arche-fossil," which describes the ancestral
past for Meillassoux.[25] To speak of the arche-fossil is obviously to
continue speaking about the *archè*. And this lexicon is somewhat
incompatible with the terminology of dates and measurements used
in *After Finitude* to talk about the age of the earth. Doesn't any *archè*
refer back to the primordial, incalculable, and undatable articulation
of the before and after? Does it ever mean anything but the pure synthesis of the before and after? A synthesis without which the before
and after would have no existence in nature itself? Again, synthesis
and correlation are not systematically reducible to one another.

First and second finitude

Another significant objection to Meillassoux's argument is that, long
before him, Heidegger also developed a critique of correlation.

There are actually two distinct moments in Heidegger's thinking
about the transcendental. In the two books that are often considered
his most important, *Being and Time* and *Kant and the Problem of
Metaphysics*, he retains the terminology of the transcendental for the
benefit of his own thought. In *Being and Time*, indeed, he describes
the ecstatic structure of temporality as "transcendental." Moreover,
many commentators have been quick to emphasize the proximity of

135

this "analytic" to Kant's analytic. It is a "reelaborated" transcendental, renamed "existential," freed of its ontological uncertainty, a post-Kantian transcendental, but one that continues to inscribe the name Kant gave it throughout *Being and Time*. We recall that the first task of the book is to develop "The Necessity, Structure, and Priority of the Question of Being."[26] *Being and Time* and *Kant and the Problem of Metaphysics* resonate with and echo one another. In both instances, the temporality at their core is the temporality of horizonal schemata. Some paragraphs in the later work sometimes even leave readers unsure about whether it is Kant or Heidegger who is speaking. Heidegger emphasized the need for a thinking "retrieval (*Wiederholung*)" of the project of the *Critique of Pure Reason*, one that simultaneously displaces it and fulfills it.

It is true that this reworking is based on bringing to light the "connection" – a synonym of correlation – that exists in Kant between the "I think" and time. Heidegger writes that in Kant "the decisive *connection* (*Zusammenhang*) between *time* and the 'I *think*' remains shrouded in complete obscurity. It did not even become a problem."[27] It is precisely this "connection" that must be illuminated, a connection that is now based on the understanding that Dasein has of its being.

Without going into the complexities of the evolution of Heidegger's thought, it is important to emphasize that the very meaning of the Turning (*Kehre*) is that Heidegger himself questions this "connectionist" perspective and vows to no longer use the term "transcendental." From that point on, the *a priori* is stored away along with all the traditional metaphysical principles.[28] In the 1927 lectures, he pronounces the "fundamental untruth" of the schematico-horizonal approach to both time and being.[29] *Being and Time*, he acknowledges, runs the risk of anthropologizing the question of being precisely because it is based on the "connection" of Dasein and time. The existential analytic is still governed by a thought of the subject. In *Contributions to Philosophy (Of the Event)*, Heidegger writes: "By this approach beyng itself is apparently still made into an object, and the most decisive opposite of that is attained which the course of the question of beyng has already opened up for itself."[30] It is therefore necessary to well and truly *relinquish the transcendental* and the associated concept of horizon. In a handwritten note in the margin of his personal copy of *Being and Time*, at §8, Heidegger announces "the surpassing of the horizon as such."[31]

From that point on, it is the *refusal* of being, its resistance and indifference to any approach, that forms the starting point of the philosophical determination of being and time from the perspective of a history that is one of withdrawal and forgetting. The distinction between authentic and vulgar time is thereby dropped, since time ceases to be a horizon of intelligibility for Dasein. The "connection" is thus abandoned en route. By the same token, the Turning challenges the entire transcendental structure. In his own way, Heidegger completes the first critique of correlationism with the *Kehre*.

Thus, in Heidegger, there is a non-correlational thinking of finitude, that of the finitude of being, which comes to replace the theme of the finitude of Dasein.[32] Certainly, the finitude of being clearly means that for Dasein being is still the fundamental question. But to think finitude for itself, in a precisely non-correlated manner, amounts to thinking the withdrawal of being and no longer only being-towards-death. The event that names the question of being from this point on is then *Ereignis*.

Meillassoux does not bother to distinguish between these decisive stages in the Heideggerian process and continues to view the dominance of correlationism through the problematic of *Ereignis*. As he writes:

> The notion of *Ereignis*, which is central in the later Heidegger, remains faithful to the correlationist exigency inherited from Kant [. . .] for the "co-propriation" which constitutes *Ereignis* means that neither being nor man can be posited as subsisting "in-themselves," and subsequently entering into relation – on the contrary, both terms of the appropriation are originally constituted through their reciprocal relation: "The appropriation appropriates man and Being to their essential togetherness."[33]

In so doing, Meillassoux says nothing about the fact that there are *two finitudes* in Heidegger. In *On Time and Being*, Heidegger could not be more explicit on this matter, stating:

> The finitude of Being was first spoken of in the book on Kant. The finitude of Appropriation (*Ereignis*), of Being, of the fourfold (*Gevier*) [. . .] is nevertheless different from the finitude spoken of in the book on Kant, in that it is no longer thought in terms of the relation to infinity, but rather as finitude in itself [. . .].[34]

What then does "*after*" finitude mean? After the first, or after the second?

Despite it all

Despite it all, and this is the reason why I did not follow Heidegger right to the end – I am returning here to my question that was left unanswered – we have to recognize that the question of time did not survive the disappearance of the "first finitude" in Heidegger's work. After the incredible Turning of *On Time and Being*, which definitively splits apart temporality and subjectivity and subordinates the presence of time to the "there is"[35] of its givenness, time quite simply vacates the philosophical scene. The time of the "second" finitude remains henceforth an enigma. Who has ever taken up this question thematically since then?

We can propose two opposing hypotheses to explain this disappearance. It could be that time cannot survive the relinquishing of the transcendental and has no future beyond *Being and Time*. In this sense, Meillassoux is right to suspect that correlation (understood as the reduction of the synthesis to the subject–object relation) remains ontologically significant in some manner from Kant to Heidegger. Alternatively, the Heideggerian relinquishing of the transcendental after the Turning is not really a relinquishing but instead paradoxically coincides with the search for a surplus transcendental, for an over-determination or an exaggeration of its purity. An excessive move that drives the thinking of time into the dead end.

Let me explain what I mean. The main problem that the reading of Kant presents between *Being and Time* and *Kant and the Problem of Metaphysics* derives from the illegitimacy of a chiasmus. Responding to the Kantian split between the transcendental and the empirical, Heidegger offers the corresponding divide between authentic temporality and leveled-down or vulgar temporality. In other words, he equates the transcendental with the authentic.

In theory, the need to relinquish the elucidation of temporality as the horizon of the question of being, the project of *Being and Time* that still guides *Kant and the Problem of Metaphysics*, officially leads Heidegger to relinquish this temporal difference after the Turning. Analyzing this transformation in "*Ousia* and *Grammè*," Derrida states that in the last instance, "perhaps there is no 'vulgar concept of time,'"[36] which, of course, means that there is perhaps no primordial time either. Relinquishing the transcendental and relinquishing this distinction of times thus appear to go hand in hand.

And yet, we can but note that the later development of Heideggerian thinking on temporality did not lead to the bringing to light of a renewed concept of time. Nor did it enable a true surpassing of the difference of the primordial and the derived or give the after-metaphysics, or "other thinking," its own chronological pulse. On the contrary, the disappearance of the question of time appears to be an exacerbation of the difference between authentic temporality and leveled-down temporality. Thus, as the approach taken by French phenomenology at the end of the twentieth century indicates, the givenness and the "*es gibt*" were quite simply understood as a new version of primordial temporality – one that is still more primordial than the one identified in *Being and Time*.[37] *Givenness has become a super transcendental*. If these readings are possible, it is only because something in the Heideggerian thinking of the "second" finitude authorizes them.

Superseding the divide between the primordial and the derived should have caused Heidegger to reconsider the conclusions of his reading of Kant. It should have caused him to revise, for example, and more than anything else, his assertion regarding the existence of a break between the two editions – and of a break, therefore, between two versions of the origin, the formative power of the imagination, on the one hand, and the logical spontaneity of the understanding, on the other. Finally, it should have caused him to reconsider the difference between time understood as ontological horizon and the objective time of appearances. The destruction-deconstruction of the transcendental as Heidegger construes it in *Being and Time* and *Kant and the Problem of Metaphysics* should have led to the bringing to light of a new, post-metaphysical unity between the ideality and naturality of time. However, instead of this, the thinking of the second finitude and of the "there is" never really clearly rid itself of the difference between the authentic and the inauthentic. It merely prolonged it.

By irremediably distinguishing primordial and derived temporality without ever being able to erase this move, without ever seeking to reconcile it in the development of the concept of a temporality of the world including both the ontological and the physical, by instead searching for a way out from the question of time itself in the mystery of a "there is" with no empirical status, Heidegger made it impossible to think together time as the pure iconic production of horizon and the time of nature. Yet this is what was begging to be done.

By splitting that which Kant presents as intimately linked, namely the dual schematic and empirical dimension of time, Heidegger had already amputated the *Critique* of its objectivity and captured the first edition in the narcissistic bubble of the pure image while clas-sifying the second edition in the register of the chronicles of derived time. Heidegger never envisaged for a moment that, as a "hidden art in the depths of the human soul," the schematism could have had a biological given as its foundation,[38] that there could have been in its structure an articulation between primordial temporality and naturality. The directions of later thought did not go beyond the split between the two ontological levels. The calling into question of the first finitude never produced a true reconciliation of time with itself.

And so, if I did not conclude my inquiry with Heidegger, if I did not grant him the last word on the subject of epigenesis, it is not because the accusation of correlationism would have prevented me from doing so. We have seen that this does not amount to a truly relevant objection. It is because Heidegger's thought never goes beyond the dualism of the authentic and the inauthentic that it is problematic. Today's time must be a time that, without going back to the time of metaphysics, is equally natural and ontological.

Tracking the motif of epigenesis thus allows us to conclude that the Heideggerian interpretation of Kant is at once unsurpassable and insufficient. It is unsurpassable in that it constitutes time as the principal problem in the *Critique of Pure Reason*. It is insufficient insofar as it has not really given post-Kantian philosophy the future promised by the bringing to light of this problem. Since Heidegger, time has remained quartered and torn between its insensibility and its materiality.

Assigned to the unceasing devalorization of beingness, continental philosophy has cut itself off from any scientific concerns, justifying Meillassoux's assertion that *"by forbidding reason any claim to the absolute, the end of metaphysics has taken the form of an exacerbated return of the religious."*[39] However, as I have also shown, it is not certain that the violence of the return to mathematics adequately interrupts this post-deconstructive religiosity. Rather, it appears that it is only its flipside. The schism continues, since we are now confronted with the spectacle of a balancing between messianic time (hyperbole for primordial time) and glacial and ancestral time (hyperbole for vulgar time). Between the two, the urgent need for an epigenetic thinking of time emerges.

Meillassoux to Heidegger: Alterity and the Critique of Property

We must continue by now asking why Meillassoux's approach, in dialogue with Heidegger above, also fails to render entirely convincing the relinquishing of the transcendental that it tries to implement.

The conclusion drawn above must certainly be nuanced somewhat by recognizing that, to its credit, *After Finitude* obviously succeeds in identifying the idea of a true post-deconstructive perspective, a philosophy liberated from self-obsession, freed from the fear of going back beyond the symbolic-transcendental line, of transgressing the forbidden. A thinking that is freed from infinite self-reflection and sent back to a time when it did not exist.

The two greatest promises of Meillassoux's book are connected first to a unique undertaking to disappropriate thinking, and second to the elaboration of the concept of *another alterity* than that of the now well-known "wholly other." We must therefore ask why we hesitate to consider these as promises kept. Let's start by examining them more closely.

On philosophy as disappropriation and as dis-propriation

The call for a radical disappropriation and dis-propriation of philosophical thought has surely never been heard as radically as in Meillassoux. Of course, in Heidegger the movement of the constitutive appropriation of *Ereignis – eigen, das Eigene*, appropriates for itself, the proper – is not separable from its apparent opposite – *Enteignis*, often translated as "dis-propriation."[40] Nevertheless, appropriation remains . . .

Meillassoux's critique of correlation clearly aligns with a critique of property. The term "disappropriation" means the fact of relinquishing a good. By extension, "disappropriation" implies a renunciation of individuality and thus becomes synonymous with depersonalization. The term "dis-propriation" is a neologism that refers to the extinction of the right of property over a thing when it ceases to exist. For Meillassoux, the relinquishing of the transcendental involves the two operations conjointly.

It is therefore first a matter of ridding oneself of a conception of thinking defined as a strategy of circumscribing and taking possession of a space. This strategy is, for instance, the one that led Kant, in the Introduction to the *Critique of the Power of Judgment*, to distinguish between the three notions of "field," "territory," and "domain" in order to define that which *belongs properly to us* in the geography of cognition and thought.

> Concepts, insofar as they are related to others, regardless of whether a cognition of the latter is possible or not, have their field, which is determined merely in accordance with the relation which their object has to

141

our faculty of cognition in general. – The part of this field within which cognition is possible for us is a territory (*territorium*) for these concepts and the requisite faculty of cognition. The part of the territory in which these are legislative is the domain (*ditio*) of these concepts and of the corresponding faculty of cognition.[41]

The legal vocabulary of property serves to reinforce these borders conceptually. We recall the distinction Kant draws between derived acquisition and originary acquisition. We should remember that originary acquisition refers to the first acquisition of a good which until then belonged to no one. The fact that for Kant appropriation is cut off from all essentialization and that the proper is not a substance changes nothing in the fact that the appropriating relation between being and thinking remains first in transcendental philosophy. It has been demonstrated on several occasions that the epigenesis of the relation between categories and objects is inseparable from a reflection on the way in which the elements of thinking become ours, the way that the subject must take ownership of the transcendental structures of truth.

In *After Finitude*, by contrast, the thinking to come is presented as the returning of a loan. It is no longer an inquiry into the acquisition of a good that until now belonged to no one, but the anonymous return of a good that we believed until now belonged only to us. A good that by the same token of dis-propriation is no longer one, and thereby ceases to exist as such. The world is not "ours."

Themes of radical contingency, the absolute, and "ancestrality" are the privileged expressions of the philosophical relinquishing at work here. Starting with "us," correlationism undertook a "disabsolutiza-tion" of philosophical thought, which, after Kant, had tightened up around the unsurpassable character of its limits. To break with this state of affairs implies "*to get out of ourselves,* to grasp the in-itself, to know what is whether we are or not."[42] To get out of ourselves is to get out *of* the ourselves, out *of* the proper. The thought of ances-trality is not even "human." "I will call 'ancestral' any reality anterior to the emergence of the human species," declares Meillassoux, and he adds, "or even anterior to every recognized form of life on earth."[43] And this "anterior" reality is equally well "posterior": the ancestral achrony and indifference are also the projections of a post-human real.[44] The existence of a "non-human" time without consciousness corresponds to the age of the earth "anterior vis-à-vis manifesta-tion,"[45] but also concerns a reality to come, capable of subsisting in the absence of all consciousness.

142

The "in-itself" which must be "grasped" is therefore not Kant's in-itself, since that, by definition, cannot exist without us. Likewise, "absolute" does not mean "unconditioned" (*unbedingt*). I have already explained that the vocabulary of the condition is the chosen lexicon of the transcendental. Here, the in-itself ceases to be the other side of finitude, and becomes instead pure separation:

> Our task [. . .] consists in trying to understand how thought is able to access the uncorrelated, which is to say, a world capable of subsisting without being given. But to say this is just to say that we must grasp how thought is able to access *an absolute*, i.e. a being whose *severance* (the original meaning of *absolutus*), and whose separateness from thought is such that it presents itself to us as non-relative to us, and hence as capable of existing whether we exist or not.[46]

The recourse to the concept of an absolute here in no way implies a return to the ontological guarantee of a foundation – whether it be the existence of God or the principle of reason – but should instead be understood as the necessity of unreason, in other words, here again, as radical contingency.

> We are thinking an absolute, but it is not metaphysical, since we are not thinking any *thing*, any (entity) that would *be* absolute. The absolute is the absolute impossibility of a necessary being. We are no longer upholding a variant of the principle of sufficient reason, according to which there is a necessary reason why everything is the way it is rather than otherwise, but rather the absolute truth of a *principle of unreason*. There is no reason for anything to be or to remain the way it is; everything must, without reason, be able not to be and/or be able to be other than it is.[47]

Speculative thinking of just such an absolute, which asserts that "contingency alone is necessary"[48] – "alone" being understood here as simultaneously an exclusivity clause, an acknowledgement of solitude (the absolute is without anyone), and disappropriation – allows us to bring to light the relation between the mathematics of the transfinite and this kind of exclusivity of emptying. Hasn't mathematics always established the ontological principles of "a world where humanity is absent; a world crammed with things and events that are not correlates of any manifestation; a world that is not the correlate of a relation to the world"?[49]

Responding to Heidegger, Meillassoux asserts that in the end "time" no longer refers to anything but the impossibility of the synthesis, its absolute destructibility or destructuration, the definitive erasure of all traces. The time of radical contingency, dispropriated time, is confounded with its own irregularity, disobedience to its own schemata. A time outside the law, "not just a time whose capacity for destroying everything is a function of laws, but a time which is capable of the *lawless destruction of every physical law.*"[50] And so, "only the time that harbours the capacity to destroy every determinate reality, while obeying no determinate law – the time capable of destroying, without reason or law, both worlds and things – can be thought as an absolute."[51]

Evidently, in this strange timeline, epigenesis appears unable to find its place anywhere. Indeed, Meillassoux continues, "to speak of 'the emergence of life' is to evoke the emergence of manifestation amidst a world that pre-existed it."[52] From then on, the attempt to situate transcendental epigenesis in Kantian thought would be only one way to grasp the birth of correlation and meaning in general. As if generation and meaning coincided and left in the shadow the thickness of the preceding inanimate and unappropriable presence. According to Meillassoux, the emergence of life in general, and the beginning of one epigenesis in particular, are nothing but events like any other in the indifferent dating of nature, in its numbers and ages. And so they lose their transcendental status.

The other alterity

The discourse of radical contingency is not apocalyptic but rather a rigorous, rational (*still* mathematics) attempt to reframe the question of absolute alterity posed ceaselessly by twentieth-century philosophy. A question that it also constantly missed since it was shut away in an artistic, poetic, or religious alternative to traditional philosophy. So long as the base structure of thought is not transformed, is not envisaged as completely transformable (non-correlational), the wholly other depends only on the fantasy or whims of messianic grace. The destruction and deconstruction of metaphysics did not go far enough in the theory and practice of dispossession, a dispossession that would forever deprive thought of a mirror and thus make it impossible for everything to come back to it one way or another, for everything to continue to come back to it.

The arrival of the wholly other is that which twentieth-century philosophy prophesied constantly from the prospect of its own demise. After so many disappointing announcements, can the wholly other finally come to pass? Can it come to pass in *reality*, without delegating the thought of its indefinite wait? To a certain degree, the speculative urgency of the question of radical contingency was prepared for negatively by Kant, who, in closing it down no sooner that it was formulated, only made its actual reopening possible. Doesn't contingency, understood as "the destruction of every form of *a priori* knowledge of why the world is as it is,"[53] in fact surface again today as the major problem, which, although it is repressed in the Transcendental Deduction, right in the heart of the *Critique of Pure Reason*, was ultimately never resolved? The problem, precisely, of the wholly other?

In the twenty-first century, it is therefore necessary to ask the question again, tirelessly but differently: can something other finally happen? Meillassoux reminds us that

> [t]he term "contingency" refers back to the Latin *contingere*, meaning "to touch, to befall," which is to say, that which happens [. . .]. The contingent, in a word, is *something that finally happens* – something other, something which, in its irreducibility to all pre-registered possibilities, puts an end to the vanity of a game wherein everything, even the improbable, is predictable. When something happens to us, when novelty grabs us by the throat, then no more calculation and no more play – it is finally time to be serious.[54]

"Serious" things are real things. The real – the fundamental question of the current movement called "speculative realism" – is that which remains when the imaginary (transcendental) and the symbolic (hermeneutic) have disappeared, in other words, *when being is really no longer anything*. Not just finished, nor even historical, just nothing. Nothing is (not) real. The nothing as the absolute undoing of the principle of reason. Nothing would have to have no reason, there would have to be no reason at all for one thing to happen rather than another, so that the wholly other might happen.

Yet nothing changes

And yet, how can we stop "conced[ing] that physical processes are indeed possessed of ultimate necessity"?[55] How can radical contingency and the lack of necessity of the laws of nature be brought to light? How can we prove that the world can change at any moment and thereby call into question Kant's famous comment on the always heavy and always red nature of cinnabar? How can we justify the wholly other understood as a set of modifiable laws?

Strangely, it is at this crucial point that Meillassoux's reasoning falls short. Indeed, against all expectation, the argument of the wholly other becomes a paradoxical defense of the stability of the world. In the end, *nothing changes*.

145

Clearly, it is not easy to rigorously rule out the "necessitarian"[56] or transcendental argument that says that if laws were in fact contingent, they would modify or would constantly be on the point of modifying. How can their necessity be contested since they do not experience modifications?[57] In the same way, if our representations were not organized by categories, our experience of the world would be pure chaos. But it's not. The unity of consciousness endures.

On the other hand, against the transcendental solution to the problem of identity and stability of the world, Meillassoux refuses to adopt a theory of chaos ("chaos can do anything whatsoever").[58] Such a theory is not satisfying. If chaos were absolutized (it can do everything), then it would become necessary and would cease to be chaos.[59]

How then can the contingency of the world be proven? This point in the reasoning is the least convincing moment in the book, for, after having enjoyed the thrill, it ultimately amounts to being content with the stability of the world. No necessity, Meillassoux says, but no chaos either. His argument is as follows:

> The only necessity proper to chaos is that it remain chaos, and hence that there be nothing capable of resisting it – that *what is* always remain contingent, and that *what is* never be necessary. However – and here we come to the crux of the matter – our conviction is that in order for an entity to be contingent and un-necessary in this way, *it cannot be anything whatsoever*.[60]

Further on he writes: "To be is necessarily to be a fact, but to be a fact is not just to be anything whatsoever."[61]

To defend this thesis, Meillassoux presents an incomprehensible argument about *"certain determinate conditions"*:

> [I]n order to be contingent and un-necessary, the entity must confirm to *certain determinate conditions*, which can then be construed as *so many absolute proprieties of what is*. We then begin to understand what the rational discourse about unreason – an unreason which is not irrational – would consist in: it would be discourse that aims to establish the constraints to which the entity must submit in order to exercise its capacity-not-to-be and its capacity-to-be-other.[62]

I grant that "contingency is such that anything might happen, even nothing at all, so that what is, remains as it is."[63] I also accept the argument that the logic of the transfinite (and the impossibility of totalizing the possibilities that come of it) is but one axiom among others, not the only, absolute one. But what I cannot accept is the critique of the anything whatsoever. If indeed anything is *"capable of actually becoming otherwise without reason,"*[64] then *why couldn't it become anything whatsoever?* Abnormal or banal, absurd or ultra-logical?

It appears that this refusal of the anything whatsoever leads precisely to the division between the authentic (rational authenticity of unreason) and the inauthentic (the vulgarity of anything whatsoever). A division that ultimately saves the order and the proper of the world, reduces radical contingency to being only "thinkable" or "mathematically possible," and in no way shakes up that which is. I reject as a sophism the "solution" claiming that *"it is necessary that there be something rather than nothing because it is necessarily contingent that there is something rather than something else."*[65]

In the end, Meillassoux's highly idiosyncratic approach fails to open up any prospect of real alterity. We were expecting an explosion. We were expecting a revolution – the revolution of the Copernican Revolution. But nothing changes. Nothing happens. Where's the surprise? Where's the metamorphosis? Above all, what's this "after" of finitude that leaves everything untouched? An "after" Kant? But the vocabulary of "certain determinate conditions" is *still* the language of the conditions of possibility, in other words, the transcendental![66] An "after" Heidegger? But in *The Principle of Reason*, Heidegger goes much further in the equivalence between "nothing is without reason"[67] and everything is "without why"![68] The notion of "play," developed at the end of that book, a play that is also without probabilities or winning formulas, unsettles the constancy of the "ground/reason (*Grund*)"[69] more effectively.

In closing, we might therefore ask what is the advantage of surpassing correlationism and relinquishing the transcendental if the power of transformation and changeability implied in and by this very surpassing are less than what is being surpassed? What's the point? "To break with the circle of correlation"[70] – but what does that change? And if it changes nothing, then why try? Above all, how? Indeed, isn't giving up the totality of the possibilities also giving up the very idea of the possible? For Kant, again, an idea is the form or rule of the totality of the conditions, that is to say, the possibilities of a thing. And so, without an idea and without an other, without the idea of the other, where does the "speculation" of contingency lead us? Shouldn't our answer be: "From nothing. For nothing"?[71]

Towards a Critique of Neurobiological Reason

Not what happens but rather what evolves

Where are we now in regard to the question regarding the equivalence of reason and the brain presented by mental Darwinism and epigenetics? What does it bring to the table for relinquishing the transcendental? In the end, why can't we follow their guiding tracks either?

Let's start by commenting on an aspect shared by Heidegger and Meillassoux: their silence on biology. We are familiar with Heidegger's mistrust of life science and the question of life in general.[72] As for Meillassoux, there is no doubt about the meaning ascribed to the "empirical science" constantly evoked in *After Finitude*. Throughout his book, "empirical science" refers exclusively to physics. Biology is the great absentee in this reflection, despite the fact that it seeks to renew "the empirical sciences' capacity to yield knowledge of the ancestral realm."[73] Given that biology is never once mentioned, we might well ask what this plural includes.

The question is important since, as the analysis of the "neo-skeptical" thesis demonstrated, it appears that *biology alone is capable of supplying reason with a plausible concept of the contingency of the laws of nature.* In this sense, contemporary biology serves the radical contingency thesis more convincingly than does mathematics. The biological perspective is brimming with a potential that is both post-metaphysical and post-critical, one that philosophers have been wrong to ignore. Let's recall that in the early twentieth century some physicists supported the idea of a possible evolution of the laws of nature, that is, they borrowed the hypothesis of a possible "mobility" of these laws from biology. I have already mentioned the positions of Helmholtz and Boltzmann on this matter. In France, philosopher Émile Boutroux also supported the evolutionary thesis. In his book *The Contingency of the Laws of Nature*, he writes the following on the principle of causality:

> [W]e must not forget that experience itself has introduced to the human mind the scientific idea of natural cause and has gradually clarified this idea. The latter is not the idea of a principle *a priori* which governs the modes of being, it is the abstract form of the relation existing between these modes. We cannot assert that the nature of things has its derivation in the law of causality. To us, this law is but the most general expression of the relations arising from the observable nature of given things.[74]

Later he continues: "[D]eductive science [. . .] determines the relations of things, once it is granted that their nature remains immobile or fixed."[75] Bouveresse comments on this remark, adding: "But of course there is absolutely no necessity that forces this nature to remain immobile."[76]

Here, the concept of a possible variability or modifiability in the laws of nature is not attained via a mathematical reading deprived of phenomenal proofs, but is based instead on the biological theory of heritage – both ontogenetic and phylogenetic. It is worth emphasizing that according to this viewpoint, contingency derives not from an axiom – whose origin is obviously always *a priori* – but instead from the idea of a constitution of the *a priori* itself by experience and adaptation.

So long as an occurrence-based understanding of contingency – in other words, a definition of contingency as that which happens – is mobilized, as in Meillassoux, only support the *hypothesis* of variability in the laws of nature can be supported. Indeed, despite what may be claimed, this kind of understanding is based on the logic of the dice throw. Contingency is reduced to the pure whim of its occurrences and is thus confounded with the pure virtuality of the frequency, rarity, or lack of modification in the order of things. Yes, indeed, the evidence indicates that this conception of the contingency *of* nature can absolutely not be verified *in* nature.

The idea of a gradual transformation of the stability of the world and laws – the laws of both nature and thought – is entirely different. The "neo-skeptical" argument is not only a transformation of Hume's argument, it also contains a transformed concept of transformation. Indeed, the occurrence-based understanding of contingency is replaced by the far more convincing idea of progressive change and changeability of the laws, based on an *empirical derivation of the a priori*.

This conception makes it possible to conjoin the concept and phenomenality of change and leads neither to the absurd supposition of a chaotic world, a versatile nature, or a shattered representation, nor to the position of a pure mathematical possibility.

And yet, it might be objected that it has been years since any physicists have supported the idea of an evolutionary modifiability of the laws of nature![77] Edelman reflects on this in *Bright Air, Brilliant Fire* when he writes: "[I]t was Einstein who first understood the significance of the invariance of the laws of physics [. . .]. Indeed, his general theory of relativity may be considered a means by which to search for conditions of *absolute* invariance!"[78]

We have seen, however, that the duality of the invariable and variable continues to disturb theories of the constitution of mental objects. A third-generation skeptical argument is at work: in neurobiology, brain epigenetics has taken the lead in the evolutionary conception of thought. The processes revealed by Darwin are studied and verified at the level of neuronal populations. Neural Darwinism transforms the assertion of the contingency of the laws of nature by orienting it towards the recognition of the selective mobility at work behind the rigidity and stability of connections and objective forms.

Let us recall the definition of mental objects proposed by Changeux in *Neuronal Man:* "The *mental object* is identified as the physical state created by correlated, transient activity, both electrical and chemical, in a large population or 'assembly' of neurons in several specific cortical areas."[79] The mental object is constituted at the point of intersection between the operation of categorization by the brain and the real object. But,

> when our brain interacts with the external world, it develops and functions according to a model of variation-selection that is sometimes called Darwinian. According to this hypothesis [. . .] variation – the generation of a diversity of internal forms – *precedes* the selection of the *adequate* form. Representations are stabilized in our brain not simply by "imprint," as though it were a piece of wax, but indirectly via a process of selection.[80]

Physical neuronal reality is subject to epigenesis. The constancy of mental objects comes from stabilization more than from stability. Their physical reality emerges constantly from a range of possibilities and their selection is highly contingent. But this contingency does not only belong to the form of the mind. Brain epigenetics is not a production apparatus of the sole "holding-true" that concerns only subjectivity. Brain activity is the natural and material capturing of nature and matter; the contingency of its epigenesis thus also engages the contingency of the world concretely. The brain is no more a subject than the world is an object. The epigenetic development of the brain affects the totality of the real.

Indeed, epigenesis involves several strata

> embedded in one another, each one subject to random variability: the evolution of species in paleontological time, together with its consequences for the genetic constitution of human beings; individual evolution, through the epigenesis of neural connections, which occurs throughout the individual's development; cultural evolution, likewise epigenetic but extracerebral, which spans not only psychological

time but also age-old memories; and finally the evolution of personal thought, which occurs in psychological time and draws upon individual and cultural memories that are both cognitive and emotional.[81]

Up to this point, in commenting on Kant's phrase "system of the epigenesis of pure reason," I have discussed epigenesis and epigenetics more than *system*. Yet, as we see in the light of Changeux's claim, it is not possible to think the different evolutionary, phylogenetic, and ontogenetic regimes of brain development other than in the form of an organized whole. Kant was therefore right when he spoke of a *system*.

Nevertheless, it bears repeating that systematic form is not transcendental and does not contest contingency. Rather, it is its paradoxical expression. The nervous system is certainly a system, but as Changeux also says, "[W]e do not evolve in a system in which imprints are rigidly propagated from one generation to another."[82] Stabilized connections can be destabilized or engaged in processes of reorganization and remodeling. *Gradual* and *non-occurrence-based* contingency is not associated with the question of what can or cannot be, may cease to be or not be all of a sudden, but rather is associated with the lability of forms of being.

What we can henceforth call the *epigenetic structure of the real* therefore reveals an entirely other meaning of contingency. It has nothing to do with the dice throw. Nor does it have anything to do anymore with the complexity of mathematical reasoning without phenomena. It refers to the adaptive pliability of the world and the metamorphic power of imprints.

Lastly, this contingency reveals another meaning of time. The postural origin of time gains consistency in mnesic replication. Time therefore ceases to be a pure somatic given and gradually becomes, through rememoration, the time of thought. Consciousness, writes Edelman, is a "remembered present."[83]

Analyzed thus, the epigenetic development of the brain allows us to situate the origin of reason in a systematic economy that goes beyond the split between "authentic" and "inauthentic." Contrary to what Heidegger claimed, it is not actually clear that the neuronal constitution of time is entirely reducible to the genesis of "vulgar" time. After all, the neuronal is also a form of "there is"...

Why the resistance to neuroscience?

We have seen that the problem is that the neurobiological viewpoint simply erases the transcendental. A bridge is thrown directly between epigenesis, understood as organic growth, and brain epigenetics, understood as a selection-stabilization process of neuronal connections, without going through the transcendental question of the formation of reason and rationality. From one skeptical argument to the next, the *a priori* never intervenes in the processes of constitution, which are declared inseparable from adaptive logic.

Why did I not come to these conclusions either? In the end, isn't the relinquishing of the transcendental implemented by neurobiology the most convincing of all? After all, doesn't it offer us a concrete and well-argued version of the epigenetic nature of thought?

Clearly, it is of the utmost necessity today to rethink relations between the biological and the transcendental, even if it is to the detriment of the latter. But who's doing so? And why do continental philosophers reject the neurobiological approach to the problem from the outset?

Why must the barrier of irreducibility be maintained by insisting that the agreement between categories and objects does not evolve, that truth does not adapt to the present state of that which it is the truth? What then is this mysterious, purely formal and symbolic place that prevents the comparison of rationality to a living system like any other, in fact, one that is subject to epigenesis? If the transcendental is the empty name of an empty place (the irreducible), if it refers only to a principled resistance to any materialization of thought, then why keep it? And if instead it defines a formal rule, a program (hyper-normativity), then why reject the integration of the transcendental to the genetic program proposed by Changeux? Why not accept taking a step back from just such a program, precisely by following the adventure of epigenetics, even against Kant if need be?

Epigenetics and the need for philosophy

At the same time, if the neurobiological approach to rationality elicits such resistance among continental philosophers, isn't it because an essential aspect of this approach is resolutely anti-philosophical? No robust theoretical discourse has yet constructed itself on the basis of contemporary epigenetics so as to conceptualize its contributions and successfully integrate its interpretative metaphors – be they readings or musical performances. We must admit, there is no epigenetic philosophy. And the fault lies with both philosophy and neurobiology.

I hypothesize that it is not certain that Kant would have been opposed to assimilating reason to the brain. There is no doubt that he would have taken the present-day neurobiological revolution seriously, that he would have been interested in all the opportunities offered by medical imagery to observe thinking caught in action, and that he would perhaps have undertaken an analysis of the philosophical implications of brain epigenesis.[84] But, of course, he would also have introduced critique to all this! If the transcendental and neuronal conflict with one another, it is less because of the supposed risk of reducing the transcendental to the neuronal than, as I suggested earlier, because of the absence of a fundamental question about the status of the philosophical consciousness of brain epigenesis among neurobiologists.

What the neurobiological perspective lacks fundamentally is the theoretical accounting for the new type of reflexivity that it enables and in which all of its philosophical interest lies. Again, the problem is not so much, as is too often assumed, the reduction of the cultural to the biological, but rather the relation of the neuronal subject to itself, the way in which it sees itself, perceives itself, or is auto-affected – a problem that has never been considered on its own count. Critique, understood here as thinking the brain, is still necessary. The task of developing a critique of neurobiological reason is urgent and is one of the fundamental challenges facing contemporary philosophy.

To Conclude

It is clear that our three opening questions are beginning to run out of steam. One lacks time. The other lacks an other. The third lacks concepts.

How then should we ultimately interpret the analogy in §27? The "system of the epigenesis of pure reason" implies an originary co-implication of *a priori* and *a posteriori*, before and after, whose paradoxical complexity and meaning have not been elucidated by any of the exegetical "keys" that we have tried so far.

Do we wish to understand transcendental epigenesis, with Heidegger, as primordial temporality? We then run into the irreducibility of the biological meaning of the notion, which refers back to a natural and objective time, one that is unthinkable in terms of authenticity and that is ontologically beyond redemption.

Or, instead, do we wish to go with biological meaning? We then face two major difficulties. Either we seek to clarify the meaning of the figure through a kind of historical recourse to the third *Critique* – but then we still fail to unify the transcendental and scientific meanings of the notion, and the problem of categorial epigenesis remains as mysterious as ever. Or we start with biology itself (evolutionary theory of the mind and contemporary epigenetics), but then the transcendental is denied by being exhausted in experience. And the critical dimension that ought to support this naturalization of reason disappears along with it.

One final possibility: we conclude that the transcendental, which no figure and no metaphor of vital growth can save, is absolute facticity, but we fail to replace the Kantian deduction of the necessity of laws with anything else, any *wholly other*.

The only way out, then, is to reframe the question, and to do so *with* Kant.

13

TOWARDS AN EPIGENETIC
PARADIGM OF RATIONALITY

It's one or the other. Is it that the breach introduced by the motif of epigenesis, illuminated and enlarged by all the contradictory readings presented up to now, including the yawning gap ripped open by speculative realism, allows us to disrupt transcendental philosophy once and for all, in which case there is no point in trying to plug the gap? Kant will obviously retain his position, but for those ultra-contemporary philosophers who are willing to see it, a crack will have appeared. This crack is that of the transcendental, inasmuch as it reveals itself to be forever unstable, unbalanced, incapable of under-girding the structural solidity that it still purports to name. From then on, there would be no choice except between the reactive restoration position – the *a priori* is flawless – and the absolutizing post-critical position – rationality has had enough of finitude, and the question of the agreement of our thought to objects, epigenetic or not, can no longer remain rational.

Or is it the second hypothesis, namely the difficulties that have appeared throughout the readings show only the failings of these readings themselves and demand that we develop a logic of epigenesis which, functioning both in and beyond Kantian philosophy, defines a new interpretative paradigm and opens a new perspective on rationality? Clearly, I have supported this second hypothesis all along, and it is this hypothesis that I shall ultimately develop by proposing, with Kant, the concept of an epigenetic paradigm of rationality.

Why a New Paradigm?

My own reading is not quite complete. Starting with an embryo – the few paragraphs in §27 – my inquiry gradually developed limbs and parts, becoming bigger and bigger, from the study of historical commentaries up to the positing of general questions that consider Kant's place in contemporary thought. But so far this trajectory has led only to aporias.

Before tomorrow, before the end of gestation, there's one last step. Kant's response. The retroactive move of his retort to posterity. No gestation without retroaction, such is the law of epigenesis. What can Kant tell us about his own tomorrows? What is his place in the generational ordering? How can he confirm the end of the dogma of the irreversibility of heritage as revealed by epigenetics?

Changeux says it loud and clear: "Let's not call Kant – a pre-evolutionist philosopher – to the rescue in a discussion of evolution [and the specific role of epigenesis, one might add]."[1] Yet that is precisely what I intend to do, by showing that Kant alone can help us construct the paradigm that today opens one of the pathways of its future to thought.

The phrase "epigenetic paradigm" echoes the "genetic paradigm" coined by Henri Atlan, who, as we saw in chapter 7, now criticizes it as being obsolete. The term "paradigm," borrowed initially from Kuhn, was adopted freely by Atlan to designate, in a general manner, "a set of ideas, concepts that form a framework in which to [. . .] imagine, plan experiments, interpret results, develop theories."[2] Understood thus, a paradigm not only is the set of principles and methods shared by a scientific community, but also acts as a reading and interpreting tool that dominates various theoretical and disciplinary fields at any given moment. Today the genetic paradigm is under reconsideration. We have seen that some scientists would prefer to no longer use the notion of program. The increasing importance of epigenetics prompts us to propose that an epigenetic paradigm is in the process of constituting itself. There is reason to believe that in the future it will also become one of the structuring tracks of philosophical rationality. A new transcendental.

I see a profound connection between Kantian thought and the contemporary rise of epigenetics. This idea has guided my research since the beginning. Consequently, to conclude, I suggest that we read the development of critique itself, from the *Critique of Pure Reason* to the *Critique of the Power of Judgment*, as an epigenetic development. This involves viewing it both as epigenesis in the classical sense of organic growth and as the economy of a relation between code, interpretation, and transformation. A meaning that Kant anticipated, even if he did not know it.

Genesis, Epigenesis, Hermeneutics: Ricœur's Contribution

Bringing together epigenesis and epigenetics, past and present, enables us to return to the distinction between genesis and epigenesis so as to refine it. A genesis measures the journey between a past and a present state of affairs. Complex or differentiated, linear or tortuous, discontinuous or unified, genesis always measures evolution starting from an origin – whether it is itself full or, as Foucault puts it, a field of various forces. By contrast, epigenesis takes place at the moving contact point between origin and the present state of affairs, until their difference disappears right into their contact – tensed origin, retrospective present, future in the making.

As I explained in chapter 3, the epicenter of an earthquake is the projection point of its focus or hypocenter. The epicenter marks the exact spot of the eruption, the place where the surface of the earth opens, cracks, bursts. Between ground and underground, the epicenter is thus in some ways the contact point of the earth with itself. Moreover, the damage of the quake is always measured from that exact spot. In this instance, the notion of an in-between base and surface is thus a decisive factor.

The logic of this in-between is also at work in epigenesis. In the *Critique of Pure Reason*, Kant situates transcendental epigenesis as the development that occurs *upon contact* between categories and experience. To wish to go back to the source of this contact, as far too many commentators do, is thus not coherent within the Kantian process, which takes place precisely at the meeting point. Again, the transcendental ground hides no treasure, and this allows me to view the transcendental as a "surface structure." The problem with the readings analyzed up to now is that one way or another they all dig for an improbable base. They look for the possibility of an always more originary instance that would somehow enable them to anchor the *a priori* in an *archè*. And if it turns out that this anchoring is impossible, they conclude that the transcendental deserves to be relinquished, that the originary and the *a priori* are simply factual and therefore unjustifiable, non-deductible. In a sense, it's true: the transcendental is not based on anything. On this point there's no change between the different editions of the first *Critique*. The productive imagination is no more founding than is the understanding.

However, clearly, this lack of a foundation is not a lack of reason. Kant warns us against this view: the originary validity of the transcendental is to be sought not in its genesis, but rather in its epigenesis. The time has come to say it: transcendental epigenesis is epigenesis *of* the transcendental itself. The transcendental is subject to epigenesis – not to foundation. The debate over whether the transcendental is innate or fabricated, and in any event factitious, is therefore pointless.

But how then can we move forward in defining a transcendental epigenesis? We don't have much to go on. The only thinker to make thematic use of the difference between genesis and epigenesis is Paul Ricœur. His temporary collaboration is very valuable in allowing us to specify the notion of meaning, which has been so omnipresent in previous discussions. Let us briefly consider this hermeneutic approach to epigenesis. Ricœur views epigenesis as both an exegetical tool and structure that allow us to question meaning in a very specific way. In *The Conflict of Interpretations*, he asks: "[I]s meaning in genesis or in epigenesis?" Where should we look for it? Does it lie "in the return [. . .] or in the rectification of the old by the new?"[3] It is precisely this distinction between "return" and "rectification of the old by the new" that helps explain the difference between genesis and epigenesis. Genesis always brings the new back to the old, while epigenesis marks the current valency of the meeting point between the old and the new, the space where they reciprocally interfere and transform one another – the embryo of a specific temporality. Once again, epigenesis situates itself in the middle, at the contact point, and is in the process of bringing the fusion of times to fruition. This median point where birth is prepared is also defined by Ricœur as the *intersection of the archaic and the teleological*.[4] Meaning therefore lies in the way in which a principle becomes its result. Teleology is a prospecting tension towards the future which rectifies after the fact the primitive or "archaic" dispositions that made it possible.

We have seen that epigenesis includes the dual dimension of regression and progression, since the embryo's formation gradually makes it more complex through the addition of new parts that complete pre-existing parts. The epigenetic economy and the hermeneutic economy thus concur, with both of them combining repetition and exploration, recapitulation and invention. It might be objected that all genesis also involves this dual dimension. This is true, but in the case of epigenesis, these dimensions are but one; they fuse together at the point of their shared impact.

Admittedly, the context in which Ricœur develops his idea of interpretative epigenesis is very different from my own.[5] But this difference is not enough to proscribe the comparison with the epigenesis of reason. Why? As we have seen, the challenge of §27 derives from the tension that it incites, rather than soothes, between preformation and transformation. It appears that the figure of epigenesis constantly sets off the conflict it is supposed to settle, the conflict between the vision of a predetermined, preformed categorial engendering and the point of view of a modification of this production by experience after the fact. There's no way out of this circle. Consequently, instead of trying in vain to break through it by remaining within the strict limits of the *Critique of Pure Reason*, instead of juxtaposing this text to other parallel texts, and, finally, instead of trying to explain the genesis of epigenesis from its first to its last occurrence, we should ask whether an epigenetic development takes place in Kant's philosophy and look for the type of hermeneutic strategy that this process requires. In other words, we should ask whether there is a gradual transformation of the transcendental, and thus of the rational itself; whether critical philosophy is organized entirely by the dual prospective and retrospective movement of epigenesis.

In fact, it turns out that the trajectory of the three *Critiques* is organized according to the rhythm of this dual dynamic. Present in embryonic form in the first *Critique*, the idea of the transformability and transformation of the transcendental comes to fruition in the last *Critique*. This process of completion simultaneously modifies the starting point and retrospectively gives the entire critical undertaking its ultimate form and meaning. The genitive in the phrase "system of the epigenesis of pure reason" must therefore be understood definitively as a subjective genitive: the epigenesis *of* reason itself.

What an epigenesis shows, says Ricœur – and this is a particularly important point – is that it "has meaning only in later figures, since the meaning of a given figure is deferred until the appearance of a new figure."[6] This new figure is neither a pure product from outside, nor the revelation of a preformed meaning. The logic of epigenesis, its own dynamic, requires that we seek out and show this place where the transcendental is "both archaic in origin and susceptible of an indefinite creation of meaning."[7] It is not therefore necessary to transgress the circularity of the *a priori* and the transcendental, which presents the structural framework of the entire rational undertaking from the first *Critique*, in order to look for its effectiveness outside of it, in experience. Nor is it appropriate to substitute an alternative model such as mental evolutionism in its place. And it is not a matter of revealing its ontological or historical assumptions. Lastly, we cannot, on the other hand, shut it up in the hermetically sealed container of predetermination.

No. Setting aside the genetic paradigm (I am deliberately playing here on both the hermeneutic and scientific meanings of the word "genetic") involves considering the idea of the system of the epigenesis of pure reason introduced in §27 as the beginning of an internal growth process which, moving by self-differentiation from one *Critique* to the next, plays with the forces *of its own outside*, starting with its creative, formative, and transformative resources. In this way we can define the core of rationality as the mobile middle between constitution and relinquishing of itself: archeology and teleology.

From the First to the Third *Critique*: The Intrication of the Transcendental and the Biological

What is this outside that is internal to critique? The new element which in the course of the critical trajectory will reveal "meaning only in later figures"[8] and demonstrate the reconciliation of the biological and the transcendental without granting either one the supremacy of a proper meaning, this element that the figure of epigenesis already introduced covertly in the first *Critique* and that profoundly transformed the entire system, is *life*. The meeting of thinking and life is the immanent outside of critique. In the *Critique of the Power of Judgment*, Kant identifies for the first time the specific question that the organized being asks reason, a question whose difficulty the first *Critique* signals, but which it does not yet try to answer.

The question that the living being and life in general address reason derives initially from their condition as outsiders. They are neither ideas, nor concepts, nor forms. They do not immediately have any transcendental status. Indeed, they appear to have come from outside. Bernard Bourgeois writes: "The concept of living being, or to put it in Kant's terms, organized being, organism, is not an *a priori* or *metaphysical* concept, is not *a fortiori* transcendental [. . .]."[9] Consequently, the real interpretative difficulty raised by §27 derives from the fact that Kant calls for help from a figure that has absolutely no transcendental meaning to illustrate the exemplary transcendental instances that are, first, the production of the objective reference of the categories, and, second, the architectonic tendency of reason.

160

The resolution of this heterogeneity between the transcendental and life is exactly that which, along with the categories and their objective reference, is also subject to epigenesis. Indeed, the structure of relation between the transcendental and life evolves, becomes more complex, and is transformed from the first to the last *Critique*. The meaning of the epigenesis of and in critical philosophy derives from the long rational maturation of the relation between the transcendental and that which appears to do without it, to resist it: the living organism, which self-forms and has no need for categories. Gradually, in the *Critique of the Power of Judgment*, Kant came to grasp these appearances which, in experience, do not present themselves as objects of experience like any other, and, in fact, do not present themselves as objects at all: the beautiful, and that which interests us the most here, the living being. Long before his twenty-first-century readers, Kant completely exposed the transcendental to the factuality of life. A series of categorial modifications resulted from this contact – epigenetic modifications whose possibility appeared to have been excluded in the first *Critique*: the specification of causality through the intermediary of purposiveness; the constitution of purposiveness as an autonomous concept; and, above all, as a result of all this, the transformation of the category of necessity.

Difference in Causality

To support this interpretation, I'll begin with the transformation in the meaning of epigenesis between the *Critique of Pure Reason* and the *Critique of the Power of Judgment*. However, its meaning appears to be identical in §27 of the first *Critique* and §81 of the third. The only difference seems to lie in a different context. In the first, epigenesis acts as an analogy of *a priori* production, while in the second it is treated according to its own meaning as the mode of growth of living beings. The philosophical debate is the same: in both instances, I repeat, it is about defending epigenesis against equivocal generation and preformationism. In §81, Kant explains that there are two main theories for the production of living beings: "occasionalism" and "prestabilism." Occasionalism claims that "the supreme world-cause, in accordance with its idea, would immediately provide the organic formation to the matter commingling in every impregnation."[10] Kant rapidly dismisses this thesis, which says that the living is endowed with no formative force at all and is always, on every occasion, created or re-created by God.

The alternative between preformation and epigenesis is presented within "prestabilism," which instead assumes that an "an organic being produces more of its kind and constantly preserves the species itself."[11] Kant writes:

> Now prestabilism can in turn proceed in two ways. Namely, it considers each organic being generated from its own kind as either the educt or the product of the latter. The system of generatings as mere educts is called that of individual preformation or the theory of evolution; the system of generatings as products is called the system of epigenesis.[12]

Kant clearly opts for the superiority or "great advantage" of epigenesis over preformation, whose "champions" "excep[t] every individual from the formative force of nature in order to allow it to come immediately from the hand of the creator."[13] Although they try not to, the advocates of preformationism share this approach with the supporters of occasionalism, who "would make impregnation a mere formality, since the supreme intelligent world-cause has decided always to form a fruit immediately with his own hand and to leave to the mother only its development and nourishment."[14]

There is no need to emphasize the similarity of the arguments in favor of epigenesis put forward by Kant in the two *Critiques*. This is clear and undeniable. The reference to Blumenbach and the formative drive at the end of §81 reinforces the advantage granted to epigenesis over the competing theories of engendering and extends the remarks made in §27.

But there is a difference, of course. Again, this difference lies not in the dissymmetry of the contexts but rather in what must be called a *difference in causality*. In the first *Critique*, the natural lawfulness that it is the mission of epigenesis to figure and validate is the mechanism. The order of nature, generated by the understanding, is the foundation of natural, that is, mechanical necessity. On the other hand, as we know, in the third *Critique* epigenesis is analyzed within the framework of the "teleological principle," which assumes "an intentionally acting cause to whose ends nature is subordinated, even in its mechanical laws."[15] But mechanism and teleology are "two entirely different kinds of causality."[16] The challenge is to arrive at their "unification."[17] The revelation of the role and importance of purposiveness – defined as a "special kind of causality"[18] – enables movement between the two regimes and effects a dramatic transformation in the categorial order.

The Order of Nature and Systematic Order: Examining Purposiveness

In the *Critique of Pure Reason*, mechanism and teleology are not yet polarized. The single difficulty that is responsible for stalling so many readings of §27 is that, as the third *Critique* clearly demonstrated, epigenesis is a form of teleological judgment and can in no way be subject to a mechanist explanation.[19] In the *Critique of Pure Reason*, epigenesis certainly has a role in representing a mode of engendering, but a mode of engendering of that which is not normally engendered: the conceptual apparatus of determinism – the identity of the laws of the understanding (categories and principles) and the laws of nature. Since the difference of mechanism and teleology as causal regime is not revealed on its own count, this makes the figure of epigenesis responsible for a symptomatic ambiguity and creates the hiatus that led exegetes to bring epigenesis back to preformation – which is more immediately compatible with mechanism – or else to simply strip it of its transcendental status. In the *Critique of Pure Reason*, the dual causal pulse of, on the one hand, the archaic or archeological (the fundamental metaphysical principles of nature, as Kant himself said) and, on the other, the teleological is not yet identified.

"System of the epigenesis of pure reason." It has been said that this phrase is as much about the understanding as about reason. As much about "nature," Kant would also say, as about the "order of nature" (*Naturordnung*)." For Kant, "nature" refers to the set of laws and the subsuming of all appearances to these laws, while the "order of nature" describes the tendency of these laws to combine together into a system. The difference between the understanding and reason thus reinforces one that exists between "nature" and the "order of nature." Nature, in its form, that is, in its *a priori* lawfulness, is subject entirely to the jurisdiction of the understanding. But this form also tends towards another order, which is the systematic order incumbent on reason: "[I]f we survey the cognitions of our understanding in their entire range, then we find that what reason quite uniquely prescribes and seeks to bring about concerning it is the systematic in cognition, i.e., its interconnection based on one principle."[20]

Kant terms this systematic tendency "purposiveness." In the *Critique of Pure Reason*, purposiveness is certainly concerned with living beings, since the regulatory principle that guides the systematic tendency of reason is present as the hierarchical ordering of nature into genera and species. And yet, quite remarkably, the concept of

teleology does not appear. Moreover, as Philippe Huneman emphasizes, in the first *Critique*, purposiveness is "strictly synonymous
with science's demands for systematicity and [. . .] is absolutely not
opposed to the explanations that are entirely given by efficient causes,
[. . .] thus [it is in keeping with] a description in terms of mechanical
determinism in which no given end has an explanatory value."[21]

Recalling the two meanings of order – the rational architectonic
and the regulation of appearances by the principle of causality –
allows us to emphasize one striking point: in the *Critique of Pure
Reason*, mechanism (necessity) and purposiveness (systematic order)
complement one another without any other form of process. The
system of pure reason is described as an "end." Indeed, its privileged
figure is the organism. And yet purposiveness does not describe the
natural living.

Certainly, the regulating idea of system is "the unity of the end,
to which all parts are related and in the idea of which they are also
related to each other."[22] The end here refers both to the goal (*Zweck*)
and to its completion (*Ende*) – the organized totality (mutual depend-
ence of the parts of the whole) – just as the *Critique of the Power of
Judgment* also claims. Moreover, once again, the three principles of
systematic unity are presented in the Appendix to the Transcendental
Dialectic as the arranging of nature into genera and species:

> Reason thus prepares the field for the understanding: 1. by a principle of
> *sameness* of kind in the manifold under higher genera, 2. by a principle
> of *variety* of what is same in kind under lower species; and in order to
> complete the systematic unity it adds 3. still another law of the *affinity*
> of all concepts, which offers a continuous transition from every species
> to every other through a graduated increase of varieties.[23]

Lastly, since the idea of the whole precedes the constitution of the
parts, the system must develop according to a law of growth analogous to that of living organisms. In the Architectonic of Pure Reason,
Kant in fact states that "[t]he whole is therefore articulated (*articulatio*) and not heaped together (*coacervatio*); it can, to be sure, grow
internally (*per intussusceptionem*), but not externally (*per appositio-
nem*), like an animal body, whose growth does not add a limb but
rather makes each limb stronger and fitter for its end without any
alternation of proportion."[24] One last passage completes the inscription of the relation between system, purposiveness, and organism in
the Architectonic:

> The systems seem to have been formed, like maggots, by a *generatio
> æquivoca*, from the mere confluence of aggregated concepts, garbled

164

at first but complete in time, although they all had their schema, as the original germ, in the mere self-development of reason, and on that account are not merely each articulated for themselves in accordance with an idea but are rather all in turn purposively united with each other as members of a whole in a system of human cognition [. . .].[25]

The contrast between growth by accumulation or "technical" arrangement and organic growth is already present, and is one of the fundamental aspects of the critique of teleological judgment.[26] We therefore have proof of the close association between purposiveness and the mode of development of organic life. Nevertheless, the systematicity of cognition analyzed in the *Critique of Pure Reason* leaves no place for biology and is therefore directly situated in the perspective opened by the *Metaphysical Foundations of Natural Science* according to which matter "in itself" is without life.[27] The first metaphysical foundations of science are the principles of movement, not those of living matter.[28] As Huneman writes, "Purposiveness is only a language to say what the natural sciences explain, and provide it with a heuristic; this language is immediately coextensive with the territory of physics."[29] From this perspective, the systematic unity of cognition, as the end of reason, matches the necessity of the mechanism perfectly.

In the *Critique of Pure Reason*, life is there without being there. It does not yet put the transcendental to the test. It has not yet emerged as a question. But the figure of epigenesis is nonetheless already inscribed in the text and thereby introduces a gap in it that is not yet mature. This is why the figure of epigenesis is, it must be said for all the reasons mentioned above, well and truly incomprehensible in the context of the Transcendental Analytic. It signals the still summary state of the difference between physics and biology, mechanism and teleology.

The perplexity of commentators of §27 is thus in one sense entirely legitimate. The difficulty returns constantly: epigenesis is unthinkable without some contingency. Yet, in the *Critique of Pure Reason*, contingency is totally excluded. *A priori* means universal and necessary (again, this explains the meaning of the discussion with Hume). At the level of reason, the architectonic tendency is entirely opposed to the contingent tendency of the "aggregate." Kant states this clearly:

If among the appearances offering themselves to us there were such a great variety – I will not say of form (for they might be similar to one another in that) but of content, i.e., regarding the manifoldness of existing beings – that even the most acute human understanding, through comparison of one with another, could not detect the least similarity (a case which can at least be thought), then the logical law of genera would not obtain at all [. . .].[30]

This "manifoldness," which was to form one of the sensitive spots of the *Critique of the Power of Judgment*, is declared here to be unimaginable, entirely outside the system. Furthermore, it is to be noted that Kant describes the principles that rule the relation between genera and species as *logical*, not *biological*.

The analogy in §27 is thus misleading if one seeks to contain it within the strict framework of the *Critique of Pure Reason*. Insofar as purposiveness does not question the structure of necessity, where the mode of organic growth does not contravene the mechanism and categories only serve determining judgments, it is difficult to see what transcendental role the figure of embryonic development by self-differentiation plays. It is difficult to contest the ambiguity of the image of the formation of the system mentioned here. As noted above, Kant describes how it may "grow internally" like a body "whose growth does not add a limb but rather makes each limb stronger and fitter for its end without any alteration of proportion." As we have seen, growth by epigenesis is exactly what changes relations of proportion. How then can we not see the unfolding of a preformed structure returning in this image? And where is self-differentiation if the constitution of systems is only the "unfolding (*Auswicklung*)" of a germ that is originarily present? We have already discussed the meaning to be attributed to the Kantian use of concepts of "germs" and "predispositions." Nothing indicates that they point entirely to preformationism. But despite it all, we have to admit that in the first *Critique* transcendental productivity has very little freedom, very little place to express its creativity. It's as if experience serves only to develop the envelope. Hindsight offers nothing but a confirmation. It is therefore practically inevitable that we conclude that the transcendental is invalid in the epigenetic analogy, an invalidity that at the same time justifies its immediate confiscation by the skeptical argument.

The Return Effect of the Third *Critique* on the First

It will be objected that I am getting caught up again in the disadvantages of the genetic approach. In fact, am I not in the process of retracing the genesis of the critique of judgment? Indeed, I could

166

simply emphasize that in the first *Critique* it is not yet a question of the reflecting power of judging, but a "hypothetical" use of reason when the universal is "problematic," and leave it at that:

> If reason is the faculty of deriving the particular from the universal, then: Either the universal is *in itself certain* and given, and only *judgment* is required for subsuming, and the particular is necessarily determined through it. This I call the "apodictic" use of reason. Or the universal is assumed only *problematically*, and it is a mere idea, the particular being certain while the universality of the rule for this consequent is still a problem; then several particular cases, which are all certain, are tested by the rule, to see if they flow from it [. . .]. This I will call the "hypothetical" use of reason.[31]

I could limit myself to pointing out again that the reflecting power of judgment that is prefigured in "the amphibology of concepts of reflection" is not yet considered or developed. I could just say that reflection is presented as a dual logical act, composed of the formation of concepts and the locating of the source of knowledge from which the representations derive. Or that the connection with the reflecting function of judgment is not yet brought to light there.

I could settle for merely stressing that the *Critique of Pure Reason* does not take up the fundamental idea of a "contingent order" developed in 1764 in *The Only Possible Argument in Support of a Demonstration of the Existence of God*. In this text, Kant states that there are "accidental harmonies" in nature *next to* the necessary systematic orders that constitute the mechanism as a whole. That if "it is inorganic nature, in particular, which furnished numberless proofs of a necessary unity,"[32] "the creatures of the plant- and animal-kingdoms everywhere offer the most admirable examples of a unity which is at once contingent [. . .]."[33] The unity of a "contingent order" is not in the purview of determinist necessity. It appears as "a unified and perfect whole [. . .] artificially devised," like the artful work of an artisan.[34] The first *Critique* also underscores the difference between systematic and technical unity. Nevertheless, in the 1764 text, the two unities are both presented as harmonious totalities (the second being in no way the result of an aggregate) that are not ruled by the same kind of causality. We still do not come across the idea of natural purposiveness or the "as if" of intentional purposiveness; however, the idea of a causality that rules non-necessary orders is present.

I might therefore conclude that in the course of a long genesis that prompted Kant to rethink "the contingent order," epigenesis did not find its place until the third *Critique*, where the thought of life and purposiveness come to fruition.

But what I intend to propose and elaborate is another reading. A reading that asks about the retroactive effect of the third *Critique* on the transcendental arrangement set up in the first and that considers that from one *Critique* to the next, it is in fact reason that is interpreted and transformed. This reading requires a different definition of the relation between reason and epigenesis from the solely linear and unilateral one that leads, like a one-way ticket, from §27 in the *Critique of Pure Reason* to §81 of the *Critique of the Power of Judgment*.

Life and Factual Rationality

Let us return specifically to the question that the first *Critique* does not ask and that becomes the leading question of the third. As I said earlier, "organized beings" immediately appear stateless in the natural order. Only the recognition of difference in causality (the difference between necessity and teleology) allows them to be identified. Kant writes: "[W]ithout this kind of causality organized beings, as ends of nature, would not be natural products."[35] The question presented by life – a question that is not developed as such in the *Critique of Pure Reason* – relates to the transgressive status of organization. The notion of an organized being eludes mechanical necessity and thereby forces reason to identify another nature for nature – purposeful nature – whose articulation it fails to understand: "[O]ur reason does not comprehend (*begreift unsere Vernunft nicht*) the possibility of a unification of two entirely different kinds of causality."[36]

The bringing to light of the reflecting aspect of teleological judgment and, consequently, the regulative aspect of the concept of "natural end" makes it possible to recognize, without understanding, that is to say, paradoxically without leading back to their cause, both the singularity and the regularity of the status of the living being among appearances. "The concept of a thing as in itself a natural end is therefore not a constitutive concept of the understanding or of reason, but it can still be a regulative concept for the reflecting power of judgment."[37]

The familiar, all too familiar, nature of these conclusions still does not mask the acuity of the rational test that they resolve. The "compatibility" of the mechanical and the teleological, which Kant

168

wrestled to achieve, in no way erases the irruption of the enigma that life presents to philosophy.

The first formulation of this is the first part of the *Critique of the Power of Judgment*, namely the critique of the power of aesthetic judgment. There are appearances which, while also subject to natural determinism, have their own form, a form that is irregular as a consequence of obeying only themselves. In this way they come to lodge themselves in all sorts of logical gaps that the categories are incapable of defining. The manifold of forms in nature is such, says Kant, that some of them remain "undetermined by those laws that the pure understanding gives *a priori* [. . .]."[38] The principle of the unity of the manifoldness that presides over these forms remains unknown to us. "The reflecting power of judgment, which is under the obligation of ascending from the particular in nature to the universal, therefore requires a principle that it cannot borrow from experience [. . .]. The reflecting power of judgment, therefore, can only give itself such a transcendental principle as a law [. . .]."[39]

What do "forms" and "manifoldness of forms" mean here? The productions of nature that enable the faculty of judgment to present as universal are specific inasmuch as they in some sense appear to categorize themselves, as if they were self-sufficient, somehow their own judges, rendering thought useless through their independence and, at the same time, thereby soliciting thought to the highest degree. If nature and freedom are reconciled with each other in the very space of this categorial desert, discovered through the use of reflective judgment, it is also, and primarily, because certain natural objects appear simultaneously *naturally free* and *necessarily autonomous.* Their "form" derives from their independence. Kant will show that natural beauty, first, then life, present reason with the enigma of factual rationality, a rationality that appears to be able to do without reason. These appearances actually appear closed in on themselves, self-formed, self-normed, dismissing our jurisdictions immediately. Factual rationality is the unique rationality in which meaning is given without us, in the chance alliance of nature and freedom.

Before its time, Kant thus discovered the power that certain appearances have to *decorrelate thought.* Once again, life organizes itself very well without us and is indifferent to the fact of being judged. But after all, one might ask, what's the problem? The problem is that indifference is the lining of meaning. It's a problem that Meillassoux never considers. That which is indifferent *makes meaning all alone.* This is just what life prompts us to think. It makes meaning in order to stand for itself alone.

In his remarkable article "Sens et fait" (meaning and fact), Eric Weil claims that the third critique is a critique of contingency, a feature that he attributes precisely to the chancy nature of meaning:

> The *Critique of the Power of Judgment* [. . .] seeks to understand *meaningful facts*, not only the meaningless facts that are organized by science, not just at the level of practical reason, a meaning that is always postulated and eternally separated from the facts [. . .]; now, meaning is a fact, facts have a meaning, this then is the fundamental position of the last *Critique*.[40]

Weil goes on to add: "We do not understand beauty, we do not understand life, we observe them."[41] Purposiveness appears precisely as the "meaning of the fortuitous existence of meaning."[42]

The Other Contingency and the Other Necessity

The reach of epigenesis thus goes far beyond a mere sensible translation of the categorial production in the *Critique of Pure Reason*. It also goes far beyond its thematic biological treatment in the *Critique of the Power of Judgment*. In the end, epigenesis defines the transformation of the transcendental that was prepared from the start and accomplished ultimately by the test of biological judgment.[43]
What does this mean? Eric Weil continues:

> The new critique emerges because Kant ran up against a new problem, which was no longer that of *a priori* judgments [. . .]. The expectation, the requirement for a coherent world, the necessary condition of all theoretical, practical, theoretical-practical orientations, is certainly *a priori*, but it is the facts that respond to it and that thereby give rise to a new fundamental problem.[44]

The "fundamental problem" is the *factual response of the world – life* – to transcendental necessity. Kant "emphasized over and over the non-necessary, non-deductible aspect of the presence of meaning."[45] Purposiveness, which Kant presents as "the lawfulness of the contingent,"[46] exceeds the framework of any transcendental deduction in general. The third *Critique* puts the transcendental deduction to the test of the non-deducible. Meillassoux is therefore wrong when he states that Kant does not take into account the factuality of the transcendental. He does nothing but! The rational path towards purposiveness is inseparable from the rational path towards the actual factuality of rationality.

170

A transcendental formative force does therefore indeed exist. The categories are not immutable. The proof of this lies in the transformation of the category of necessity that takes place in the third *Critique*. As we have seen, this is prepared for by the specification – and thus already the modification – of causality as purposiveness (intentional causality). At the same time, this specification reveals another meaning of purposiveness itself. According to the transcendental definitions offered in the two first *Critiques*, purposiveness simply refers to "the causality of a concept in regard to its object," the way that the object is thought as the possible effect of a concept.[47] Thus understood, purposiveness requires no specification of causality, of which it is only a representation. On the other hand, the possibility of a thing such as a "natural end" assumes that this thing in itself is an end, without the causality of concepts intervening in any way. "As a natural product, [it] is nevertheless to contain *in itself* and its *internal possibility* a relation to ends [. . .]."[48] Self-organization, according to which "its parts be combined into a whole,"[49] is not a law of the mind. It is factual, self-sufficient, and has no need to be thought.

The specification of causality and the increasing complexity of purposiveness prompt the taking into account of another necessity. The third *Critique* confronts the thought of the existence of *different types of lawfulness in nature*, beginning with a new structure of the concept of necessity. A passage in §66 demonstrates clearly the coexistence of the two necessities:

> It might always be possible that in, e.g., an animal body, many parts could be conceived as consequences of merely mechanical laws (such as skin, hair and bones). Yet the cause that provides the appropriate material, modifies it, forms it, and deposits it in its appropriate place must always be judged teleologically, so that everything in it must be considered as organized, and everything is also, in a certain relation to the thing itself, an organ in turn.[50]

Traditionally, the necessary is that whose opposite is impossible, while the contingent is that whose opposite is possible. These definitions are valid only for mechanical causality. They are in no way operative in defining organization. As Weil also wrote quite rightly: "[T]he necessary is that which cannot be denied without contradiction, [yet] the beautiful and the living being are not such that their negation, their real negation, their absence, would introduce a contradiction to natural science."[51] This passage is key. What we will call the *other* necessity has no opposite. To deny it would not lead to any contradiction, any logical threat, any risk of instability or irregularity in the laws. And yet it changes everything since its discovery is that which prompts the modification of the transcendental. *The question that life asks thought is about necessity defined as transcendental contingency.* Kant says as much clearly: "[T]here is such a manifold of forms in nature, as it were so many *modifications of the universal transcendental concepts* of nature (*so viele Modificationen der allgemeinen transzendentalen Naturbegriffe*) [. . .]."[52] It is the manifold of forms that modifies the transcendental!

Clearly, this categorial change is not therefore simply epistemological, which would only be attached to the move, from one critique to the next, of mechanism to teleology or from physics to biology. According to Kant, it is not about the biological adaptability of the categories, their gradual evolution. It is about the fact that reason encounters itself *as a fact* in nature and discovers a meaning of necessity that is no longer tied to determinism.

Indeed, reason discovers that the other necessity is its own contingency. The structure of our mind is such that it is "neither necessary, nor understandable starting from itself alone."[53] The distinction between contingency and necessity is only meaningful in relation to the contingency of our thinking. Paragraph 70 of the *Critique of the Power of Judgment* asserts the "contingent unity of particular laws."[54] But this is clearly not separable from "a certain contingency in the constitution (*eine gewisse Zufälligkeit der Beschaffenheit*)" of our understanding and our mind in general.[55] Kant explains that this contingency results from the discursive nature of our understanding, forced to start from concepts to go towards the particular, whose diversity it in no way determines.[56] An intuitive understanding would grasp the whole and the linkages of the parts to the whole, the unity and the manifold of forms, in a single necessity. By contrast, our understanding cannot reduce the diversity of appearances to the unity of knowledge except "through the correspondence of natural characteristics (*Naturmerkmale*) with our faculty of concepts, which is quite contingent (*sehr zufällig*) [. . .]."[57]

And here the agreement between categories and objects, the *Übereinstimmung* that we started with in §27, which appeared to Kant as the very structure of *a priori* necessity, the very one whose opposite is impossible and that therefore allows for no contradiction, here this agreement, in its very necessity, is said to be *quite contingent!* Subject, if you like, to the other contingency, that is to say, again, the other necessity. The necessity of its factuality. Kant allows us, from finitude, to discover a meaning of contingency that is more innovative and radical than the one that Meillassoux proposes when he believes himself to be announcing his after. The epigenetic transformation of necessity and causality, starting from reason itself, reveals that contingency derives less from a possible modification of the laws of physics than from the existence of different levels of necessity or lawfulness in which physical necessity is but one dimension.

The epigenesis of reason: it is therefore important to understand the genitive in the phrase as a subjective genitive. It is indeed about an epigenesis, that is, about the gestation and embryogenesis of reason itself. Throughout the itinerary of the three *Critiques*, reason is transformed, and the last stage of the trajectory organizes the reflection of reason on this transformation *a posteriori*. The transformation does not come from outside, nor is it linked, or no longer only linked, to the type of object examined; it responds to a fundamental internal demand of reason, one that is already present, as a germ in the first *Critique*, and already manifest in the idea – unacceptable to many, even if it is incontestable – of a certain changeability of the categories.

Structure and Evolution

We recall Kant's comment in the Transcendental Analytic that we took as our starting point:

> We will therefore pursue the pure concepts into their first germs and predispositions in the human understanding, where they lie ready, until with the opportunity of experience they are finally developed and exhibited in their clarity by the very same understanding, liberated from the empirical conditions attaching to them.[58]

The discussion continued at length about these "first germs" and "predispositions" that are the entirely "ready" forms of the categories of the understanding. We can now accept that the problem is no longer the source of the source, or knowing what role is played by the innateness of the constitution of cognitive power for this power itself. In the third *Critique*, Kant effectively answers these questions in his own way. The reason that could never be provided is the reason of life. It is never the thing in itself that is mysterious for Kant, and we have to ask why so many readers stop there. The real difficulty is life. The fact that thought belongs simultaneously to a transcendental subject *and* to a living being – which is something other than an empirical subject.

The relation between transcendental subjectivity and empirical subjectivity is examined and settled in the Transcendental Deduction.

But the difference between transcendental subjectivity, empirical subjectivity, and living subjectivity is what appears between the lines in the third *Critique*. It is organization that makes the difference between that which is simply empirical and that which is living. Organization appears to be the reply to thought – Kant speaks of a "mirror" – it orders and organizes itself like it, and similarly its form is systematic. And yet life can do without thought, it has no need to be thought, even if the subject of thought is living and, as the object of thought that is different from others, encounters the factuality of its life. In the last analysis, the innate part of cognitive power thus refers back to the living naturalness of thought.

We can now say that the epicenter is in some senses stratified, as if it were becoming more complex. The objective reference of the categories no longer concerns only the objects of nature ruled by mechanism, but also organized beings. We see it now: epigenesis unfolds at the very place of this dual objectivity. On the one hand, it refers to the production of the categories and their "correspondence" with the objects (first *Critique*), but, on the other, it refers to the categorial modification that arises with teleological judgment and brings to light the need for another agreement with other objects (third *Critique*). From one dimension of epigenesis to the next, it is the entire rational enterprise that matures and finds its definitive form.

The Kantian critical enterprise combines a structural and an evolutionary view of reason in a whole. There's no need to choose between the two. The dynamic of transcendental philosophy proceeds both from the formal anteriority of the *a priori* – the archeological dimension – and from its modifiability through successive corrections – the teleological dimension. The permanence and mobility of form are thus combined in a single economy: the system of the epigenesis of pure reason.

— 14 —

CAN WE RELINQUISH THE TRANSCENDENTAL?

The End of the Divorce between Primordial Temporality and Leveled-Down Time

Understood as a transcendental formative force, epigenesis allows us to conceive of time in terms of the germinative relation that the understanding and reason each develop with themselves. Another meaning of the before-and-after relation emerges, which, in the constant shift between prospective and retrospective perspectives, reflects the development of rationality from one *Critique* to the next. Because he was convinced that the eviction of the imagination from the second edition of the *Critique of Pure Reason* amounted to a triumph for the traditional concept of time, Heidegger did not see the deconstructive resource that the motif of epigenesis harbored in Kant's work. This resource offered no less than a means to be done with the difference between primordial temporality and leveled-down or "vulgar" time. Epigenesis is not a genesis, but nor is it a succession or connection of events taking place in a linear fashion starting from a given, identifiable point. The unique temporality of epigenesis places it "above" or "at the surface" of genesis and is instead the temporality of a synthetic continuum within which all of the parts are presented together in a movement of growth whereby the whole is formed through self-differentiation. Synthesis in Kant must be understood as productive and generative in the strong sense, as a movement to produce its posterity, without which it would remain forever premature.

Epigenesis can thus be thought as a process of temporalization within which ontological horizon and biological maturation, coming into presence and natural growth, are no longer distinguished from

175

one another. Epigenetic temporality is transcendental without being primordial, natural without being derived. It is impossible to separate epigenetic temporality from the biological process it refers to, from organic growth, from the future of the living being. However, insofar as its movement is *also* the movement of the reason that thinks it, insofar as there is no rationality without epigenesis, without self-adjustment, without the modification of the old by the new, the natural and objective time of epigenesis may also be considered to be the subjective and pure time of the formation of horizon by and for thought.

In this way, there would no longer be a difference between primordial temporality and objective temporality. Natural productivity and ontological productivity meet at the site of one and the same moment, without any difficulty arising from the acceptance that primordial temporality might also unfold according to the ages of biological-archeological dating. Between an authentic temporality without maturation and a chronological vulgarity without ecstasy, epigenetic temporality unfolds at its own rhythm. Henceforth, all it asks is to be conceptualized.

Regarding the Possible Non-World

To limit himself strictly to the first *Critique*, to restrict the Kantian inquiry into the necessity of the laws of physics – following the specific example of cinnabar – without ever tackling the problem of purposiveness, Meillassoux keeps to the traditional definition of contingency as the hypothesis of the possible wholly other world. We have seen the extent to which this hypothesis was difficult, if not well-nigh impossible, to justify. All the more so since, as Eric Weil comments, "while it is true that concrete science would become inconceivable in a non-organized and non-directed world, it does not follow that a non-structured nature, non-world, non-cosmos, is a contradictory concept (in his cosmogonic hypothesis, Kant himself had imagined just such a nature ...)."[1] Kant therefore never contested the very idea of a wholly other world on its own count. A world that would cease to obey physical necessity is not inconceivable. But for him, the problem of the relation between necessity and contingency occurs elsewhere. Not in the passage through the absurd – the relativization of the laws of physics – but in the *recognition of different regimes of necessity*, physical necessity being, once again, only one of them.[2]

Insofar as he does not take into account the biological question as Kant formulates it, Meillassoux appears not to see that the analytic

176

of the life sciences "replaces the classic metaphysical question of the contingency of that which is."[3] The epigenetic development of reason reveals precisely the different levels of necessity while also bringing about a transformation in the meaning of contingency. Contingency is no longer synonymous solely with a power to be other, but indeed also with an irremissible factuality of being, which is not at all one and the same. The question that the living, organized individual addresses to reason is not then about a possible alternative to the necessary order of nature, but rather about an independence of order in relation to reason. This possibility of decorrelation, which Kant saw very clearly, opens the door not to the thought of a modification in the laws of physics or natural laws in general, but rather to the thought of a factual rationality – which reason alone can somehow "come upon" – namely the self-sufficiency of life. The spontaneity of life is without reason.

It is true that from this Kant deduces that this contingency echoes the contingency of *our* mind and, once again, the inexplicable nature of the constitution of our cognitive power. It is certainly because our mind is contingent that it can consider the question of contingency. We have seen that the rational grasp of the contingency of rationality led back to finitude, to which the discursive nature of our understanding must also be attributed. There's no doubt about this point: contingency and necessity are the categories of *our* relation to appearances.

But, as we have shown, finitude does not exist in the singular. The concept of finitude, just like the concepts of necessity and contingency, is plural. We have referred to Heidegger's distinction between two elaborations of finitude. But the finitude analyzed in the third *Critique* also has its own, highly specific, meaning.

Unlike the *Critique of Pure Reason*, the teleological critique of judgment does not emphasize the notion of finitude understood as a limit. This critique requires that finitude be thought of starting from life. After Kant, the relation between life and finitude is only ever taken up and developed in the twentieth century to the benefit of existential finitude, never life. To be finite, it is necessary not only to live but rather to exist; this is what we were told for a century. Today, what we must undertake is a philosophical thinking of finite life, not finite existence. Epigenesis can help us to do just that.

Not that Kant grants the living being any special privilege. Unlike Dasein, the living being is not exemplary. The emergence of life can be understood entirely in his work as a banal event that is part of mechanical regularity since it "reigns over all the other creatures,"[4] that is, living beings. Human beings can very well be "included."[5] But

177

despite it all, if the judgment of organized beings in no way prevents consideration of inorganic nature and never contravenes the mechanism, it still makes it possible to consider it in a non-mechanistic manner, as a memory. Thus the earth always appears as a collection of traces. According to Kant, it cannot include any "history of nature," that is, any "description of nature," without an "archaeology." The archeology concerns the "remaining traces of its oldest revolutions" in nature.[6]

For Kant, it is not possible to date the past of the earth, which he calls its history, without using the archeological calendar, without which what happens means nothing. What is archeology? It in no way counters objectivity, but it does prohibit the neutrality of the look. Indeed, it makes possible a "representation of the primitive condition of the earth" as a play of signs, a perspective "to which nature itself invites and summons us."[7] However, archeology is not, for all that, a mere anthropologization. It is about petrified "fossils," rather than "carved stones" made by humans. This is not therefore an anthropologization of the ancestral past, but rather a reckoning of this past as an abundance of clues. In other words, to use a vocabulary that is not his, for Kant the arche-fossil is always an architrace. And the architrace is always a trace of life.[8]

Kant would criticize speculative realism for avoiding life and biological judgment entirely just when, as Eric Weil says, it "turns towards the real to address it as its problem,"[9] and thereby misses a new meaning of contingency that appears in his thought: (1) the real of a finitude of the living being, (2) factuality as meaning, (3) the archeological link of meaning and the past.

Biological Reason

Now, what relation can we establish between the Kantian meaning of the epigenetic development of reason presented above and the contemporary approach to brain development? What relation does it establish between epigenesis and epigenetics? If our emphasis on the Kantian definition of life is correct, it must then be confronted with contemporary biological judgment.

Throughout this analysis, I have faced the difficult question of a biologization of the transcendental. In every instance where it has been a matter of exploring it, the two terms appear to be incompatible. On several occasions, we have in fact seen that the neurobiological approach to the origin of the categories of thought immediately confiscated the motif of epigenesis from philosophy and severed from its transcendental meaning. We noted that the transcendental dissolved in some sense into the evolutionary perspective that supports the theory of brain epigenesis – a dual perspective that is simultaneously ontogenetic and phylogenetic. On the one hand, it is a matter for neurobiologists to explain the individual development of the brain by taking into account the influence of non-genetic factors such as experience and learning. On the other hand, it is a matter of inscribing this very process within the wider framework of a revisited theory of evolution that now takes the view that heredity depends not only on genetic factors, but also on epigenetic factors.[10] Yet, as we have already noted, these types of perspectives on adaptation, evolution, and heredity appear to be totally incompatible with any idea of an *a priori* or transcendental structure. If the agreement of the categories with the objects of experience follows an evolutionary line and transforms according to adaptive imperatives, then the existence of *a priori* epigenesis cannot be supported.

And yet, clearly, Kant does not use the term "epigenesis" just by chance in §27. This use cannot but bring up the question of the close relation between reason and living organism that unfolds throughout the critical enterprise. In Kant, the organism is not only an object of thought, it also refers its own image in thought. Life is the "as if" of thought, while thought is the "as if" of life. Beyond paralogisms, beyond any attempt at substantialization, there is no doubt that biology is the most relevant field for supporting the investigation into the *identity* of reason. This is all the more the case given that Kant's developments in regard to the living being are striking for their present-day relevance. We cannot but be impressed by the way in which his philosophy appears to have anticipated the turn to epigenetics in contemporary biology. Despite the intervening centuries, in his description of "the organization where everything is an end and reciprocally a means,"[11] it is entirely possible to see in Kant a prefiguring of the mode of formation of the phenotype by cellular differentiation made possible by epigenetic mechanisms. As Huneman rightly emphasizes, Kant asks the question of how both the whole and the parts can be engendered simultaneously, especially in §66 of the *Critique of the Power of Judgment*. His description announces the "theory of cellular differentiation, which considers the whole organism to ask why, given that all the cells have the same genotype, [it is, for example,] a neuron that is expressed."[12]

What then does reason see in living factuality? I have suggested that it sees itself in it. I would like to take another step in this direction by arguing that what neurobiology makes possible today through its increasingly refined description of brain mechanisms and its use of increasingly effective imaging techniques is the *actual taking into account, by thought, of its own life.* Reason not only sees itself in the mirror of the living being, it also sees its own life: it sees itself living. Now, more than ever, this vision needs the resources of a critique of biological judgment. This is the case not because, in this objective and subjective grasping of thought by itself, the transcendental marks a bar of invisibility (something in thought that must remain hidden away from the discovery of its biological functioning), but rather because the visibility of thought quite simply calls to be not just observed, but, rather, conceptually elaborated. Indeed, the fact that reason sees itself living has effects on reason, thereby provokes thought, calls for critique, and never amounts simply to an observation.

As the heirs of Kant receiving his thought from within the specific state of contemporary philosophy, we can again imagine that he would have been opposed neither to the idea of a neuronal inscription of the activities of thinking and rationality in general, nor to that of an evolutionary process of truth. Here again, he would not necessarily have contested the assimilation of reason to the brain, since, far from being a rigidly programmed organ, the brain is open to the adventure of epigenetics. He would not necessarily have rejected any adaptive view of the transcendental, since he himself accepts a categorial modifiability. The epigenetic development of reason coincides with the modifiable – and modified – form of the transcendental, just as the form of a brain coincides with the modifiable development of its connections.

On the other hand, Kant would not have accepted the unquestioning dogmatism of cognitivism that never interrogates the return effect of the biology of thinking on thought itself. The taking into account of this effect is a task that contemporary philosophy can no longer avoid if it is to escape the new *Kampfplatz* between idealism and skepticism, which, as I have tried to show, is setting up its stage before our very eyes today.

The Thorny Problem of Analogy

But aren't I going too far? After all, epigenesis is presented as an analogy in §27. By transforming it into a paradigm, aren't I wrongfully transgressing the limits of this analogy and, consequently, the limits of reflective judgment? Isn't it a stretch to claim that today reason sees itself living and that Kant can help us think this state of affairs? Lastly, is it legitimate to postulate the existence of an epigenetic mode of transmission and heritage of philosophy – a mode for which I offer an example here with the reception of Kantian thought via the interplay of readings and interpretative dialogues developed throughout my analysis?

The meaning to be attributed to the analogical status of epigenesis in Kant is a point that was deferred in my approach, and one which I must now explain. I deliberately waited until the end to deal with this question, on which the validity of all my work depends. If it turns out that epigenesis is only an image with nothing other than an exoteric, pedagogic, or illustrative role, then my entire elaboration is meaningless.

The value of the analogy of epigenesis in §27 is signaled by the phrase "as it were (*gleichsam*)" in "as it were a system of the epigenesis of pure reason."[13] In this paragraph, "analogy" should be understood in its general sense, not in the technical meaning presented during the examination of the principle in the "Analogies of Experience."[14]

Here the analogy between epigenesis and the production of the categories does not correspond to either mathematical analogy or philosophical analogy. The four terms of which it is composed are present and can be readily related to one another: epigenesis is to the theory of generation what the production of categories is to transcendental philosophy. At the same time, it is not a matter either of mathematical equality, since the proportion remains undetermined. Analogy should therefore be understood here as a simple case of hypotyposis, that is, the sensible presentation of a concept.

In the *Critique of the Power of Judgment*, Kant says that this type of sensible presentation has two possible expressions:

> either *schematic*, where to a concept grasped by the understanding [. . .] the corresponding intuition is given *a priori*; or *symbolic*, where to a concept which only reason can think, and to which no sensible intuition can be adequate, an intuition is attributed with which the power of judgment proceeds in a way merely analogous to that which it observes in schematization.[15]

Epigenesis is not the schema of a category, since it represents the production process of the relation of categories to objects in general, but nor is it the symbol of an idea. It might appear that it is situated somewhere between the two: it can count as an example of the empirical concept of production, but it can also be considered as the schema of the idea of system, a symbolic representation of the whole. In the Architectonic of Pure Reason, Kant writes:

> For its execution the idea needs a *schema*, i.e., an essential manifoldness and order of the parts determined *a priori* from the principle of the end. A schema that is not outlined in accordance with an idea, i.e. from the chief end of reason, but empirically, in accordance with aims occurring contingently [. . .], yields *technical* unity, but that which arises only in consequence of an idea (where reason provides the ends *a priori* and does not await them empirically) grounds *architectonic* unity.[16]

As an example of the production or schema of the idea of system, with a pedagogic or symbolic value, epigenesis finds itself between several registers of the sensible presentation. What it is important to emphasize here is that its status as hypotyposis in no way detracts from its logical effectiveness. Indeed, the last lines of the passage cited above state this clearly: an authentic schema of reason "arises" from the idea. It is not forged technically. In other words, it is author-less, automatically produced by the concept or idea of which it is the image. Hypotyposis is not of the order of subjective creation or invention. It refers to the logical process of the sensible translation of concepts (of the understanding or reason) and is not initially an act of free creation. Thus, it does not depend on the good will of the philosopher. The image springs up "in consequence" of the concept and establishes itself as most apt to illustrate it. It therefore has no rhetorical value. Hence, the epigenesis analogy is *constitutive*, the illustrated expression of the concept that springs up spontaneously from the concept. It is the sensible translation that imposes itself most immediately and most legitimately upon thought as the biological image of categorial production. It would not be relevant to reduce it to its metaphorical meaning, as if it had no objective importance.

Invariance and Reorganization

There is nothing to stop us, therefore, from expanding this motif into a paradigm. A morphological invariance held at the cost of constant redevelopment and micro-reorganizations of the base structure: this is the meaning of the epigenetic paradigm.

Reason shares a dual economy with living organization. As a total-ity that generates order and stability, reason necessarily pre-exists the elements it orders, just as the "germs" or "predispositions" ensure the invariance of the morphogenesis of the species. The "transcendental faculty" of reason is the "faculty of principles,"[17] which proceeds "to comprehend all the actions of the understanding in respect of every object into an *absolute whole*."[18] This "rational concept of the form of a whole"[19] is systematic unity as it first presents itself, *a priori*, as "the outline (*monogramma*)" or the "articulated (*articulatio*)" whole, "a single supreme and inner end" that rules "its affinity and [...] its derivation."[20]

The unfolding of this systematic program also assumes the malleability – the property of transformation, accommodation, and rectification – of the structure, which is ensured by the growth of new parts. This suppleness is the condition of the equilibrium of the system. Ultimately, my argument is that in Kantian philosophy, *the transcendental is that which ensures both the stability and the transformability of the whole.*

The question of the foundational solidity of the transcendental thus appears to be false as soon as we stop looking for its supposed "focus," or hypocenter, and instead consider its specific mobility, namely its value as a *passage* and *conductor* between invariance and modification.

This vector role of the transcendental is illuminated specifically in the *Critique of the Power of Judgment*. As we know, in the last instance, Kant asked what it is that enables the articulation – the contact point – between nature and freedom, without which they would remain separated by "an incalculable gulf."[21] It is important to look for what authorizes "the transition from the manner of thinking in accordance with the principles of the one to that in accordance with the principles of the other."[22] Since it is immediately impossible to observe "the determining grounds of causality in accordance with the concept of freedom"[23] in nature, it is therefore necessary to manage to bring the two "into association"[24] or to "throw a bridge"[25] between them. This is the task of the third *Critique*, which locates the epicenter of their encounter in purposiveness. Indeed, "the power of judgment provides the mediating concept between the concepts of nature and the concepts of freedom, which makes possible the transition from the purely theoretical to the purely practical [reason]."[26] The fact that some appearances only seem to be possible as ends allows us to think about nature "in such a way that the lawfulness of its form is at least in agreement with the possibility of the ends that are to be realized in it in accordance with the laws of freedom."[27] The epigenesis of critical philosophy thus comes to fruition, ultimately, through the development of the concept of purposiveness, through the revelation of the conductor power of the transcendental. It was necessary to stretch the transcendental enough to include in its jurisdiction (the faculty of judgment) that which excludes it (the beautiful and the living being) and to integrate that which does not depend on it in its own economy.[28] As we have seen, this extension or development assumes a differentiation of causality, an increased complexity in the concept of purposiveness, and a modification of necessity – in other words, as announced in §27, *an epigenesis of categories.*

Kant Tomorrow

The perspective of a transcendental in constant negotiation with itself enables Kant's philosophy to rediscover the fluidity that too many polarized readings have petrified. Drawn between two regimes of temporalization (Heidegger), two logical and biological options (preformationism and the evolutionism of cognition), two understandings of the *a priori* (formal and historical), ultimately it could appear only as the exhausted expression of finitude.

It is true that it was time to speak out against the contemporary impoverishment of philosophy, condemned for so long to poetic-messianic waiting, ignoring the most serious scientific revolutions of our time. But, as I have sought to demonstrate, the positivist or reductionist temptation is none other than the flipside of the same failure.

Against this, I have not proposed a revivalist attempt to save the integrity of the transcendental or critical rationality. What I have tried to say is as follows. In the *Critique of Pure Reason*, when discussing the schema of the triangle, Kant asserts that there are realities that "can never exist anywhere except in thought."[29] If we share this view, as I do, then the validity of the transcendental is upheld. Yes, there are realities that exist nowhere but in thought. But we must add immediately that thought is nothing without its reality – both material and objective. By describing epigenesis as a paradigm of rationality, I never forget the scientific meaning and I support the equivalence and interchangeability of its two dimensions, the biological and the philosophical.

Tomorrow, biology will prove that epigenetic modifiability is a more important evolutionary factor than genetics. Tomorrow, the order of precedence between program and its translation will be inverted. As Kant clearly understood, the task initiated by the introduction of the epigenetic motif into the heart of reason is to restore time to the transformation of the *a priori*.

Today, before tomorrow, a non-existential concept of finitude is dawning. The shadow of the living being, the moment of a new thought.

CONCLUSION

This moment might be called "historic," if we stop taking history for the absolute other of nature, and meaning for the result of their difference. The question of a new state of history and meaning in the age of the epigenetic paradigm is fundamental. It announces a deep displacement of the relation between the symbolic and the biological, which is no longer one of mutual irreducibility, but instead is one of exchange.

In his discussion with Changeux, Ricœur says: "I very particularly appreciate the contribution neuroscience makes to our debate when it introduces, beyond the genetic composition of functions, the 'epigenetic' development of the brain, thus making individual histories of development possible." But, he continues, "that doesn't mean that any advance will have been made in understanding the link between this underlying epigenetic development and the individual history of the human subject."[1]

Personally, I disagree. Some advance will have been made. To the point where perhaps we can no longer really understand what, for so long, kept them apart.

186

NOTES

Translator's Foreword: Epigenesis of Her Texts

1 Peter Connor, conversation, "Translation in Transition" conference, Barnard College, May 2015.
2 Lori Chamberlain, "Gender and the Metaphorics of Translation," *Signs: Journal of Women in Culture and Society*, vol. 13, 1988, pp. 454–72; James St André, ed., *Thinking through Translation with Metaphors*, New York: Routledge, 2014.

Epigraphs

1 Georges Canguilhem, Georges Lapassade, Jacques Piquemal, and Jacques Ulmann, *Du Développement à l'évolution au XIXe siècle*, Paris: Presses Universitaires de France, coll. "Pratiques Théoriques," 1962, p. 26. My translation.
2 Immanuel Kant, *Critique of the Power of Judgment*, trans. Paul Guyer and Eric Matthews, Cambridge: Cambridge University Press, 2000, §75, p. 269. Hereafter *CPJ*.

Preface

1 Catherine Malabou, *The Future of Hegel: Plasticity, Temporality and Dialectic*, trans. Lisabeth During, London: Routledge, 2004.

Introduction

1 Martin Heidegger, *On Time and Being*, trans. Joan Stambaugh, New York: Harper and Row, 1972, p. 22. Translation modified.
2 Jean-Pierre Changeux and Paul Ricœur, *What Makes Us Think? A*

Neuroscientist and a Philosopher Argue about Ethics, Human Nature, and the Brain, trans. M. B. DeBevoise, Princeton, NJ: Princeton University Press, 2000, p. 47. My emphasis.

3 Quentin Meillassoux, *After Finitude: An Essay on the Necessity of Contingency*, trans. Ray Brassier, London: Continuum, 2008.

4 Immanuel Kant, *Critique of Pure Reason*, trans. Paul Guyer and Allen W. Wood, Cambridge: Cambridge University Press, 1998, p. 137, B4. Hereafter *CPR*.

5 *After Finitude*, p. 5.

6 *After Finitude*, p. 5.

7 *After Finitude*, p. 27. While "relinquishing of *transcendentalism*" is the published translation of "*abandon du transcendantal*," we have modified this translation by referring to "relinquishing *the transcendental.*"

8 Cf. *After Finitude*, p. 28: "break with the transcendental tradition."

9 On the many different meanings of "transcendental," see Roger Verneaux's article, "La notion kantienne d'analyse transcendantale," *Revue philosophique de Louvain*, Année 52, vol. 50, no. 27, pp. 394–428.

10 *CPR*, p. 137, B3.

11 *CPR*, p. 149, A11–12.

12 *CPR*, p. 196, A56/B81.

13 *After Finitude*, p. 38.

14 Jacques Derrida, *Glas*, trans. John P. Leavy, Jr and Richard Rand, Lincoln/London: University of Nebraska Press, 1986, p. 162.

15 Immanuel Kant, *Kant's Inaugural Dissertation of 1770*, trans. William J. Eckoff, New York: Columbia College, 1894, section II, §8, p. 54, AK (II:345). Translation modified.

16 Immanuel Kant, *On a Discovery According to Which Any New Critique of Pure Reason Has Been Made Superfluous by an Earlier One*, trans. Henry E. Allison, Baltimore; London: Johns Hopkins University Press, 1973, p. 135. This text is also known as the *Response to Eberhard*, AK (VIII:221–3).

17 Kant, *On a Discovery*, p. 135. AK (VIII:221–3). Translation modified.

18 *CPJ* §75, p. 268.

19 J.G. Schlosser, *Plato's Briefe nebst einer historischen Einleitung und Anmerkungen*, Königsberg, 1795, p. 182.

20 Immanuel Kant, *On a Recently Prominent Tone of Superiority in Philosophy*, in *Theoretical Philosophy after 1781*, eds Henry Allison and Peter Heath, trans. Gary Hatfield et al., Cambridge: Cambridge University Press, 2004, p. 444, AK (VIII:404). On these comments by Schlosser and Kant's response, see Roger Verneaux, *Le Vocabulaire de Kant*, Paris: Aubier-Montaigne, 1967, p. 103.

21 On Kantian philosophy as the foundation of the identity of continental philosophy, see Tom Rockmore, *In Kant's Wake: Philosophy in the Twentieth Century*, Malden, MA/Oxford: Blackwell, 2006 and Lee Braver, *A Thing of This World: A History of Continental Anti-Realism*, Evanston, IL: Northwestern University Press, 2007.

22 Martin Heidegger, *Kant and the Problem of Metaphysics*, trans. Richard Taft, Bloomington: Indiana University Press, 1997.

23 Heidegger, *Kant and the Problem of Metaphysics*, p. 99.

24 *Kant and the Problem of Metaphysics*, p. 99.

25 Cf. *Kant and the Problem of Metaphysics*, pp. 58 and 90.

26 *Kant and the Problem of Metaphysics*, p. 99.
27 *Kant and the Problem of Metaphysics*, p. 97.
28 *Kant and the Problem of Metaphysics*, p. 95.
29 *Kant and the Problem of Metaphysics*, p. 46.
30 *Kant and the Problem of Metaphysics*, p. 116.
31 *Kant and the Problem of Metaphysics*, p. 137.
32 *Kant and the Problem of Metaphysics*, p. 114.
33 *Kant and the Problem of Metaphysics*, p. 113.
34 Jean-Pierre Changeux, *Du vrai, du beau, du bien: Une nouvelle approche neuronale*, Paris: Odile Jacob, 2008. While an English version exists, translated and revised by Laurence Garey, *The Good, the True and the Beautiful: A Neuronal Approach*, New Haven, CT: Yale University Press, 2012, my translation here and below is directly from the French since the English version is a reworking of the French text.
35 Changeux, *Du Vrai, du beau, du bien*, pp. 422–3. René Descartes, *Philosophical Essays: Discourse on Method; Meditations; Rules for the Direction of the Mind*, trans. Laurence J. Lafleur, Indianapolis/New York/ Kansas City: Bobbs-Merrill Company Inc., 1964, p. 119.
36 *Du Vrai, du beau, du bien*, p. 423.
37 *Du Vrai, du beau, du bien*, p. 7.
38 *Du Vrai, du beau, du bien*, p. 7.
39 *Du Vrai, du beau, du bien*, p. 77.
40 *Du Vrai, du beau, du bien*, p. 472.
41 Meillassoux, *After Finitude*, p. 39.
42 *After Finitude*, p. 40.
43 Cf. "break with the transcendental tradition," *After Finitude*, p. 28.
44 *After Finitude*, p. 26.
45 *After Finitude*, p. 62.
46 *After Finitude*, p. 29.
47 Cf. Immanuel Kant, *The Metaphysics of Morals*, trans. Mary Gregor, Cambridge: Cambridge University Press, 1996, AK (IV:452).
48 *CPR*, p. 533, A533/B561.
49 *CPR*, p. 533, A533/B561.
50 *After Finitude*, p. 26.
51 *CPR*, p. 205, B93.
52 *CPR*, p. 265, B167.
53 *CPR*, p. 265, B167. Translation modified.
54 *CPR*, p. 265, B167.
55 Aristotle, *Generation of Animals*, trans. A.L. Peck, London: Heinemann, 1943.
56 Aristotle, *Generation of Animals*, Book II, chap. 6, 743 *b*, p. 225.
57 William Harvey, *Observations on the Generation of Animals* (*Exercitationes de generatione animalium*), London, 1651, Ex. 46. Republished: Ann Arbor, MI: Edwards, 1943, p. 366. Quoted by John Zammito in "Kant's Persistent Ambivalence toward Epigenesis, 1764–1790," in Philippe Huneman, ed., *Understanding Purpose: Collected Essays on Kant and Philosophy of Biology* (*North American Kant Society Studies in Philosophy*, Vol. VIII), Rochester, NY: University of Rochester Press, 2007, pp. 51–74, p. 54.
58 Buffon develops the theory of the "inner mold," which is a reformulation of Harvey's "formative faculty": *Œuvres complètes, Histoire des animaux*,

Paris: F.-D. Pillot, 1830, Vol. 11, "Expériences au sujet de la génération," pp. 7–8. See Maupertuis' book: *Essai sur la formation des corps organisés*, Paris/Berlin, 1754.

Chapter 1 Paragraph 27 of the *Critique of Pure Reason*

1 *CPR*, Architectonic of Pure Reason, p. 691, A833/B861.
2 *CPR*, Architectonic of Pure Reason, p. 691, A833/B861.
3 Immanuel Kant, *Metaphysical Foundations of Natural Science*, trans. Michael Friedman, in *Theoretical Philosophy after 1781*, pp. 171–270, p. 188.
4 Kant, *Metaphysical Foundations of Natural Science*, p. 190.
5 *CPR*, §27, pp. 264–5, B167.
6 *CPR*, §27, p. 264, B167.
7 *CPR*, §27, p. 264, B167.
8 *CPR*, §27, p. 265, B167.
9 Not Leibniz, as might have been expected. On this point, see Günter Zöller, "Kant on the Generation of Metaphysical Knowledge," in Hariolf Oberer and Gerhard Seel, eds, *Kant, Analysen – Probleme – Kritik*, Würzburg: Königshausen and Neumann, 1988, pp. 71–90, p. 76.
10 *Prolegomena to Any Future Metaphysics That Will Be Able to Come Forward as a Science*, trans. Gary Hatfield, in *Theoretical Philosophy after 1781*, pp. 29–169, AK (4:320).
11 *Prolegomena to Any Future Metaphysics*, pp. 111–12.
12 *Prolegomena to Any Future Metaphysics*, p. 112. Christian August Crusius (January 10, 1715–October 18,1775), professor of philosophy and theology at Leipzig, author of *Advice for a Rational Life* (1744), *Sketch of the Necessary Truths of Reason* (1745), and *The Way to the Certainty and Dependability of Human Knowledge* (1747). Crusius played a key role in forming Kant's system. He was the first to put forward the idea that physical necessity is different to logical necessity. As Cassirer commented: "Crusius [. . .] lays the utmost emphasis on the fact that the principle of contradiction, as a purely formal principle, can of itself alone yield no specific and concrete knowledge, but that a set of original and underivable, but nevertheless certain, 'material principles' is unconditionally necessary for that." Ernst Cassirer, *Kant's Life and Thought*, trans. James Haden, New Haven, CT: Yale University Press, 1981, p. 74.
13 *Metaphysical Foundations of Natural Science*, p. 190.
14 *Metaphysical Foundations of Natural Science*, p. 190.
15 David Hume, *An Enquiry Concerning Human Understanding*, reprinted from the posthumous edition of 1777, third edition, L.A. Selby-Bigge, ed., Oxford: Clarendon Press, section IV "Sceptical Doubts Concerning the Operations of the Understanding," section V "Sceptical Solution of These Doubts."
16 Hume, *An Enquiry Concerning Human Understanding*, section V, part II, pp. 54–5.
17 *Metaphysical Foundations of Natural Science*, p. 190.
18 *Metaphysical Foundations of Natural Science*, p. 190.
19 *CPR*, p. 265, B168.

NOTES TO PP. 25–8

20 Cf. Hans Werner Ingensiep, "Die biologischen Analogien und die erkenntnistheoretischen Alternativen in Kants Kritik der reinen Vernunft B§27," *Kant-Studien* 85, vol. 85, no. 4, 1994, pp. 381–3, p. 383.

21 François Duchesneau, "Épigenèse de la raison pure et analogies biologiques," in François Duchesneau, Guy Lafrance, and Claude Piché, *Kant actuel: Hommage à Pierre Laberge*, Paris: Bellarmin-Vrin, 2000, pp. 233–56, p. 234. My translation of this article is used throughout.

22 Caspar Friedrich Wolff, *Theoria generationis* [1764], Hildesheim: Georg Olms Verlag, 1966. Johann Friedrich Blumenbach: "Über den Bildungstrieb (Nisus formativus) und seinen Einfluß auf die Generation und Reproduction," in Georg Christoph Lichtenberg and Georg Forster, eds, *Göttingisches Magazin der Wissenschaften und Litteratur*, vol. 1, no. 5, 1780, pp. 247–66. The essay then appeared in a monograph (*Über den Bildungstrieb und das Zeugnungsgeschäfte*, Göttingen: Dietrich, 1781). The revisions were incorporated in the second and subsequent editions of the *Handbuch der Naturgeschichte* (first edition: Göttingen: Dietrich, 1779, *Manual of the Elements of Natural History* [1781], trans. R.T. Gore, London: W. Simpkin and R. Marshall, 1825).

The term *Bildungstrieb* is usually translated as "formative force" or "formative impulse" (as in the Cambridge edition of the *Critique of the Power of Judgment*). We choose to translate it here as "formative drive," following (among others) Peter McLaughlin, "The Impact of Newton on Biology on the Continent in the Eighteenth Century," in Scott Mandelbrote and Helmut Pulte, eds, *The Reception of Isaac Newton in Europe*, London: Bloomsbury Academic, 2014, pp. 1–23; Helmut Müller-Sievers, *Self-Generation: Biology, Philosophy, and Literature Around 1800*, Stanford, CA: Stanford University Press, 1997, p. 43; and Iain Hamilton Grant, *Philosophies of Nature after Schelling*, London: Continuum, 2006, p. 98.

23 *CPR*, §27, p. 265, B167S.

Chapter 2 Caught between Skeptical Readings

1 *CPR*, p. 203, A66/B91. Translation modified. I have translated "*Keime und Anlagen*" as "germs and predispositions" throughout. This translation follows Phillip R. Sloan, who stresses "the importance of [. . .] the terms *Keim*, commonly rendered in English translations as 'seed,' but which I consider best rendered within its historical context by the term 'germ,' and *Anlage*, usually translated as 'disposition,' 'predisposition,' 'aptitude,' or 'capacity.' I have settled on the term 'predisposition' as the best contextualized rendition." "Performing the Categories, Eighteenth-Century Generation Theory and the Biological Roots of Kant's *A Priori*," *Journal of the History of Philosophy*, vol. 40, no. 2, April 2002, pp. 229–53, p. 232. See also Edgar Landgraf, "The German word '*Anlagen*' implies talent, aptitude, and, more generally, predispositions, while retaining the meaning of something of concrete design (and in this regard indeed comes close to the modern idea of the gene). '*Keime*' means germs, seeds, or buds." "The Education of Humankind: Perfectibility and Discipline in Kant's Lectures *Über Pädagogik*," *Goethe Yearbook* 14, pp. 39–60, p. 44.

2 As we shall see later in Zöller, "Kant on the Generation of Metaphysical

Knowledge," p. 72. Cf. also A.C. Genova, "Kant's Epigenesis of Pure Reason," *Kant-Studien*, vol. 65, no. 3, 1974, pp. 259–73. According to Genova, most of the misunderstandings about transcendental idealism derive from a lack of attention to "a very much ignored passage" in which Kant expresses "a clue to the correct understanding." "I have reasons to believe," Genova concludes, that "the principle of epigenesis serves as a key to the interpretation of each of Kant's *Critiques* as well as their interrelation," p. 259.
3 *CPJ*, p. 292.
4 *CPJ*, p. 246.
5 Duchesneau, "Épigenèse de la raison pure et analogies biologiques," p. 254.
6 Canguilhem et al., *Du Développement à l'évolution au XIXe siècle*, p. 6. All translations from this work cited here are mine.
7 *Du Développement à l'évolution au XIXe siècle*, p. 15.
8 *Du Développement à l'évolution au XIXe siècle*, p. 44.
9 *Du Développement à l'évolution*, p. 8.
10 *Du Développement à l'évolution*, p. 8.
11 *Du Développement à l'évolution*, p. 20.
12 Alain Boyer, *Hors du temps : Un essai sur Kant*, Paris : Vrin, 2001, p. 63. My translation.
13 Cf. Christian Godin, "La figure et le moment du scepticisme chez Hegel," *Les Études philosophiques*, vol. 3, no. 70, 2004, pp. 341–56, p. 342. My translation.
14 Gérard Lebrun, *Kant et la fin de la métaphysique*, Paris: Armand Colin, 1970. All translations from this work are mine.
15 "What Is Enlightenment?," in Paul Rabinow, ed., *The Foucault Reader*, amended trans. Catherine Porter, New York: Pantheon Books, 1984, pp. 32–50.
16 Jacques Bouveresse, "Le problème de l'*a priori* et la conception évolutionniste des lois de la pensée," *Revue de théologie et de philosophie*, vol. 123, 1991, pp. 353–68. My translation here and below.

Chapter 3 The Difference between Genesis and Epigenesis

1 Seismic waves follow the shortest route to reach the surface of the earth. In this way they lose less energy because they travel through fewer rocks. Since they have more energy at the epicenter, the destruction caused at this point is greater than elsewhere.
2 *CPR*, p. 398, A319/B376.
3 *CPR*, p. 203, A66/B91.
4 Immanuel Kant, *Critique of Practical Reason*, trans. Werner S. Pluhar, Indianapolis/Cambridge, MA: Hackett Publishing Company, 2002, Analytic, chapter 1, p. 67, AK (V:48).

Chapter 4 Kant's "Minimal Preformationism"

1 "Kant on the Generation of Metaphysical Knowledge," p. 89.
2 "Kant on the Generation of Metaphysical Knowledge," p. 87.
3 "Kant on the Generation of Metaphysical Knowledge," p. 85.
4 "Kant on the Generation of Metaphysical Knowledge," p. 84.

5 Note 4275, AK (XVII: 492): "Crusius erklärt die reale Grundsätze der Vernunft [vor] nach dem *systemate praeformationis* (aus subjectiven *principiis*), Locke nach dem *influxu physico* wie Aristoteles, Plato und Malebranche aus dem *intuitu intellectuali*, wir nach der epigenesis aus dem Gebrauch der natürlichen Gesetzte der Vernunft." *Notes and Fragments*, ed. Paul Guyer, trans. Curtis Bowman, Paul Guyer, and Frederick Rauscher, Cambridge: Cambridge University Press, 2005, p. 124. Translation modified.

6 Cf. also Note 4865, in which Kant writes: "The important fundamental truths of morality and religion are grounded on the natural use of reason [. . .]." *Notes and Fragments*, p. 197, thereby inducing the idea of an epigenesis of these truths themselves.

7 "Kant on the Generation of Metaphysical Knowledge," p. 87.

8 "Kant on the Generation of Metaphysical Knowledge," p. 87.

9 *CPR*, pp. 220–1, A86/B119.

10 Judy Wubnig, "The Epigenesis of Pure Reason: A Note on *the Critique of Pure Reason*, B sec. 27, 165–167," *Kant-Studien*, vol. 60, no. 2, 1969, pp. 147–52.

11 Wubnig, "The Epigenesis of Pure Reason," p. 151.

12 "The Epigenesis of Pure Reason," p. 151.

13 "The Epigenesis of Pure Reason," p. 151.

14 "The Epigenesis of Pure Reason," p. 151.

15 "The Epigenesis of Pure Reason," p. 151.

16 "Kant on the Generation of Metaphysical Knowledge, p. 84.

17 Cf. Genova, "Kant's Epigenesis of Pure Reason," p. 264.

18 Cf. "Kant's Epigenesis of Pure Reason," pp. 269–70 in particular.

19 "Kant's Epigenesis of Pure Reason," p. 270.

20 "Kant's Epigenesis of Pure Reason," p. 269.

21 "Kant's Epigenesis of Pure Reason," pp. 270–1.

22 "Kant on the Generation of Metaphysical Knowledge," p. 85.

23 Herman Jan de Vleeschauwer, *La Déduction transcendantale dans l'œuvre de Kant*, 3 vols, Antwerp/Paris/The Hague: De Sikkel/Ernest Leroux/ Martinus Nijhoff, 1934–7.

24 See p. 5 above.

25 Immanuel Kant, *The Metaphysics of Morals, The Doctrine of Right*, §10, "How to Acquire Something External," pp. 47–8.

26 *The Metaphysics of Morals*, p. 47.

27 *The Metaphysics of Morals*, p. 47.

28 Zöller says that de Vleeschauwer falsely attributes this term to Kant. See "Kant on the Generation of Metaphysical Knowledge," note 51, p. 86.

29 *La Déduction transcendantale dans l'œuvre de Kant*, Vol. III, p. 270. Cf. Zöller, "Kant on the Generation of Metaphysical Knowledge," note 50, p. 86.

30 "Kant on the Generation of Metaphysical Knowledge," p. 87.

31 "Kant on the Generation of Metaphysical Knowledge," p. 73.

32 "Kant on the Generation of Metaphysical Knowledge," p. 73.

33 "Kant on the Generation of Metaphysical Knowledge," p. 73.

34 *CPR*, §26, p. 261, B159.

35 "Kant on the Generation of Metaphysical Knowledge," p. 90.

36 "Kant on the Generation of Metaphysical Knowledge," p. 88. The Metaphysical Deduction covers all of the Analytic, not just the Analytic of Concepts. Cf. "Kant on the Generation of Metaphysical Knowledge," p. 89.

37 *CPR*, p. 254, B145.
38 *CPR*, p. 256, B150.
39 "Kant on the Generation of Metaphysical Knowledge," p. 89.
40 "Kant on the Generation of Metaphysical Knowledge," p. 89.
41 "Kant on the Generation of Metaphysical Knowledge," p. 90.

Chapter 5 Germs, Races, Seeds

1 It is nevertheless worth mentioning that Kant refers to Blumenbach in a note in his response to Forster in *On the Use of Teleological Principles in Philosophy*, published in 1788 and written in the fall of 1787, in *Anthropology, History, and Education*, eds Robert B. Louden and Günter Zöller, trans. Mary Gregor et al., Cambridge: Cambridge University Press, 2007, pp. 192–218, p. 214. The note refers to Blumenbach's 1779 *Handbuch der Naturgeschichte* (*Handbook of Natural History*), of which Kant had a copy.
2 Immanuel Kant, *Gesammelte Schriften*, Berlin: Königlich Preussischen Akademie der Wissenschaften, 1902–97, Vol. XVII, p. 416 (Note 4104); p. 92 (Note 4275); p. 554 (Note 4446); Vol. XVIII, p. 8 (Note 4851); p. 12 (Note 4859); Vol. XXVIII, p. 684, p. 760. See *Notes and Fragments*.
3 Immanuel Kant, *The Only Possible Argument in Support of a Demonstration of the Existence of God*, in *Theoretical Philosophy 1755–1770*, ed. and trans. David Walford, Cambridge: Cambridge University Press, 1992, pp. 107–201, AK (II:68).
4 Immanuel Kant, *Review of J.G. Herder's Ideas for the Philosophy of the History of Humanity*, in *Anthropology, History, and Education*, pp. 121–42. Johann Godfried Herder, *Ideen zur Philosophie der Geschichte der Menschheit*, in *Herders Sämtliche Werke*, ed. V.B. Suphan, Vol. 13, Berlin: Weidmann, 1887, republished Berlin/Weimar: Aufbau-Verlag, Vol. I, 1965.
5 Zöller translates *Anlagen* as "dispositions."
6 *CPJ*, §81, p. 291.
7 "Kant on the Generation of Metaphysical Knowledge," p. 77.
8 Since Blumenbach was against the idea of "germs," Kant removed all references to them in *CPJ*.
9 On this topic, see Robert J. Richards *The Romantic Concept of Life: Science and Philosophy in the Age of Goethe*, Chicago: University of Chicago Press, 2002, p. 225.
10 Blumenbach, *Manual of the Elements of Natural History*, p. 10. Here I use the retranslation of this passage by Grant, *Philosophies of Nature after Schelling*, p. 98. The conclusion of the passage is slightly different in the second edition (Göttingen: Dietrich, 1789). An English translation of this second edition (which was the one which Kant owned) is available as J. Blumenbach, *An Essay on Generation*, trans. Alexander Crichton, London: Cadell, 1792. On general relations between Kant and Blumenbach, see Sloan, "Performing the Categories," and Timothy Lenoir, "Kant, Blumenbach, and Vital Materialism in German Biology," *Isis*, vol. 71, no. 256, 1980, pp. 77–108.
11 "Review of J.G. Herder's Ideas," p. 127. Kant cites Herder here: "Just as the plant itself is organic life, so the polyp is also organic life. There are therefore

many organic forces, those of vegetation, of the muscular stimuli of sensation [. . .]. The *animal soul* is the sum of all the effective forces in one organization," p. 127.

12 Johann Godfried Herder, *Ideen zur Philosophie der Geschichte der Menschheit*, p. 50, cited by Zöller, "Kant on the Generation of Metaphysical Knowledge," p. 81.

13 "Review of J.G. Herder's Ideas," p. 139.

14 "Review of J.G. Herder's Ideas," p. 140. Note that "self-forming faculty" has also been translated as "self-structuring capacity." Cf. Sloan "Performing the Categories," p. 244.

15 "Review of J.G. Herder's Ideas," p. 139.

16 "Review of J.G. Herder's Ideas," p. 139.

17 Zammito, 'Kant's Persistent Ambivalence toward Epigenesis," p. 58.

18 'Kant's Persistent Ambivalence toward Epigenesis," p. 59.

19 "Review of J.G. Herder's Ideas," pp. 132–3.

20 Zammito, "Kant's Persistent Ambivalence toward Epigenesis," pp. 59–60.

21 Immanuel Kant, *Of the Different Races of Human Beings*, in *Anthropology, History, and Education*, pp. 82–97, pp. 85, 89. On this point, see Raphaël Lagier, *Les Races humaines selon Kant*, Paris: Presses Universitaires de France, 2004.

22 *Of the Different Races of Human Beings*, p. 90.

23 Immanuel Kant, *Determination of the Concept of a Human Race*, in *Anthropology, History, and Education*, pp. 145–59, p. 152.

24 Kant, *On the Use of Teleological Principles in Philosophy*, p. 201.

25 *On the Use of Teleological Principles in Philosophy*, p. 214.

26 Zöller, "Kant on the Generation of Metaphysical Knowledge," p. 82.

27 Cf. "Kant on the Generation of Metaphysical Knowledge," pp. 83–4.

28 See p. 42 above.

29 Note 4851, *Notes and Fragments*, p. 194, AK (XIII:8).

30 Note 4859, AK (XIII:12), not included in *Notes and Fragments*. My translation. See Alexander Baumgarten, *Metaphysics: A Critical Translation with Kant's Elucidations, Selected Notes, and Related Materials*, ed. and trans. Courtney D. Fugate and John Hymers, New York: Bloomsbury Academic, 2013, p. 45.

31 *CPJ*, p. 291.

32 *CPJ*, p. 292.

33 *CPJ*, p. 292.

34 *CPJ*, p. 292.

35 *CPJ*, p. 292.

36 Cf. "Kant on the Generation of Metaphysical Knowledge," p. 89.

37 Zammito, "Kant's Persistent Ambivalence toward Epigenesis," p. 57. Zammito is referring to the passage from the Analytic mentioned above: "We will therefore pursue the pure concepts into their first germs and predispositions in the human understanding, where they lie ready [. . .]," *CPR*, p. 203, A66/B91.

38 "Kant's Persistent Ambivalence toward Epigenesis," p. 65.

39 "Kant's Persistent Ambivalence toward Epigenesis," p. 51.

40 *CPR*, p. 265, B167.

41 *CPR*, p. 265, B168.

Chapter 6 The "Neo-Skeptical" Thesis and Its Evolution

1 Genova, "Kant's Epigenesis of Pure Reason," p. 263.
2 Bouveresse, "Le problème de l'*a priori*."
3 "Le problème de l'*a priori*," p. 354. In this quotation, Bouveresse cites Ross Harrison, "Transcendental Arguments and Idealism," in Godfrey Vesey, ed., *Idealism Past and Present*, Cambridge: Cambridge University Press, 1982, pp. 211–24, p. 211.
4 Bouveresse, "Le problème de l'*a priori*," pp. 354–5.
5 "Le problème de l'*a priori*" p. 354.
6 *CPR*, p. 242, A126.
7 *CPR*, p. 242, A127.
8 Bouveresse, "Le problème de l'*a priori*," p. 357.
9 Charles Sanders Peirce, *Principles of Philosophy*, in *Collected Papers of Charles Sanders Peirce*, eds Charles Hawthorne and Paul Weiss, Cambridge, MA: The Belknap Press of Harvard University Press, 1965, Vol. I, section 12, "Il Lume Naturale," §81, p. 33. Cited by Bouveresse in "Le problème de l'*a priori*," p. 357.
10 Peirce, "Principles of Philosophy," §81, p. 33.
11 Bouveresse, "Le problème de l'*a priori*," p. 357.
12 Quotes cited in notes 12–15 are taken from the fuller version of Bouveresse's text in *Essais V – Descartes, Leibniz, Kant*, Marseille: Agone, 2006, pp. 113–28. Bouveresse, "Le problème de l'*a priori*," in *Essais V*, p. 117. My translation.
13 Bouveresse, "Le problème de l'*a priori*," in *Essais V*, p. 116.
14 "Le problème de l'*a priori*," in *Essais V*, p. 116.
15 "Le problème de l'*a priori*," in *Essais V*, p. 116.
16 Ludwig Boltzmann, *Principien der Naturfilosofi. Lectures on Natural Philosophy 1903–1917*, ed. Ilse M. Fasol-Boltzmann, Berlin/Heidelberg: Springer, 1990, p. 160. My translation. Cited by Bouveresse, "Le problème de l'*a priori*," p. 364 (here and henceforth from *Revue de théologie et de philosophie*).
17 Boltzmann, *Principien der Naturfilosofi*, p. 160
18 Bouveresse, "Le problème de l'*a priori*," p. 365.
19 In one of his notebooks, Robert Musil writes, in a manner very similar to Boltzmann: "The laws of nature: the cause of natural events; this can but mean that they systematically render them comprehensible in the causal form. They do not condition that which happens; rather they are merely an abstraction drawn from them. The causal conception says only that we are internally constrained by a change to presuppose a cause. From the phylogenetic point of view, this constraint may derive from experience; from the ontogenetic point of view, it is a category." Robert Musil, *Tagebücher*, ed. Adolf Frisé, Rowohlt: Reinbek bei Hamburg, 1976, Vol. 1, p. 119. Cited by Bouveresse in, "Le problème de l'*a priori*," p. 364. English translation from Bouveresse's loose translation to French from the German.
20 Genova, "Kant's Epigenesis of Pure Reason," p. 267.
21 Boltzmann, *Principien der Naturfilosofi*, p. 222. Cited by Bouveresse in "Le problème de l'*a priori*," p. 364.
22 "Le problème de l'*a priori*," p. 357.

23 Gottlob Frege, *Posthumous Writings*, trans. Peter Long and Roger M. White, Chicago: University of Chicago Press, 1979, p. 4.

24 Gottlob Frege, *The Foundations of Arithmetic: A Logico-Mathematical Inquiry into the Concept of Number*, trans. J.L. Austin, second revised edition, Evanston, IL: Northwestern University Press, 1980, p. vi.

25 Frege, *The Foundations of Arithmetic*, p. vi.

26 *The Foundations of Arithmetic*, p. vi.

27 *The Foundations of Arithmetic*, p. 6.

28 Cited by Bouveresse in "Le problème de l'*a priori*," p. 361. Frege, *17 Key Sentences on Logic*, in *Posthumous Writings*, p. 174.

29 Bouveresse, "Le problème de l'*a priori*," p. 366. On this point, it is impossible not to refer to the polemic between Frege and Husserl on the topic of transcendental idealism. Bouveresse reminds us that for Husserl, only an exploration of transcendental interiority could allow for situating the *source* of truth. In *Formal and Transcendental Logic*, Husserl actually states: "Only by virtue of a fundamental clarification, penetrating the depths of the inwardness that produces cognition and theory, the *transcendental* inwardness, does what is produced as genuine theory and genuine science become understandable. Only by virtue of such a clarification, moreover, does the true sense of that being become understandable, which science has labored to bring out in its theories as true being, as true Nature, as the true cultural world." Edmund Husserl, *Formal and Transcendental Logic*, trans. Dorion Cairns, The Hague: Martinus Nijhoff, 1969, pp. 15–16. Cited by Bouveresse, in "Le problème de l'*a priori*," p. 366. For a full and detailed study of the problem, see Jacques Derrida's major study in his work *The Problem of Genesis in Husserl's Philosophy*, trans. Marian Hobson, Chicago: University of Chicago Press, 2003, "The Polemic with Frege," pp. 23–4.

30 Bouveresse, "Le problème de l'*a priori*," p. 366.

31 "Le problème de l'*a priori*," p. 368. In arguing for this position, Bouveresse counters Hans D. Sluga's interpretation developed in his work *Gottlob Frege*, London: Routledge & Kegan Paul, 1980. He explains this position on p. 368.

32 "Le problème de l'*a priori*," p. 354.

33 *CPR*, p. 263, B164.

Chapter 7   From Epigenesis to Epigenetics

1 Conrad Hal Waddington, "The Basic Ideas of Biology," in *Towards a Theoretical Biology*, Vol. 1, *Prolegomena*, Edinburgh: Edinburgh University Press, 1968, pp. 1–32, pp. 9–10.

2 Thomas Morgan, "The Relation of Genetics to Physiology and Medicine," Nobel lecture, 1935, p. 323 (http://www.nobelprize.org/nobel_prizes/medi cine/laureates/1933/morgan-lecture.pdf).

3 One of the ways that gene expression is regulated is through the state of the chromatin. Chromatin is either uncondensed or "open" (euchromatin), thereby allowing access to transcription and gene expression activity; or it is condensed or "closed" (heterochromatin), which prevents gene expression. The state of chromatin is dictated by post-translational modifications of the histone proteins linked to DNA.

NOTES TO PP. 80–3

This modification involves the addition of a methyl group (-CH3) in place of a hydrogen atom. Although the four types of base can be methylated, cytosine is most frequently affected by the process.

5 Thomas Pradeu, "Qu'est-ce qu'un individu biologique?," in Pascal Ludwig and Thomas Pradeu, eds, *L'Individu: perspectives contemporaines*, Paris: Vrin, 2008, pp. 97–125, p. 120. Cf. also Henri Atlan, *La Fin du tout génétique? Vers de nouveaux paradigmes en biologie*, Paris: INRA Editions, 1999, p. 58: "We are witnessing a return of extreme preformationism, in the form of a new avatar, in which everything is contained in the genes." All translations of Atlan's work are mine.

6 Changeux, *The Good, the True and the Beautiful*, p. 372.

7 *Nature, International Weekly Journal of Science*, February 2001, online edition.

8 Cf. *Le Monde*, February 13, 2001, "Le génome humain cache de 'vastes déserts'," online edition.

9 Henri Atlan, *La Fin du "tout génétique"?*, p. 16.

10 Henri Atlan, "Programme de Recherche Inter-Centres Biologie et société," 2009, website.

11 *La Fin du "tout génétique"? Vers de nouveaux paradigmes en biologie*, p. 16. See also *La Recherche*, no. 463, April 2012, "Épigénétique: L'hérédité au-delà des gènes," pp. 38–54.

12 "Post-genomic" biology assumes an interdisciplinary approach that expands the field of molecular biology in order to study element systems (DNA, proteins, supramolecular structures, small molecules) interacting with each other.

13 François Jacob, *The Logic of Life: A History of Heredity*, trans. Betty E. Spillmann, New York: Pantheon, 1982, pp. 9–10.

14 Research on certain types of cress has, for example, demonstrated that being exposed to cold during the winter led to structural changes in the chromatin, which silenced the flowering genes. These genes are reactivated in the spring when the longer and warmer days become suitable for reproduction. The environment may also provoke changes that have effects on future generations.

15 With supplements rich in methyl such as folic acid and vitamin B12.

16 Cf. Mae-Wan Ho, *Living with the Fluid Genome*, London/Penang: Institute of Science in Society/Third World Network, 2003, and "Epigenetic Inheritance: 'What Genes Remember,'" *Science in Society*, vol. 41, 2009, pp. 4–5.

17 Thomas Pradeu, "Philosophie de la biologie," in Anouk Barberousse, Denis Bonnay, and Mikaël Cozic, eds, *Précis de philosophie des sciences*, Paris: Vuibert, 2011, pp. 378–403, p. 398. My translation here and below.

18 For instance, in their fundamental text, Eva Jablonka and Marion J. Lamb write: "The idea that DNA alone is responsible for all the hereditary differences between individuals is now so firmly fixed in people's minds that it is difficult to get rid of it. When it is suggested that information transmitted through non-genetic inheritance systems is of real importance for understanding heredity and evolution, two problems arise." *Evolution in Four Dimensions: Genetic, Epigenetic, Behavioral, and Symbolic Variation in the History of Life*, Cambridge, MA: MIT Press, 2005, p. 109.

19 Mary-Jane West-Eberhard, *Developmental Plasticity and Evolution*, New York: Oxford University Press, 2003, p. 34.

20 Jean-Pierre Changeux, Philippe Courrège, and Antoine Danchin, "A Theory

of Epigenesis of Neuronal Networks by Selective Stabilization of Synapses," *Proceedings of the National Academy of Sciences, USA*, vol. 70, no. 10, Oct. 1973, pp. 2974–8 and *Neuronal Man: The Biology of the Mind*, trans. Laurence Garey, New York: Pantheon, 1985.

21 Jean-Pierre Changeux and Antoine Danchin, "Selective Stabilization of Developing Synapses as a Mechanism for the Specification of Neural Networks," *Nature*, December 23–30, 1976, vol. 264, no. 5588, pp. 705–12.

22 Pradeu, "Philosophie de la biologie," p. 400. 23 Again, on this point, see Jablonka and Lamb, *Evolution in Four Dimensions*.

24 Changeux continues: "It is no longer possible then to identify one gene with one function." *The Good, the True and the Beautiful*, p. 372.

25 Jeffrey M. Schwarz and Sharon Begley, *The Mind and the Brain: Neuroplasticity and the Power of Mental Force*, New York: HarperCollins, 2002, p. 365. The authors write: "Although it would be perfectly reasonable to posit that genes determine the brain's connections, just as a wiring diagram determines the connections on a silicon computer chip, that is a mathematical impossibility. As the Human Genome Project drew to a close in the early years of the new millennium, it became clear that humans have something like 35,000 different genes. About half of them seem to be active in the brain, where they are responsible for such tasks as synthesizing a neurotransmitter or a receptor. The brain, remember, has billions of nerve cells that make, altogether, trillions of connections. If each gene carried an instruction for a particular connection, we'd run out of instructions long before our brain reached the sophistication of a banana slug's. Call it the genetic shortfall: too many synapses, too few genes. Our DNA is simply too paltry to spell out the wiring diagram for the human brain" (pp. 111–12).

26 Jean-Pierre Changeux and Alain Connes, *Conversations on Mind, Matter, and Mathematics*, trans. M. B. DeBevoise, Princeton, NJ: Princeton University Press, 1995, p. 104.

27 Changeux and Connes, *Conversations on Mind, Matter, and Mathematics*, p. 108.

28 *Conversations on Mind, Matter, and Mathematics*, p. 128.

29 *Conversations on Mind, Matter, and Mathematics*, p. 14.

30 *Conversations on Mind, Matter, and Mathematics*, p. 59. The biologization of the transcendental leads to "mental Darwinism," cf. p. 80.

31 *Conversations on Mind, Matter, and Mathematics*, p. 128.

32 *Conversations on Mind, Matter, and Mathematics*, p. 35.

33 *Conversations on Mind, Matter, and Mathematics*, p. 40.

34 See, for instance, Gerald M. Edelman, *Bright Air, Brilliant Fire: On the Matter of the Mind*, New York: Basic Books, p. 119.

35 *Bright Air, Brilliant Fire*, p. 64.

36 See the example of the immune system.

37 *Bright Air, Brilliant Fire*, p. 119.

38 *Bright Air, Brilliant Fire*, p. 120.

39 *Bright Air, Brilliant Fire*, p. 161.

40 See http://www.epigenome.eu/en/1.1.0. See also C. David Allis, Marie-Laure Caparros, Thomas Jenuwein, and Danny Reinberg, eds, *Epigenetics*, second edition, New York: Cold Spring Harbor Press, 2015.

41 "The transmission of information through the genetic system is analogous to the transmission of music through a written score, whereas transmitting

information through non-genetic systems, which transmit phenotypes, is analogous to recording and broadcasting, through which particular inter-pretations of the score are reproduced. [. . .] What we are interested in now is how the two ways of transmitting music interact. Biologists take it for granted that changes made in genes will affect future generations, just as changes introduced into a score will affect future performances of the music. Rather less attention is given to the alternative possibility, which is that epi-genetic variants may affect the generation and selection of genetic variation." *Evolution in Four Dimensions*, p. 245.

Chapter 8 From Code to Book

1 "Kant on the Generation of Metaphysical Knowledge," p. 72.
2 Cf. Catherine Malabou, "Pour une critique de la raison neurobiologique," *La Quinzaine littéraire*, no. 984, January 2009, pp. 4–6.
3 Germs are more explicitly responsible for the development of the parts, while dispositions are at work in relations between the parts.
4 Duchesneau, "Épigenèse de la raison pure et analogies biologiques," p. 244. Phillip R. Sloan adopts a similar approach when he says that in the third *Critique*, Kant's preformationism "is of a novel kind. It is a preformationism of *Anlagen*, now conceived as dynamic, purposive predispositions that function in relation to the *Bildungstrieb*." "Preforming the Categories," p. 249.
5 Duchesneau, "Épigenèse de la raison pure et analogies biologiques," p. 245.
6 Kant (AK [II:435]) cited in Duchesneau, "Épigenèse de la raison pure et analogies biologiques," p. 246.
7 "Épigenèse de la raison pure et analogies biologiques," p. 247.
8 *CPJ*, §65, p. 245.
9 *CPJ*, §81, p. 292.
10 "Épigenèse de la raison pure et analogies biologiques," p. 248.
11 "Épigenèse de la raison pure et analogies biologiques," p. 237. See pp. 236–7 on the topic of Wolff and Haller's influence on Blumenbach.
12 "Épigenèse de la raison pure et analogies biologiques," p. 251.
13 Lebrun, *Kant et la fin de la métaphysique*, p. 716.
14 *Kant et la fin de la métaphysique*, p. 708.
15 *Kant et la fin de la métaphysique*, p. 704.
16 *Kant et la fin de la métaphysique*, p. 704.
17 *Kant et la fin de la métaphysique*, p. 708.
18 *Kant et la fin de la métaphysique*, p. 713.
19 *Kant et la fin de la métaphysique*, p. 705.
20 *Kant et la fin de la métaphysique*, p. 707.
21 *Kant et la fin de la métaphysique*, p. 708.
22 *Kant et la fin de la métaphysique*, p. 707.
23 *On the Use of Teleological Principles in Philosophy*, p. 198.
24 *Kant et la fin de la métaphysique*, p. 708.
25 *CPR*, p. 76, AK (V:56).
26 *CPR*, p. 178, AK (V:141).
27 *CPR*, p. 179, AK (V:141).
28 Lebrun, *Kant et la fin de la métaphysique*, p. 706.
29 *Kant et la fin de la métaphysique*, p. 706.

30 *Kant et la fin de la métaphysique*, p. 717, citing Friedrich Nietzsche, *The Will to Power*, trans. Walter Kaufmann and R.J. Hollingdale, New York: Vintage, 1967, p. 351.

31 Except perhaps Evelyn Fox Keller, in "Rethinking the Meaning of Genetic Determinism," The Tanner Lectures on Human Values 15, pp. 113–39, University of Utah, February 18, 1993. http://tannerlectures.utah.edu/_documents/a-to-z/k/keller94.pdf.

Chapter 9 Irreducible Foucault

1 "What Is Critique?" in Michel Foucault, *The Politics of Truth*, eds Sylvère Lotringer and Catherine Porter, trans. Lysa Hochroth, Los Angeles: Semiotext(e), 1997, pp. 23–82. Lecture given to the French Society of Philosophy on May 27, 1978 and published in *Bulletin de la Société française de philosophie*, vol. LXXXIV, 1990, pp. 35–63.

2 Foucault, "What Is Enlightenment?" This text is available both in *The Foucault Reader* (pp. 32–50) and in *The Politics of Truth* (pp. 7–20). I refer here primarily to Catherine Porter's version in the former volume. The second version of "Qu'est-ce que les Lumières ?" was published in *Magazine littéraire*, no. 207, May 1984, pp. 35–9 (extract from the lecture at the Collège de France, January 5, 1983) and published in English as "What Is Revolution?" in *The Politics of Truth*, pp. 83–100.

3 Immanuel Kant, "An Answer to the Question: What Is Enlightenment?" in *Practical Philosophy*, trans. Mary J. Gregor, Cambridge: Cambridge University Press, 1996, pp. 15–22.

4 Foucault, "What Is Enlightenment?" p. 32.

5 Foucault asks: "What is happening today? What is happening right now?" in "What is Revolution?," p. 84.

6 Michel Foucault, *The Hermeneutics of the Subject: Lectures at the Collège de France, 1981–1982*, trans. Graham Burchell, New York: Picador, 2006, p. 15.

7 This is also the central theme in *The Hermeneutics of the Subject*. See especially pp. 15ff.

8 "What Is Enlightenment?," p. 50.

9 "What Is Enlightenment?," p. 34.

10 "What Is Enlightenment?," p. 38.

11 Cf. *The Hermeneutics of the Subject*, pp. 15–19.

12 "What Is Enlightenment?," p. 35.

13 "What Is Enlightenment?," p. 44.

14 "What Is Revolution?," p. 85.

15 "What Is Revolution?," p. 84.

16 "What Is Revolution?," p. 85.

17 "What Is Revolution?," p. 85.

18 "What Is Enlightenment?," p. 48.

19 "What Is Enlightenment?," p. 49.

20 Foucault, "What Is Enlightenment?," p. 35. Kant, "An Answer to the Question: What Is Enlightenment?," p. 17. The translation says: "*Sapere aude!* Have courage to make use of your *own* understanding! is thus the motto of Enlightenment."

21 Kant, "An Answer to the Question: What Is Enlightenment?," p. 17.
22 "An Answer to the Question: What Is Enlightenment?," p. 17.
23 Foucault, "What Is Enlightenment?," p. 38.
24 "What Is Enlightenment?," p. 38.
25 "What Is Enlightenment?," p. 42.
26 Michel Foucault, "Nietzsche, Genealogy, History," in *The Foucault Reader*, pp. 76–100, p. 78.
27 "Nietzsche, Genealogy, History," p. 80.
28 "Nietzsche, Genealogy, History," p. 81.
29 "Nietzsche, Genealogy, History," p. 83.
30 "Nietzsche, Genealogy, History," p. 82.
31 "Nietzsche, Genealogy, History," p. 83.
32 "Nietzsche, Genealogy, History," p. 82.
33 "Nietzsche, Genealogy, History," p. 46.
34 "Nietzsche, Genealogy, History," p. 46.
35 "Nietzsche, Genealogy, History," pp. 45–6.
36 Michel Foucault, "On the Archeology of the Sciences: Response to the Epistemology Circle," in *Essential Works, Volume Two: Aesthetics, Method and Epistemology*, eds James Faubion and Paul Rabinow, New York: New Press, 1998, pp. 297–335, pp. 331–2.
37 "On the Archeology of the Sciences," p. 332.
38 "An Historian of Culture," debate with Giulio Preti (1972) in Michel Foucault, *Foucault Live (Interviews, 1961–1984)*, ed. Sylvère Lotringer, trans. Jared Becker and James Cascaito, New York: Semiotext(e), 1989, pp. 95–104, p. 98.
39 "Nietzsche, Genealogy, History," p. 87.
40 Michel Foucault, *The Archaeology of Knowledge*, trans. A.M. Sheridan Smith, New York: Pantheon Books, 1972, p. 127.
41 *The Archaeology of Knowledge*, p. 127.
42 *The Archaeology of Knowledge*, p. 128.
43 *The Archaeology of Knowledge*, p. 128.
44 *The Archaeology of Knowledge*, p. 128.
45 "What Is Enlightenment?," p. 46.
46 Foucault, "An Historian of Culture," pp. 98–9.

Chapter 10 Time in Question

1 Zammito, "Kant's Persistent Ambivalence toward Epigenesis," p. 65.
2 "Kant's Persistent Ambivalence toward Epigenesis," p. 65.
3 On this point, see also Martin Heidegger, *Phenomenological Interpretation of Kant's Critique of Pure Reason*, trans. Parvis Emad and Kenneth Maly, Bloomington: Indiana University Press, 1997.
4 Heidegger, *Kant and the Problem of Metaphysics*, p. 78.
5 *Kant and the Problem of Metaphysics*, p. 78.
6 *Kant and the Problem of Metaphysics*, p. 74.
7 *Kant and the Problem of Metaphysics*, p. 74.
8 *Kant and the Problem of Metaphysics*, p. 74.
9 *Kant and the Problem of Metaphysics*, p. 74.
10 *Kant and the Problem of Metaphysics*, p. 54.

11 *Kant and the Problem of Metaphysics*, p. 102.
12 *Kant and the Problem of Metaphysics*, p. 134.
13 *Kant and the Problem of Metaphysics*, p. 141.
14 *Kant and the Problem of Metaphysics*, p. 139.
15 *Kant and the Problem of Metaphysics*, pp. 137–8.
16 Edelman, *Bright Air, Brilliant Fire*, p. 105. See the entire section on "Memory" in chapter 10: "Memory and Concepts: Building a Bridge to Consciousness."
17 *Bright Air, Brilliant Fire*, p. 105.

Chapter 11 No Agreement

1 Meillassoux, *After Finitude*, p. 123.
2 *After Finitude*, p. 16.
3 *After Finitude*, p. 8.
4 *After Finitude*, p. 123.
5 *After Finitude*, p. 123.
6 *After Finitude*, p. 16. It would therefore be necessary to renounce the philosophical position that consists in speaking about time from the position of a retrojected present, in other words, in fact, a future anterior. It will be necessary to stop thinking from the "retrojection of the diachronic past on the basis of the living present in which it is given" (*After Finitude*, p. 122).
7 *After Finitude*, p. 6.
8 *After Finitude*, p. 37.
9 *After Finitude*, p. 127.
10 *After Finitude*, p. 39.
11 *After Finitude*, p. 85.
12 *After Finitude*, p. 90.
13 *After Finitude*, p. 91.
14 *After Finitude*, p. 80.
15 *After Finitude*, p. 79.
16 *After Finitude*, p. 83.
17 *After Finitude*, p. 83.
18 *After Finitude*, p. 89.
19 *After Finitude*, p. 93. The reference to cinnabar comes from note 13, pp. 135–6.
20 *After Finitude*, p. 100.
21 *After Finitude*, p. 101.
22 *After Finitude*, p. 99.
23 *After Finitude*, p. 99.
24 *After Finitude*, pp. 102–3.
25 *After Finitude*, p. 104.
26 *After Finitude*, p. 104.
27 *After Finitude*, p. 99.
28 *After Finitude*, p. 53.

Chapter 12 The Dead End

1 According to Meillassoux, Kant did nothing but distort the meaning of the "Copernican revolution." By introducing it to philosophy, he inverted its meaning: "Yet this is where we encounter a rather disconcerting paradox. This paradox is the following: when philosophers refer to the revolution in thought instituted by Kant as the 'Copernican revolution,' they refer to a revolution *whose meaning is the exact opposite of the one we have just identified*. For as everyone knows, in the Preface to the second edition of the *Critique of Pure Reason*, Kant presents his own revolution in thought under the banner of the revolution wrought by Copernicus – instead of knowledge conforming to the object, the Critical revolution makes the object conform to our knowledge. Yet it has become abundantly clear that a more fitting comparison for the Kantian revolution in thought would be to a 'Ptolemaic counter-revolution,' given that what the former asserts is not that the observer whom we thought was motionless is in fact orbiting around the observed sun, but on the contrary, that the subject is central to the process of knowledge." *After Finitude*, pp. 117–18.

2 *After Finitude*, p. 126.

3 The term was coined by Jacques Derrida, who defines the "quasi-transcendental" as a condition of possibility whose only content is the impossibility of our doing without it. On the different uses of this concept in Derrida's work, see Geoffrey Bennington, "Derridabase," in *Jacques Derrida*, Chicago/London: University of Chicago Press, 1993, pp. 267–70.

4 On this topic, see, for example, Alexander R. Galloway, *Les Nouveaux Réalistes*, trans. Clémentine Duzer and Thomas Duzer, Paris: Éditions Léo Scheer, 2012.

5 *After Finitude*, p. 9. Translation modified.

6 *After Finitude*, p. 16.

7 Martin Heidegger, "The Origin of the Work of Art," in *Off the Beaten Track*, trans. Julian Young and Kenneth Haynes, Cambridge: Cambridge University Press, 2002, pp. 1–56, p. 37.

8 "The Origin of the Work of Art," p. 37.

9 *After Finitude*, p. 9.

10 Aristotle, *Physics*, trans. Robin Waterfield, Oxford: Oxford University Press, 1996, p. 106.

11 Aristotle writes: "But 'number' is ambiguous: we describe not only that which is numbered and numerable as number, but also that by which we number. So time is number in the sense of that which is numbered, not in the sense of that by which we number. That by which we number is not the same as that which is numbered." *Physics*, p. 106.

12 Rémi Brague, *Du Temps chez Platon et Aristote: Quatre Études*, Paris: Presses Universitaires de France, 1982, pp. 134–5. My translation.

13 *Du Temps chez Platon et Aristote*, pp. 134–5.

14 Cf. Aristotle, *Physics*, Book IV, 223a 28, p. 115.

15 *After Finitude*, p. 34.

16 *After Finitude*, p. 108.

17 Martin Heidegger, "Anaximander's Saying," in *Off the Beaten Track*, pp. 242–81, p. 276.

18 Jacques Derrida, "*Ousia* and *Grammè*: Note on a Note from *Being and Time*," in *Margins of Philosophy*, trans. Alan Bass, Chicago: University of Chicago Press, 1982, pp. 29–68. See in particular pp. 48ff., in which Derrida "compares the 'Transcendental Exposition of the Concept of Time to *Physics IV*."
19 Heidegger, *On Time and Being*, p. 15.
20 *On Time and Being*, p. 15.
21 *On Time and Being*, p. 14.
22 *After Finitude*, p. 13.
23 *On Time and Being*, p. 14.
24 *On Time and Being*, p. 14.
25 Cf. *After Finitude*, pp. 10ff.
26 Martin Heidegger, *Being and Time*, trans. Joan Stambaugh, revised and with a foreword by Dennis J. Schmidt, Albany: SUNY Press, 2010. Title of the first part of the book, see the table of contents, p. vii.
27 *Being and Time*, §6, p. 23 [24].
28 Cf., for example, *Contributions to Philosophy (of the Event)*, trans. Richard Rojcewicz and Daniela Vallega-Neu, Bloomington: Indiana University Press, 2012, no. 111 ("The '*Apriori*' and φύσις"), no. 112 ("The '*Apriori*'"), p. 174.
29 Martin Heidegger, *The Basic Problems of Phenomenology*, trans. Albert Hofstadter, Bloomington: Indiana University Press, 1982, p. 322.
30 Heidegger, *Contributions to Philosophy (of the Event)*, no. 262, p. 355.
31 Mentioned by Jean Grondin in *L'Horizon herméneutique de la pensée contemporaine*, Paris: Vrin, 1993, p. 65. My translation.
32 A "finitude," which, it should be noted, appears explicitly only four times in *Being and Time*. Cf. Grondin, *L'Horizon herméneutique de la pensée contemporaine*, p. 66.
33 *After Finitude*, p. 8.
33 Heidegger, *On Time and Being*, p. 54.
35 "*Es gibt*" is translated as "there is," but sometimes also as "it gives." Cf. *On Time and Being*, p. 8.
36 Derrida, "*Ousia* and *Grammè*," p. 63.
37 Cf., for example, Jean-Luc Marion, *Being Given: Toward a Phenomenology of Givenness*, trans. Jeffrey L. Kosky, Stanford, CA: Stanford University Press, 2002. Marion certainly refuses to equate givenness and transcendental. But this refusal leads to thinking givenness as a still more primitive principle, in this sense as a "super" or "hyper" transcendental that comes before all the befores. Both first and last. Ultimate. Marion writes, "The privilege of givenness [. . .] comes to it from its definition. Since givenness always beats a hasty retreat before its given, its very withdrawal confirms it; its absence – not being, object, I, or transcendental – attests its activity. It is indeed posited as principle, but on condition that it remain the last" (p. 61).
38 *CPR*, p. 273, A141.
39 *After Finitude*, p. 45.
40 Cf. Jacques Derrida, *Given Time: I, Counterfeit Money*, trans. Peggy Kamuf, Chicago: University of Chicago Press, 1992, p. 19.
41 *CPJ*, introduction, section II, "On the Domain of Philosophy in General," pp. 61–2.
42 *After Finitude*, p. 27.
43 *After Finitude*, p. 10.
44 Meillassoux writes: "The problem of the arche-fossil is not confined to

ancestral statements. For it concerns every discourse whose meaning includes a *temporal discrepancy* between thinking and being – thus, not only statements about events occurring prior to the emergence of humans, but also statements about possible events that are *ulterior* to the extinction of the human species." *After Finitude*, p. 112.
45 *After Finitude*, p. 31.
46 *After Finitude*, p. 28.
47 *After Finitude*, p. 60.
48 *After Finitude*, p. 65.
49 *After Finitude*, p. 26.
50 *After Finitude*, p. 62.
51 *After Finitude*, p. 62.
52 *After Finitude*, p. 15.
53 *After Finitude*, p. 124.
54 *After Finitude*, p. 108.
55 *After Finitude*, p. 90.
56 *After Finitude*, p. 94.
57 See *After Finitude*, p. 98: "[T]he Humean-Kantian inference is an instance of probabilistic reasoning applied not to an event in our universe, but rather to our universe itself considered as merely one among a totality of possible universes. The nub of the argument consists in registering the immense numerical gap between those possibilities that are conceivable and those that are actually experienced, in such a way as to derive from this gap the following probabilistic aberration (which provides the source for the frequentalist implication): if physical laws *could actually change for no reason*, it would be extraordinarily improbable if they did not change *frequently*, not to say frenetically. Indeed, they would change so frequently that we would have to say – and here we move from Hume to Kant – not just that we would have noticed it already, but that we would never have been here to notice it in the first place [. . .]."
58 *After Finitude*, p. 81.
59 Cf. the argument presented in *After Finitude*, pp. 66–7.
60 *After Finitude*, p. 66.
61 *After Finitude*, p. 79.
62 *After Finitude*, p. 66.
63 *After Finitude*, p. 63.
64 *After Finitude*, p. 53.
65 *After Finitude*, p. 76.
66 Cf. *After Finitude*, p. 67.
67 Martin Heidegger, *The Principle of Reason*, trans. Reginald Lilly, Bloomington: Indiana University Press, 1991, p. 125.
68 *The Principle of Reason*, p. 126.
69 "The 'because' withers away in play. The play is without 'why.' It plays since it plays. It simply remains a play: the most elevated and the most profound." *The Principle of Reason*, p. 113.
70 *After Finitude*, p. 9.
71 *After Finitude*, p. 110. Translation modified.
72 Heidegger's interest in biology is certainly genuine, as a number of key texts indicate, especially *The Fundamental Concepts of Metaphysics: World, Finitude, Solitude*, trans. William McNeill and Nicholas Walker,

Bloomington: Indiana University Press, 1995. Nevertheless, in his work, the status of life is always *derived* as compared to higher instances of being or existence.

73 *After Finitude*, p. 26.
74 Émile Boutroux, *The Contingency of the Laws of Nature*, trans. Fred Rothwell, Chicago: Open Court, 1920, p. 26. Cited by Bouveresse in "Le problème de l'*a priori*," p. 359.
75 *The Contingency of the Laws of Nature*, p. 156. Cited in Bouveresse, "Le problème de l'*a priori*," p. 359.
76 "Le problème de l'*a priori*," p. 359.
77 Cf. Poincaré's point of view, which is entirely opposed to any idea of the evolution of the laws of nature. See Bouveresse, "Le problème de l'*a priori*," p. 360.
78 Edelman, *Brilliant Air, Brilliant Fire*, p. 202.
79 Changeux, *Neuronal Man*, p. 137.
80 Changeux and Ricœur, *What Makes Us Think?*, p. 91.
81 *What Makes Us Think?*, p. 239.
82 *What Makes Us Think?*, p. 209.
83 Edelman, *Bright Air, Brilliant Fire*, title of chapter 11, p. 111.
84 Of course, there will be objections that draw attention to the famous remarks in the preface to *Anthropology from a Pragmatic Point of View* whereby: "He who ponders natural phenomena, for example, what the causes of the faculty of memory may rest on, can speculate back and forth (like Descartes) over the traces of impressions remaining in the brain, but in doing so he must admit that in this play of his representations he is a mere observer and must let nature run its course, for he does not know the cranial nerves and fibers, nor does he understand how to put them to use for his purposes. Therefore all theoretical speculation about this is a pure waste of time." *Anthropology, History, and Education*, p. 231, AK (VII:119). Of course, this naïve realism is not the one I am arguing for here, and one might imagine that in the light of recent discoveries Kant would have accepted that contemporary neurobiology does indeed allow for the opening up of new theoretical speculation.

Chapter 13 Towards an Epigenetic Paradigm of Rationality

1 Changeux and Ricœur, *What Makes Us Think?*, p. 217.
2 Atlan, *La Fin du "tout génétique"?*, pp. 11–12.
3 Paul Ricœur, *The Conflict of Interpretations: Essays in Hermeneutics*, ed. Don Idhe, Evanston, IL: Northwestern University Press, 1974, pp. 146–47. See also *Freud and Philosophy: An Essay on Interpretation*, trans. Denise Savage, New Haven, CT: Yale University Press, 1970, especially book III, chapter III: "Dialectic: Archeology and Teleology," pp. 459ff. Ricœur draws a very clear distinction between genesis and epigenesis: on this point, see in particular *The Conflict of Interpretations*, pp. 109ff. See also the fine work of Øystein Brekke: "On the Subject of Epigenesis: An Interpretive Figure in Paul Ricœur," in Marius Timmann Mjaaland, Ulrik Houlind Rasmussen, and Philipp Stoellger, eds, *Impossible Time: Past and Future in the Philosophy of Religion*, Tübingen: Mohr Siebeck, 2013, pp. 73–82.
4 Ricœur, *Freud and Philosophy*.

5 In fact, for Ricœur, in both *The Conflict of Interpretations* and *Freud and Philosophy*, it is a matter of bringing to light an "epigenesis of religious feeling" (*Freud and Philosophy*, p. 534), the intermediary between the Freudian approach of the primordial event of the killing of the father, which, inasmuch as it repeats itself without alteration through time, authorizes no evolution, but instead "sempiternal treading" (p. 534), and the Hegelian vision of a constant dialectical transformation of meaning that renders religion nothing but a simple moment of the mind. The unconscious and consciousness pull meaning in two opposing directions. Ricœur sets out to show that there is actually no "antinomy" between the two, and that archeology and teleology share solidarity: all archeology is waiting, and all teleology proceeds from the archeological traces of the past.

6 *The Conflict of Interpretations*, p. 113.

7 *Freud and Philosophy*, p. 548.

8 *The Conflict of Interpretations*, p. 113.

9 Bernard Bourgeois, *L'Idéalisme allemand*, Paris: Vrin, 2000, p. 109. Later he writes: "The concept of living being has no place in the doctrine of reason: the *Critique of Judgment* refuses it any objectivity, any value that is *constitutive* of the object, and sends it back, as a merely *regulative* concept, to the explorative subjectivity of objective nature" (p. 109). My translation.

10 *CPJ*, §81, p. 291.

11 *CPJ*, §81, p. 291.

12 *CPJ*, §81, p. 291.

13 *CPJ*, §81, p. 291.

14 *CPJ*, §81, p. 292.

15 *CPJ*, §81, p. 290.

16 *CPJ*, §81, p. 290.

17 *CPJ*, §81, p. 290.

18 *CPJ*, §84, p. 301.

19 Paragraph 65 of the *Critique of the Power of Judgment* demonstrates this point explicitly.

20 *CPR*, p. 591, A645/B673.

21 Philippe Huneman, "La place de l'analytique de la biologie dans la philosophie transcendantale," in Sophie Grapotte, Mai Lequan, and Margit Ruffing, eds, *Kant et les Sciences: un dialogue philosophique avec la pluralité des savoirs*, Paris: Vrin, 2011, pp. 253–65, p. 257. My translation.

22 *CPR*, Architectonic of Pure Reason, p. 691, A832/B860.

23 *CPR*, Appendix to the Transcendental Dialectic, p. 598, A657/B685.

24 *CPR*, p. 691, A833/B861.

25 *CPR*, p. 692, A835/B863.

26 Kant also distinguishes the growth of organic life from the "accretion" of minerals that takes place through the addition of successive layers, rather than through internal self-differentiation.

27 "The inertia of matter is, and means, nothing else than its *lifelessness*, as matter in itself," *Metaphysical Foundations of Natural Science*, in *Theoretical Philosophy after 1781*, p. 251, AK (IV:544).

28 *Metaphysical Foundations of Natural Science* is concerned with studying the principles of movement, not those of matter endowed with life, an absurd idea that is the basis of the hylozoism that Kant criticizes harshly.

29 Huneman, "La place de l'analytique de la biologie, " p. 257.

30 *CPR*, p. 596, A653/B681.
31 *CPR*, Appendix to the Transcendental Dialectic, p. 592, A646/B674.
32 Kant, *The Only Possible Argument*, p. 150.
33 *The Only Possible Argument*, p. 149.
34 *The Only Possible Argument*, p. 150.
35 *CPJ*, §81, p. 290.
36 *CPJ*, §81, p. 290.
37 *CPJ*, §65, p. 247.
38 *CPJ*, introduction, section IV, p. 67.
39 *CPJ*, introduction, section IV, p. 67.
40 Eric Weil, "Sens et fait," in *Problèmes kantiens*, Paris: Vrin, 1970, pp. 57–107, pp. 64–5. My translation here and below.
41 "Sens et fait," p. 76.
42 "Sens et fait," p. 80.
43 It is now widely accepted that the critique of teleological judgment is an analytic of biological judgment. Cf. Huneman, "La place de l'analytique de la biologie."
44 Weil, "Sens et fait," p. 64.
45 "Sens et fait," p. 67.
46 *CPJ*, §76, p. 274.
47 Cf. *CPJ*, §10 "On Purposiveness in General," p. 105.
48 *CPJ*, §65, p. 245. My emphasis.
49 *CPJ*, §65, p. 245.
50 *CPJ*, §66, p. 249.
51 Weil, "Sens et fait," p. 104.
52 *CPJ*, introduction, section IV, p. 67. My emphasis.
53 "Sens et fait," p. 60.
54 *CPJ*, p. 258.
55 *CPJ*, §77, p. 275.
56 See *CPJ*, §77, p. 275.
57 *CPJ*, §77, p. 276.
58 *CPR*, p. 203, A66/B91.

Chapter 14 Can We Relinquish the Transcendental?

1 Weil, "Sens et fait," p. 104.
2 Weil adds, moreover, that "with the concept of entropy, nor does post-Kantian physics see any logical or material impossibility in it." "Sens et fait," p. 104.
3 Huneman, "La place de l'analytique de la biologie," p. 265.
4 *CPJ*, §82, p. 296, English translation modified following changes to the French translation.
5 *CPJ*, §82, p. 296.
6 *CPJ*, §80, p. 288.
7 *CPJ*, §82, note, p. 296, English translation modified following changes to the French translation.
8 Moreover, it is surprising that Meillassoux chose never to speak about the problem of the trace, even though he mobilizes the figure of the fossil and the arche-fossil so strongly. Admittedly, he does specify, "I will call 'arche-fossil,'

or 'fossil-matter,' not just materials indicating the traces of past life, according to the familiar sense of the term 'fossil,' but materials indicating the existence of an ancestral reality or event." *After Finitude*, p. 10. Nevertheless, it seems difficult, to say the least, to think the one without the other!

9 Weil, "Sens et fait," p. 105.
10 See the "synthetic" theory of evolution.
11 *CPJ*, §66, p. 247, English translation modified following changes to the French translation.
12 Huneman, "La place de l'analytique de la biologie," p. 262.
13 *CPR*, §27, p. 265, B167.
14 Kant says that an analogy is either mathematical or philosophical. He expands: "In philosophy analogies signify something very different from what they represent in mathematics. In the latter they are formulas that assert the identity of two relations of magnitude, and are always *constitutive*, so that if two members of the proportion are given the third is also thereby given, i.e., can be constructed. In philosophy, however, analogy is not the identity of two quantitative but of two qualitative relations, where from three given members I can cognize and give *a priori* only the *relation* to a fourth number but not *this* fourth *member* itself." *CPR*, Analogies of Experience, pp. 297–8, A180/B223.
15 *CPJ*, §59, p. 225.
16 *CPR*, pp. 691–2, A833/B861.
17 *CPR*, p. 387, A299/B356.
18 *CPR*, p. 402, A326–7/B383.
19 *CPR*, p. 691, A833/B861.
20 *CPR*, p. 692, A834/B862.
21 *CPJ*, introduction, section II, p. 63.
22 *CPJ*, introduction, section II, p. 63.
23 *CPJ*, introduction, section IX, p. 81.
24 *CPJ*, introduction, section III, p. 64.
25 *CPJ*, introduction, section IX, p. 81.
26 *CPJ*, introduction, section IX, pp. 81–2.
27 *CPJ*, introduction, section II, p. 63.
28 This integration is only possible due to the fact that "the principle of the purposiveness of nature [. . .] is a transcendental principle." *CPJ*, introduction, section V, p. 69.
29 The expression of reality that only exists for thought comes from *CPR*, "On the Schematism of the Pure Concepts of the Understanding," regarding the schema of the triangle: "[T]he schema of the triangle can never exist anywhere except in thought [. . .]." *CPR*, p. 273, A141/B180.

Conclusion

1 Changeux and Ricœur, *What Makes Us Think?*, p. 75.

BIBLIOGRAPHY

Works by Kant

In German

Gesammelte Schriften, Berlin: Königlich Preussischen Akademie der Wissenschaften, 1902–97. (AK with the volume listed in roman numerals and the page in arabic numerals.)

English translations used

Anthropology, History, and Education, eds Robert B. Louden and Günter Zöller, trans. Mary Gregor et al., Cambridge: Cambridge University Press, 2007. Includes "Of the Different Races of Human Beings"; "Determination of the Concept of a Human Race"; "Review of J.G. Herder's Ideas for the Philosophy of the History of Humanity"; "Anthropology from a Pragmatic Point of View"; and "On the Use of Teleological Principles in Philosophy."

Critique of the Power of Judgment [*CPJ*], trans. Paul Guyer and Eric Matthews, Cambridge: Cambridge University Press, 2000.

Critique of Practical Reason, trans. Werner S. Pluhar, Indianapolis/Cambridge, MA: Hackett Publishing Company, 2002.

Critique of Pure Reason [*CPR*], trans. Paul Guyer and Allen W. Wood, Cambridge: Cambridge University Press, 1998.

Kant's Inaugural Dissertation of 1770, trans. William J. Eckoff, New York: Columbia College, 1894.

Metaphysics: A Critical Translation with Kant's Elucidations, Selected Notes, and Related Materials, Alexander Baumgarten, ed. and trans. Courtney D. Fugate and John Hymers, New York: Bloomsbury Academic, 2013.

The Metaphysics of Morals, trans. Mary Gregor, Cambridge: Cambridge University Press, 1996.

Notes and Fragments, ed. Paul Guyer, trans. Curtis Bowman, Paul Guyer, and Frederick Rauscher, Cambridge: Cambridge University Press, 2005. Includes *Notes on Metaphysics*.

On a Discovery According to Which Any New Critique of Pure Reason Has

211

Been Made Superfluous by an Earlier One, trans. Henry E. Allison. Baltimore/London: Johns Hopkins University Press, 1973.

Practical Philosophy, trans. Mary J. Gregor, Cambridge: Cambridge University Press, 1996. Includes "An Answer to the Question: What Is Enlightenment?"

Theoretical Philosophy 1755–1770, trans. David Walford, Cambridge: Cambridge University Press, 1992.

Theoretical Philosophy after 1781, eds Henry Allison and Peter Heath, trans. Gary Hatfield et al., Cambridge: Cambridge University Press, 2004. Includes *Prolegomena to Any Future Metaphysics That Will Be Able to Come Forward as a Science* and *Metaphysical Foundations of Natural Science*.

Works on Kant

Benoist, Jocelyn, *Kant et les limites de la synthèse: Le sujet sensible*, Paris: Presses Universitaires de France, 1996.

Bouveresse, Jacques, *Essais V – Descartes, Leibniz, Kant*, Marseille: Agone, 2006.

Bouveresse, Jacques, "Le Problème de l'*a priori* et la conception évolutionniste des lois de la pensée," *Revue de théologie et de philosophie*, vol. 123, 1991, pp. 353–68.

Boyer, Alain, *Hors du temps: Un essai sur Kant*, Paris: Vrin, 2001.

Cassirer, Ernst, *Kant's Life and Thought*, trans. James Haden, New Haven, CT: Yale University Press, 1981.

de Vleeschauwer, Herman Jan, *La Déduction transcendantale dans l'œuvre de Kant*, 3 vols, Antwerp/Paris/The Hague: De Sikkel/Ernest Leroux/Martinus Nijhoff, 1934–7.

Duchesneau, François, "Épigénèse de la raison pure et analogies biologiques," in François Duchesneau, Guy Lafrance, and Claude Piche, *Kant actuel: Hommage à Pierre Laberge*, Paris: Bellarmin-Vrin, 2000, pp. 233–56.

Foucault, Michel, "What Is Critique?," in *The Politics of Truth*, eds Sylvère Lotringer and Catherine Porter, trans. Lysa Hochroth, Los Angeles: Semiotext(e), 1997, pp. 23–82.

Foucault, Michel, "What Is Enlightenment?," in Paul Rabinow, ed., *The Foucault Reader*, New York: Pantheon Books, 1984, pp. 32–50.

Foucault, Michel, "What Is Revolution?," in *The Politics of Truth*, eds Sylvère Lotringer and Catherine Porter, trans. Lysa Hochroth, Los Angeles: Semiotext(e), 1997, pp. 83–100.

Genova, A.C. "Kant's Epigenesis of Pure Reason," *Kant-Studien*, vol. 65, no. 3, 1974, pp. 259–73.

Heidegger, Martin, *Kant and the Problem of Metaphysics*, trans. Richard Taft, Bloomington: Indiana University Press, 1997.

Heidegger, Martin, *Phenomenological Interpretation of Kant's Critique of Pure Reason*, trans. Parvis Emad and Kenneth Maly, Bloomington: Indiana University Press, 1997.

Huneman, Philippe, *Métaphysique et biologie: Kant et la constitution du concept d'organisme*, Paris: Vrin, 2008.

Huneman, Philippe, "La place de l'analytique de la biologie dans la philosophie transcendantale," in Sophie Grapotte, Mai Lequan, and Margit Ruffing, eds, *Kant et les Sciences: un dialogue philosophique avec la pluralité des savoirs*, Paris: Vrin, 2011, pp. 253–65.

Ingensiep, Hans Werner, "Die biologischen Analogien und die erkenntistheoretischen Alternativen in Kants Kritik der reinen Vernunft B§27," *Kant-Studien*, vol. 85, no. 4, 1994, pp. 381–93.

Landgraf, Edgar, "The Education of Humankind: Perfectibility and Discipline in Kant's Lectures *Über Pädagogik*," *Goethe Yearbook* 14, pp. 39–60.

Lebrun, Gerard, *Kant et la Fin de la métaphysique*, Paris: Armand Colin, 1970.

Lenoir, Timothy, "Kant, Blumenbach, and Vital Materialism in German Biology," *Isis*, vol. 71, no. 256, 1980, pp. 77–108.

Longuenesse, Beatrice, *Kant et le Pouvoir de juger: Sensibilité et discursivité dans l'Analytique transcendantale de la Critique de la raison pure*, Paris: Presses Universitaires de France, 1993.

Löw, Reinhard, *Philosophie des Lebendingen: Der Begriff des Organischen bei Kant, sein Grund und seine Aktualität*, Frankfurt: Suhrkamp, 1980.

McLaughlin, Peter, *Kant's Critique of Teleology in Biological Explanation: Antinomy and Teleology*, Lewiston, NY: Edwin Mellen Press, 1990.

Mensch, Jennifer, *Kant's Organicism: Epigenesis and the Development of Critical Philosophy*, Chicago: University of Chicago Press, 2013.

Rockmore, Tom, *In Kant's Wake: Philosophy in the Twentieth Century*, Malden, MA/Oxford: Blackwell, 2006.

Sandford, Stella, "Spontaneous Generation: The Fantasy of the Birth of Concepts in Kant's *Critique of Pure Reason*," *Radical Philosophy*, no. 179, May–June 2013, pp. 15–26.

Sloan, Phillip R., "Performing the Categories: Eighteenth-Century Generation Theory and the Biological Roots of Kant's *A Priori*," *Journal of the History of Philosophy*, vol. 40, no. 2, 2002, pp. 229–53.

Verneaux, Roger, "La notion kantienne d'analyse transcendantale," *Revue philosophique de Louvain*, vol. 50, no. 27, 1952, pp. 394–428.

Verneaux, Roger, *Le Vocabulaire de Kant*, Paris: Aubier-Montaigne, 1967.

Weil, Eric, "Sens et fait," in *Problèmes kantiens*, Paris: Vrin, 1970, pp. 57–107.

Wubnig, Judy, "The Epigenesis of Pure Reason: A Note on the *Critique of Pure Reason*, B sec. 27, 165–167," *Kant-Studien*, vol. 60, no. 2, 1969, pp. 147–52.

Zammito, John H., *The Genesis of Kant's Kritik der Urteilskraft*, Chicago: University of Chicago Press, 1992.

Zammito, John H., "Kant's Persistent Ambivalence toward Epigenesis, 1764–1790," in Philippe Huneman, ed., *Understanding Purpose: Collected Essays on Kant and Philosophy of Biology* (*North American Kant Society Studies in Philosophy*, Vol. VIII), Rochester, NY: University of Rochester Press, 2007, pp. 51–74.

Zöller, Günter, "Kant on the Generation of Metaphysical Knowledge," in Hariolf Oberer and Gerhard Seel, eds, *Kant, Analysen – Probleme – Kritik*, Würzburg: Königshausen und Neumann, 1988, pp. 71–90.

Works on Biology

Allis, C. David, Marie-Laure Caparros, Thomas Jenuwein, and Danny Reinberg, eds, *Epigenetics*, second edition, New York: Cold Spring Harbor Press, 2015.

Aristotle, *Generation of Animals*, trans. A.L. Peck, London: Heinemann, 1943.

Atlan, Henri, *La Fin du "tout génétique"? Vers de nouveaux paradigmes en biologie*, Paris: INRA Éditions, 1999.

BIBLIOGRAPHY

Atlan, Henti, "Programme de Recherche Inter-Centres *Biologie et société*," 2009. http://www.ehess.fr/fileadmin/template/images/documents_pdf/PRI-Biologie.pdf

Blumenbach, Johann Friedrich, *The Institutions of Physiology* [1797], trans. John D. Elliotson, London: E. Cox and Sons, 1817, section 40: "Of the Nissus Formativus," paragraph 591, p. 337.

Blumenbach, Johann Friedrich, *Manual of the Elements of Natural History* [1781], trans. R.T. Gore, London : W. Simpkin and R, Marshall, 1825.

Blumenbach, Johann Friedrich, "Über den Bildungstrieb (Nisus formativus) und seinen Einfluß auf die Generation und Reproduction," in Georg Christoph Lichtenberg, Georg Forster, eds, *Göttingisches Magazin der Wissenschaften und Litteratur*, vol. 1, no. 5, 1780, pp. 247–66.

Blumenbach, Johann Friedrich, *Über den Bildungstrieb und das Zeugungsgeschäfte*, Göttingen: Dietrich, 1781.

Boutroux, Émile, *The Contingency of the Laws of Nature*, trans. Fred Rothwell, Chicago: Open Court, 1920.

Buffon, Georges-Louis Leclerc, comte de, *Œuvres complètes*, *Histoire des animaux*, Paris: F.-D. Pillot, Vol. 11, 1830.

Canguilhem, Georges, Lapassade, Georges, Piquemal, Jacques, and Ulmann, Jacques, *Du Développement à l'évolution au XIXe siècle*, Paris: Presses Universitaires de France, coll. "Pratiques Théoriques," 1962.

Changeux, Jean-Pierre, *Du Vrai, du beau, du bien: Une nouvelle approche neuronale*, Paris: Odile Jacob, 2008.

Changeux, Jean-Pierre, *The Good, the True and the Beautiful: A Neuronal Approach*, trans. and revised Laurence Garey, New Haven, CT: Yale University Press, 2012.

Changeux, Jean-Pierre, *Neuronal Man: The Biology of the Mind*, trans. Laurence Garey, New York: Pantheon, 1985.

Changeux, Jean-Pierre and Connes, Alain, *Conversations on Mind, Matter and Mathematics*, trans. M.B. DeBevoise, Princeton, NJ: Princeton University Press, 1995.

Changeux, Jean-Pierre, Courrège, Philippe, and Danchin, Antoine, "A Theory of Epigenesis of Neuronal Networks by Selective Stabilization of Synapses," *Proceedings of the National Academy of Sciences USA*, vol. 70, no. 10, Oct. 1973, pp. 2974–8.

Changeux, Jean-Pierre and Danchin, Antoine, "Selective Stabilization of Developing Synapses as a Mechanism for the Specification of Neural Networks," *Nature*, December 23–30, 1976, vol. 264, no. 5588, pp. 705–12.

Changeux, Jean-Pierre and Ricœur, Paul, *What Makes Us Think? A Neuroscientist and a Philosopher Argue about Ethics, Human Nature, and the Brain*, trans. M.B. DeBevoise, Princeton, NJ: Princeton University Press, 2000.

Dupré, John and Parry, Sarah, eds, *Nature after the Genome*, London: Wiley-Blackwell, 2010.

Edelman, Gerald M., *Bright Air, Brilliant Fire: On the Matter of the Mind*, New York: Basic Books, 1992.

Harvey, William, *On the Generation of Animals* [1651], Ann Arbor, MI: Edwards, 1943.

Ho, Mae-Wan, "Epigenetic Inheritance: 'What Genes Remember,'" *Science in Society*, vol. 41, 2009, pp. 4–5.

214

Ho, Mae-Wan, *Living with the Fluid Genome*, London/Penang: Institute of Science in Society/Third World Network, 2003.
Jablonka, Eva and Lamb, Marion J., *Evolution in Four Dimensions: Genetic, Epigenetic, Behavioral, and Symbolic Variation in the History of Life*, Cambridge, MA: MIT Press, 2005.
Jacob, François, *The Logic of Life: A History of Heredity*, trans. Betty E. Spillmann, New York: Pantheon, 1982.
Keller, Evelyn Fox, "Rethinking the Meaning of Genetic Determinism," The Tanner Lectures on Human Values 15, pp. 113–39, University of Utah, February 18, 1993. http://tannerlectures.utah.edu/_documents/a-to-z/k/keller94.pdf
Lenoir, Timothy, *The Strategy of Life: Teleology and Mechanism in Nineteenth-Century German Biology*, Dordrecht: Reidel, 1982.
Lewontin, Richard, *The Triple Helix: Gene, Organism, and Environment*, Cambridge, MA: Harvard University Press, 2000.
McLaughlin, Peter, "The Impact of Newton on Biology on the Continent in the Eighteenth Century," in Scott Mandelbrote and Helmut Pulte, eds, *The Reception of Isaac Newton in Europe*, London: Bloomsbury Academic, 2014, pp. 1–23.
Malabou, Catherine, "Pour une critique de la raison neurobiologique," *La Quinzaine littéraire*, no. 984, January 2009, pp. 4–6.
Maupertuis, Pierre-Louis Moreau de, *Essai sur la formation des corps organisés*, Paris: A. Berlin, 1754.
Morgan, Thomas Hunt, "The Relation of Genetics to Physiology and Medicine," Nobel Lecture, June 4, 1934. http://www.nobelprize.org/nobel_prizes/medicine/laureates/1933/morgan-lecture.pdf
Pradeu, Thomas, "Philosophie de la biologie," in Anouk Barberousse, Denis Bonnay, and Mikaël Cozic, eds, *Précis de philosophie des sciences*, Paris: Vuibert, 2011, pp. 378–403.
Pradeu, Thomas, "Qu'est-ce qu'un individu biologique?," in Pascal Ludwig and Thomas Pradeu, eds, *L'Individu: perspectives contemporaines*, Paris: Vrin, 2008, pp. 97–125.
La Recherche, "Épigénétique: l'hérédité au-delà des gènes," no. 463, April 2012, pp. 38–54.
Schwarz, Jeffrey M. and Begley, Sharon, *The Mind and the Brain: Neuroplasticity and the Power of Mental Force*, New York: HarperCollins, 2002.
Waddington, Conrad Hal, "The Basic Ideas of Biology," in *Towards a Theoretical Biology*, Vol. 1, *Prolegomena*, Edinburgh: Edinburgh University Press, 1968, pp. 1–32.
West-Eberhard, Mary-Jane, *Developmental Plasticity and Evolution*, New York: Oxford University Press, 2003.
Wolff, Caspar Friedrich, *Theoria generationis* [1764], Hildesheim: Georg Olms Verlag, 1966.

Other

Aristotle, *Physics*, trans. Robin Waterfield, Oxford: Oxford University Press, 1996.
Badiou, Alain, *Logics of Worlds (Being and Event, 2)*, trans. Alberto Toscano, London/New York: Continuum, 2009.

Bennington, Geoffrey, "Derridabase," in Jacques Derrida and Geoffrey Bennington, *Jacques Derrida*, Chicago/London: University of Chicago Press, 1993, pp. 267–70.

Boltzmann, Ludwig, *Principien der Naturfilosofi. Lectures on Natural Philosophy 1903–1917*, ed. Ilse M. Fasol-Boltzmann, Berlin/Heidelberg: Springer, 1990.

Bourgeois, Bernard, *L'Idéalisme allemand*, Paris: Vrin, 2000.

Brague, Rémi, *Du Temps chez Platon et Aristote: Quatre Études*, Paris: Presses Universitaires de France, 1982.

Braver, Lee, *A Thing of This World: A History of Continental Anti-Realism*, Evanston, IL: Northwestern University Press, 2007.

Brekke, Øystein, "On the Subject of Epigenesis: An Interpretive Figure in Paul Ricœur," in Marius Timmann Mjaaland, Ulrik Houlind Rasmussen, and Philipp Stoellger, eds, *Impossible Time: Past and Future in the Philosophy of Religion*, Tübingen: Mohr Siebeck Verlag, 2013, pp. 73–82.

Derrida, Jacques, *Given Time: I, Counterfeit Money*, trans. Peggy Kamuf, Chicago: University of Chicago Press, 1992.

Derrida, Jacques, *Glas*, trans. John P. Leavy, Jr and Richard Rand, Lincoln/ London: University of Nebraska Press, 1986.

Derrida, Jacques, "*Ousia* and *Grammè*: Note on a Note from *Being and Time*," in *Margins of Philosophy*, trans. Alan Bass, Chicago: University of Chicago Press, 1982, pp. 29–68.

Derrida, Jacques, *The Problem of Genesis in Husserl's Philosophy*, trans. Marian Hobson, Chicago: University of Chicago Press, 2003.

Descartes, René, *Philosophical Essays: Discourse on Method; Meditations; Rules for the Direction of the Mind*, trans. Laurence J. Lafleur, Indianapolis/New York/Kansas City: Bobbs-Merrill Company Inc., 1964.

Foucault, Michel, *The Archaeology of Knowledge*, trans. A.M. Sheridan Smith, New York: Pantheon Books, 1972.

Foucault, Michel, *Essential Works, Volume Two: Aesthetics, Method and Epistemology*, eds James Faubion and Paul Rabinow, New York: New Press, 1998.

Foucault, Michel, *Foucault Live (Interviews, 1961–1984)*, ed. Sylvère Lotringer, trans. Jared Becker and James Cascaito, New York: Semiotext(e), 1989.

Foucault, Michel, *The Hermeneutics of the Subject: Lectures at the Collège de France, 1981–1982*, trans. Graham Burchell, New York: Picador, 2006.

Foucault, Michel, "Nietzsche, Genealogy, History," in Paul Rabinow, ed., *The Foucault Reader*, New York: Pantheon Books, 1984, pp. 76–100.

Frege, Gottlob, *The Foundations of Arithmetic: A Logico-Mathematical Inquiry into the Concept of Number*, trans. J.L. Austin, second revised edition, Evanston, IL: Northwestern University Press, 1980.

Frege, Gottlob, *Posthumous Writings*, trans. Peter Long and Roger M. White, Chicago: University of Chicago Press, 1979.

Galloway, Alexander R., *Les Nouveaux Réalistes*, trans. Clementine Duzer and Thomas Duzer, Paris: Éditions Leo Scheer, 2012.

Godin, Christian, "La figure et le moment du scepticisme chez Hegel," *Les Études philosophiques*, vol. 3, no. 70, 2004, pp. 341–56.

Grant, Iain Hamilton, *Philosophies of Nature after Schelling*, London: Continuum, 2006.

Grondin, Jean, *L'Horizon herméneutique de la pensée contemporaine*, Paris: Vrin, 1993.

Harrison, Ross, "Transcendental Arguments and Idealism," in Godfrey Vesey, ed., *Idealism Past and Present*, Cambridge: Cambridge University Press, 1982, pp. 211–24.

Heidegger, Martin, *The Basic Problems of Phenomenology*, trans. Albert Hofstadter, Bloomington: Indiana University Press, 1982.

Heidegger, Martin, *Being and Time*, trans. Joan Stambaugh, revised and with a foreword by Dennis J. Schmidt, Albany: SUNY Press, 2010.

Heidegger, Martin, *Contributions to Philosophy (of the Event)*, trans. Richard Rojcewicz and Daniela Vallega-Neu, Bloomington: Indiana University Press, 2012.

Heidegger, Martin, *The Fundamental Concepts of Metaphysics: World, Finitude, Solitude*, trans. William McNeill and Nicholas Walker, Bloomington: Indiana University Press, 1995.

Heidegger, Martin, *Off the Beaten Track*, trans. Julian Young and Kenneth Haynes, Cambridge: Cambridge University Press, 2002.

Heidegger, Martin, *On Time and Being*, trans. Joan Stambaugh, New York: Harper and Row, 1972.

Heidegger, Martin, *The Principle of Reason*, trans. Reginald Lilly, Bloomington: Indiana University Press, 1991.

Herder, Johann Godfried, *Ideen zur Philosophie der Geschichte der Menschheit*, in *Herders Sämtliche Werke*, ed. V.B. Suphan, Vol. 13, Berlin: Weidmann, 1887, republished Berlin/Weimar: Aufbau-Verlag, Vol. I, 1965.

Hume, David, *An Enquiry Concerning Human Understanding*, republished from the 1777 edition, third edition, ed. L.A. Selby-Bigge, Oxford: Clarendon Press, 1975.

Husserl, Edmund, *Formal and Transcendental Logic*, trans. Dorion Cairns, The Hague: Martinus Nijhoff, 1969.

Johnston, Adrian, *Prolegomena to Any Future Materialism, Volume One: The Outcome of Contemporary French Philosophy*, Evanston, IL: Northwestern University Press, 2013.

Marion, Jean-Luc, *Being Given: Toward a Phenomenology of Givenness*, trans. Jeffrey L. Kosky, Stanford, CA: Stanford University Press, 2002.

Meillassoux, Quentin, *After Finitude: An Essay on the Necessity of Contingency*, trans. Ray Brassier, London: Continuum, 2008.

Müller-Sievers, Helmut, *Self-Generation: Biology, Philosophy, and Literature Around 1800*, Stanford, CA: Stanford University Press, 1997.

Musil, Robert, *Diaries 1899–1941*, trans. Philip Payne, New York: Basic Books, 1976.

Nietzsche, Friedrich, *The Will to Power*, trans. Walter Kaufmann and R.J. Hollingdale, New York: Vintage, 1967.

Peirce, Charles Sanders, *Principles of Philosophy*, in *Collected Papers of Charles Sanders Peirce*, eds Charles Hawthorne and Paul Weiss, Cambridge, MA: Belknap Press of Harvard University Press, 1965.

Richards, Robert J., *The Romantic Concept of Life: Science and Philosophy in the Age of Goethe*, Chicago: University of Chicago Press, 2002.

Ricœur, Paul, *The Conflict of Interpretations: Essays in Hermeneutics*, ed. Don Idhe, Evanston, IL: Northwestern University Press, 1974.

Ricœur, Paul, *Freud and Philosophy: An Essay on Interpretation*, trans. Denise Savage, New Haven, CT: Yale University Press, 1970.

Schlosser, J.G., *Plato's Briefe nebst einer historischen Einleitung und Anmerkungen*, Königsberg, 1795.

Sluga, Hans D., *Gottlob Frege*, London: Routledge & Kegan Paul, 1980.

INDEX

a priori
    and condition of possibility 3–5,
        12, 107
    epigenesis 9–12, 17–18, 64, 73
    formal and historical 107–8, 109,
        117–18
    innatism 10, 70, 71–2, 74
    and the transcendental 3–4, 5–6, 9,
        10–11, 13–14
acquisition, original and derived
    46–7
adaptation 45, 67
    see also evolution; "neo-skeptical"
        thesis
aesthetic judgment 169
alterity and critique of property 140–7
analogy, problem of 112–14, 180–2
anthropological variety 58–60
archeology/genealogy 105–6, 178
Aristotle 16–17, 133, 134
Atlan, Henri 81, 156

Baudelaire, Charles 104
Baumgarten, Alexander 61
Blumenbach, Johann 25, 45, 53, 56,
    62, 63, 64, 93–4, 95
Boltzmann, Ludwig 72
Bourgeois, Bernard 160
Boutroux, Émile 148–9
Bouveresse, Jacques 33, 67–70, 71–2,
    73, 74–5, 76, 85, 149
Boyer, Alain 30
Brague, Rémi 133

brain *see* neurobiology/brain and
    reason
Buffon, Georges-Louis Leclerc 17, 54

Canguilhem, Georges 29–30
categories
    and experience 16, 31, 122, 157
    origin of 20–1
causality
    difference in 161–2
    and "purposiveness" 171
chance and contingency 126–7
changeability/mutability of the
    transcendental 3–4, 32–4, 124–8
Changeux, J.-P. 1, 10–11, 80, 83, 85,
    86, 130, 150–1, 156, 186
cognitive structures *see* neurobiology/
    brain and reason
condition of possibility 3–5, 12, 107
contingency/radical contingency 2–3,
    7, 11–12, 14, 122–3, 124–5, 128
    and alterity 142, 143–7
    and chance 126–7
    Critique of Pure Reason 165–6,
        167–8
    of laws of nature 148–9, 150, 151
    and necessity 170–3, 176–7
correlation/correlationism 2, 3, 11,
    12, 16, 50
    and articulation 133
    and "connection" 136–7
    and temporality 120–1, 134–5, 147
Crusius, Christian August 23, 42

219

INDEX

dating and mathematics 131–5
de Vleeschauwer, Herman Jan 46,
47
Derrida, Jacques 4, 134, 138
disappropriation/dis-propriation,
philosophy as 141–4
DNA 36, 79–80, 81, 88
Duchesneau, François 25, 29, 92

Edelman, Gerald 86–8, 118, 149,
151
embryonic development 16–17, 25,
28, 118, 158
as unpredictable 29–31
empiricism
and innatism 31, 39, 47
rejecting 44–7
and the transcendental 15–16,
173–4
Enlightenment 100–2
environment
"epistemological environment"
44–6
importance of 81–2
epigenesis: "system of the epigenesis
of pure reason" 16–17, 20–6
epigenetic paradigm of rationality 155
difference in causality 161–2
genesis, epigenesis, hermeneutics
157–60
intrication of the transcendental
and biological 160–1
life and factual rationality 168–70
order of nature and systematic
order 163–6, 167
other contingency and other
necessity 170–3
reason for new paradigm 156–7
structure and evolution 173–4
third and first *Critique* 166–7
epigenetics
defining 78–80
and genetics, difference between
35–9, 88–9, 157–60
human genome sequencing and
"genetic paradigm" 80–1
importance of environment 81–2
"epistemological environment" 44–6
equivocal generation 21–4, 25–6, 69,
161–2

evolution
neural/mental Darwinism 78, 83,
86, 88, 150–1
and structure 173–4
variability of laws of nature
148–51
see also "neo-skeptical" thesis
experience
and categories 16, 31, 122, 157
opportunity of 38, 40, 43–4, 47
experimental philosophy 106

fabricated/acquired vs innate
transcendental 5–6, 7–9, 10–11,
13, 15, 17
facticity 11, 45, 51–2, 95, 124–5
factual rationality 168–70
finitude 131–40, 177
"formation without preformation"
28–30
formative drive 29, 45, 54, 58, 62–3
limits of 55–7
"forms of the materials" and
"epistemological environment"
44–6
Foucault, Michel 33, 98, 100–10,
113, 117, 118, 157
Frege, Gottlob 74–7, 85

genealogy/archeology 105–6, 178
generative production 21
genesis and epigenesis, difference
between 35–9, 88–9, 157–60
"genetic paradigm" 80–1
Genova, A.C. 45–6, 66, 73
geology 35–6
germs and predispositions 38–9, 41,
54, 55, 59, 68, 93, 166
gradual harmonization 67–9, 70

Harvey, William 17
Hegel, George Wilhelm Friedrich 3,
31, 67
Heidegger, Martin 1, 7–9, 13, 111–14,
116–19, 175
and Meillassoux 120–1, 131–47,
148
Helmholtz, Herman von 71–2
Herder, Johann Godfried 53, 54,
55–7, 58, 60, 62, 63

220

hermeneutics/interpretation 88–9, 91,
  94–9, 157–60
history
  archeology/genealogy 105–6, 178
  Enlightenment 100–2
  as field of interpretation 94–9
  historical and formal *a priori*
    107–8, 109, 117–18
  new state of 186
  problem of 94–9
human/anthropological variety 59–60
human genome sequencing 80–1
Hume, David 23–4, 31, 34, 68–9, 97,
  123–4, 125–6
Huneman, Philippe 164, 165, 179
hylozoism 58, 62–3
hyper-normative and hypo-normative
  transcendental 130–1, 152

innate/innatism 10, 13
  a priori 10, 70, 71–2, 74
  analysis of 67–8
  and empiricism 31, 39, 47
  and "evolutionary paradox" 84
  vs fabricated/acquired
    transcendental 5–6, 7–9, 10–11,
    13, 15, 17
  "intellectual" epigenesis 61–2
interpretation/hermeneutics 88–9, 91,
  94–9, 157–60
invariance/immutability
  of mathematics 73, 75
  and reorganization 182–4
  see also variability/variety

Jacob, François 81
Jenuwein, Thomas 88, 99

Kant, Immanuel *see* epigenesis:
  "system of the epigenesis of pure
  reason"

laws of nature 23, 148–51, 171
Lebrun, Gérard 33, 94, 95–6, 97–8
life *see* nature/life
localization and surface 35–7, 38–9
Locke, John 43

mathematics 12, 14, 15, 127, 128
  dating and 131–5

immutability of 73, 75
  mental objects and representation
    85–6
Maupertuis, Pierre-Louis Moreau de
  17, 54
"maximal" preformationism 64–5
Meillassoux, Quentin 2–3, 4, 11,
  13–14, 34, 122–7, 129, 176–7
  and Heidegger 120–1, 131–47, 148
mental Darwinism *see* neural/mental
  Darwinism
mental objects and representation
  85–6, 150–1
metaphysical knowledge and
  deduction 48, 49–50
methodological principles and details
  19–20, 32–4
"minimal preformationism" 40–2, 51,
  90, 92–3, 118
metaphysical knowledge 48
metaphysical and transcendental
  deduction 48, 49–50
objective genitive hypothesis 42
preformed epigenesis 50–2
"pure" readings 40–2
reductive division of source 43–4
rejecting "empiricist" readings
  44–7
Morgan, Thomas 79

"nativism", critique of 71–4
"natural laws of reason" 42
nature/life
  and factual rationality 168–70
  intrication of the transcendental
    and 160–1
  laws of 23, 148–51, 171
  systematic order and order of
    163–6, 167
necessity and contingency 170–3,
  176–7
"neo-skeptical" thesis 66, 124
  analysis of innatism 67–8
  another version of sources 69–71
  critique of "nativism" 71–4
  eclipse of transcendental idealism
    74–7
  pre-established and gradual
    harmony 67–9, 70
  role reversal 67

221